Gongs and Pop Songs

Ohio University Research in International Studies

This series of publications on Africa, Latin America, Southeast Asia, and Global and Comparative Studies is designed to present significant research, translation, and opinion to area specialists and to a wide community of persons interested in world affairs. The editors seek manuscripts of quality on any subject and can usually make a decision regarding publication within three months of receipt of the original work. Production methods generally permit a work to appear within one year of acceptance. The editors work closely with authors to produce high-quality books. The series is distributed worldwide. For more information, consult the Ohio University Press website, ohioswallow.com.

Books in the Ohio University Research in International Studies series are published by Ohio University Press in association with the Center for International Studies. The views expressed in individual volumes are those of the authors and should not be considered to represent the policies or beliefs of the Center for International Studies, Ohio University Press, or Ohio University.

Gongs and Pop Songs

*Sounding Minangkabau
in Indonesia*

Jennifer A. Fraser

Ohio University Research in International Studies
Southeast Asia Series No. 127
Ohio University Press
Athens

© 2015 by the
Center for International Studies
Ohio University
All rights reserved

To obtain permission to quote, reprint, or otherwise reproduce or distribute material from Ohio University Press publications, please contact our rights and permissions department at (740) 593-1154 or (740) 593-4536 (fax).
www.ohioswallow.com

Printed in the United States of America
The books in the Ohio University Research in International Studies Series are printed on acid-free paper ♾ ™

25 24 23 22 21 20 19 18 17 16 15   5 4 3 2 1

Library of Congress Cataloging-in-Publication Data
Fraser, Jennifer A.
 Gongs and pop songs : sounding Minangkabau in Indonesia / Jennifer A. Fraser.
       pages cm. — (Ohio University research in international studies. Southeast Asia series ; No. 127)
   Includes bibliographical references and index.
   ISBN 978-0-89680-294-0 (hc : alk. paper) — ISBN 978-0-89680-295-7 (pb : alk. paper) — ISBN 978-0-89680-490-6 (pdf)
   1. Music—Indonesia—Sumatera Barat—History and criticism. 2. Minangkabau (Indonesian people)—Music—History and criticism. 3. Talempong—Indonesia—Sumatera Barat. I. Title.
   ML3758.I537S83 2015
   780.9598'13—dc23
                                2015013620

Contents

List of Illustrations	vii
Map	vii
Figures	vii
Tables	viii
Music Examples	viii
Preface and Acknowledgments	ix
Technical Notes	xiii

ONE	Ethnicity, Gongs, and Pop Songs	1
TWO	Talempong and Community	37
THREE	Institutionalizing Minangkabau Arts	89
FOUR	Reforming Talempong	133
FIVE	Talempong in the Marketplace	176
SIX	Multiple Ways of Sounding Minangkabau	216

Notes	225
Glossary	231
References	241
Discography	251
Interviews by the Author	253
Online Resources	255
Audio Examples	255
Video Examples	256
Web Figures	257
Web Map	258
Index	259

Illustrations

Map

1.1. West Sumatra — 13

Figures

1.1. Talempong — 24
1.2. Nurlaili playing *talempong kayu* — 25
1.3. *Talempong jao* — 26
2.1. Women playing *talempong* at a wedding in Paninjauan — 38
2.2. *Talempong pacik* as part of a *gandang tambua* ensemble with *pupuik solo*, Paninjauan — 51
2.3. *Talempong duduak* in Paninjauan — 52
2.4. Mardiani playing *aguang* with a young jackfruit — 54
2.5. Asma playing *gandang* — 55
2.6. Samsinar playing *botol* — 56
2.7. Rosani playing *giriang* — 56
2.8. *Talempong pacik* in a wedding procession in Pesisir Selatan — 62
2.9. Alternative ensemble in Paninjauan — 65
2.10. Wedding procession in Paninjauan — 67
3.1. The institute in Padang Panjang when it was known as STSI — 90
3.2. Computer-generated notation for the piece "Sambalado lah tatunggang" — 123
3.3. Cipher notation for "Sambalado lah tatunggang" — 124
4.1. *Orkes talempong* with *talempong jao* — 145

4.2.	The *bansi* and *saluang* take a solo in *orkes talempong*	171
5.1.	Halim with Alfa Musik, Padang Panjang	200
5.2.	Alfa Musik looking like a rock band with *talempong*, Padang Panjang	201

Tables

2.1.	Structure of "Tupai bagaluik"	54
2.2.	*Talempong duduak* tunings from three *nagari* with absolute pitch	59
2.3.	Intervallic structure of *talempong duduak* tunings from three *nagari*, illustrating variation within a *nagari*	61
3.1.	List of state- and province-funded arts institutions in Indonesia	94
4.1.	Instrumentation of *orkes talempong*	143
5.1.	Instrumentation of *talempong kreasi* at the arts institutions	187
5.2.	Tuning of the *talempong* in Alfa Musik	202

Music Examples

2.1.	The "Tupai bagaluik" melody with *talempong pambao* and the supporting parts	57
3.1.	"Gua cak din din" with basic parts	125
3.2.	Notated variations for the *panyaua* in "Gua cak din din"	125
4.1.	Transcription of the *orkes talempong* piece "Kambang cari"	149
4.2.	Structural outline of "Kambang cari"	169
4.3.	Accompaniment patterns for *dendang* "Indang Payakumbuah" in "Tak tontong"	172
5.1.	Transcription of the *talempong kreasi* piece "Minangkabau"	188

Also see Online Resources (p. 255) for lists of audio examples, video examples, and additional images available online.

Preface and Acknowledgments

In 1998, I traveled to West Sumatra for the first time and enrolled for a year at Akademi Seni Karawitan Indonesia (glossed for now as Academy of Indonesian Traditional Music) in Padang Panjang under the Dharmasiswa exchange program. I had become interested in working outside the canon of the ethnomusicology of Indonesia focused on the islands of Java and Bali and was particularly fascinated with *talempong,* a gong chime ensemble of the Minangkabau, the people who populate the province of West Sumatra, in part because there were some villages where women played and men did not. As a student at the academy, I became fascinated with the institution itself, its pedagogical methods, and its influence on music in the region. I returned in 2003 for fourteen months of fieldwork and then again in the summer of 2010. In January 2014, faculty colleague and friend Jan Miyake and I led a group of ten Oberlin College students to Indonesia for three weeks. When the rest of the group left Indonesia, I returned to West Sumatra for several more weeks of research, including follow-up research in Paninjauan regarding the ceremony to install a lineage chief that the group had witnessed. The book is therefore a culmination of more than two years of research in West Sumatra lasting over a sixteen-year period.

All the audiovisual material accompanying this book, along with color versions of the figures and additional photographs, can be found through links on the following website: http://www.ohioswallow.com/book/Gongs+and+Pop+Songs. Unless otherwise indicated, I took all the photographs, recordings, and videos.

This book would not have been possible without the support of numerous individuals. I am most deeply indebted to the people I worked with in the field. Over the years, I have encountered and received the generosity of time and knowledge from hundreds of individuals. This includes faculty, staff, and students at the arts institution in Padang Panjang known over the years by several names, along with its sister high school in Padang. I also worked with officials in the national, provincial, and regional levels of the bureaus dealing with education, tourism, and culture, along with officials at the Culture Park in Padang and the West Sumatra Pavilion at the Beautiful Indonesia in Miniature theme park in Jakarta. I am also indebted to freelance performers, composers, and choreographers; directors and members of performance troupes and companies; and musicians in several villages. Invited to attend events by musicians, I received the generosity of hosts that I sometimes never even met. These individuals are too numerous to name here, but their generosity is evident in the pages of the text that follows.

In 2003–4 my research was sponsored by a grant from the Social Science Research Council, along with a grant from the Presser Foundation. It was facilitated by the support of Lembaga Ilmu Pengetahuan Indonesia (Indonesian Academy of Sciences) and sponsored by the arts institution in Padang Panjang. In 2010 a Powers Travel Grant and Research Status from Oberlin College supported my trip. As I traveled around the province, many people opened up their homes to me. My deepest debt is to my host family with whom I resided both in 1998–99 as an exchange student and each subsequent trip to West Sumatra. I felt truly embraced as a member of the family. Pak Arzul Jamaan is not only my "father" but also my mentor and adviser in the field. He helped with texts and translations, answered endless questions, and introduced me to musicians and people. Bu Suryanti, my "mother," was my closest friend, always understanding and generous, treating me as one of her own siblings. Their children were equally generous welcoming me into their home and were willing to put up with the quirks of living with a foreigner. Other hosts to whom I am grateful include Bu Zuryati Zoebir and family in Padang, Bu Siti Aisah and family in Unggan, Bu Asma and family in Paninjauan, and Pak Syahrial in Bukittinggi. I also thank Pak Zulkifli, director of the arts institution in Padang Panjang in 2003–4, along with Pak I Dewo Nyoman Supenida and Pak Hanefi who were variously heads of the Department of Traditional Music during my fieldwork. Other individuals with whom I repeatedly worked or were gracious to invite me to special events include Admiral, Alfalah, Anusirwan, Arnailis, Asnam Rasyid, Asril, Ediwar, Edy Utama, Elizar, Erianto, Hajizar, Halim, Herawati, Jenni Aulia, Murad, Musliwardinal, Suharti, Sulastri Andras, and Zahara Kamal. I am also grateful to Victoria Randa Ayu, Tony Riyaldi, and Wil for their transcriptions of interviews, song texts, or speeches in Indonesian and Minangkabau.

Special thanks goes to Margaret Kartomi for allowing me access to her Sumatra Music Archive, housed at Monash University in Melbourne, Australia, where I found the only extant recordings of *orkes talempong* from the 1970s, along with rare photographs, which she has generously allowed me to make use of here. I am grateful to Jack Thomas for making the map, Stephen Larson for making the staff notation examples of "Minangkabau," and several Oberlin students, some of whom have now graduated, for their work on the "Kambang cari" transcription, including Seán Hanson and Maurice Cohn. Most of the credit for the final product goes to Christian James, especially for picking it up at the late hour.

Over the years, I have had the great fortune to be mentored by an inspiring group of people, including Sarah Weiss, the person who initially inspired me to pursue a career in the ethnomusicology of Indonesia, and Charles Capwell, Thomas Turino, Donna Buchanan, and Clark Cunningham at the University of Illinois at Urbana-Champaign. My discovery of an Indonesia beyond Java and Bali in large part is thanks to the influence of Marc Perlman, my adviser when I was at Brown University; Philip Yampolsky through the Smithsonian Folkways Music of Indonesia series; and the nuanced feminist analyses of anthropologist Evelyn Blackwood. Their collective contributions led me to talempong in West Sumatra and I have not looked back since.

The project also would not have come to fruition without the continued support of friends, colleagues, and family. I am particularly grateful for the advice and friendship of Evelyn Blackwood, Wendy

Gaylord, Catherine Sylstra, and Alice Trend in the field in 2003–4. I thank the many friends, colleagues, and students at the University of Illinois at Urbana-Champaign and Oberlin College for their intellectual and personal support since. Special thanks to Roderic Knight and Andrew Pau, who consulted on tuning systems; Erika Hoffmann-Dilloway, Jason Haugen, and Danny Yee, who consulted on questions of ethnicity and language; and Tanya Lee and Kathryn Metz, who read parts of earlier drafts. Philip Yampolsky and anonymous reviewers gave many constructive comments to make this a better book. Any mistakes and weaknesses that remain are entirely mine.

Kok ado langkah nan salah, rila jo maaf.

If there steps that are wrong, please forgive me.

Technical Notes

Languages in the Field and Translations

Many people I worked with are conversant in both the Indonesian and Minangkabau languages. In chapter 1, I explain why people might prioritize one language over the other, but most of my interviews were in a mix of the two languages. A few were exclusively in Minangkabau, while some in Indonesian used Minangkabau only for terms, genres, and practices, or reference to aphorisms. All translations from Indonesian and Minangkabau are mine unless otherwise noted. All emphasis in quoted material appears in the original unless otherwise noted.

Orthography and Abbreviations

For the Indonesian language I use the standardized system of spelling implemented in 1972. There is no such officially accepted standardized system for spelling in Minangkabau, although orthography is becoming increasingly standard. I have followed the most common conventions, including those in *Kamus umum bahasa Minangkabau* (Usman 2002). When I first use a non-English term, in addition to providing a definition, I will identify whether it is Minangkabau (M) or Indonesian (I), unless it is obvious from the context. Terms used more than once are in the glossary. Indonesian and Minangkabau noun plurals are often identical to the singular forms.

Personal Names

I retain the most common spelling for a name, which sometimes means employing the older orthographic system: for example, Boestanoel instead of Bustanul or Irsjad instead of Irsyad. The matter of naming also is complex in Indonesia, with people switching between legal names as stated on one's identity card or in official documents, nicknames, stage names, or names augmented with honorifics and degrees. Indonesians often use titles to indicate relative social position when referring to someone, such as *Bapak* or *Pak* (I, an older or important man), *Ibu* (I, a woman), and so on. There are a series of Minangkabau equivalents, which can vary from one village or region to the next. In Paninjauan, for instance, my former hostess in the village was *Uaik* (older woman) Asma. But I avoid this practice in the text, aiming instead for clarity.

In Minangkabau practice, men who have been appointed a *pangulu* (M, lineage or clan leader) have a title. For example, my host father's legal name is Arzul Jamaan but he is also a pangulu, which comes with the title Datuak (Dt.) Endah Kayo nan Kuniang. Although people are often best known by nicknames, for the purposes of clarity in this text I have emphasized legal names, except when I am discussing contexts where it would be disrespectful to not use men's titled names.

Transcriptions and Recordings

For the most part the notational system I employ is the kind of cipher notation used at the arts institutions, which is well suited to talempong.

Example:

$$\overline{54\ 54\ 34}\ \ \overline{5\ 55\ 43\ {}^{2}1\ 23\ 34}$$

Each number represents a relative pitch in the scale, with 1 being the lowest pitch. Unlike cipher notation, used for Javanese gamelan, in West Sumatra, this notational system is used in institutional contexts without any presumption of particular scales or intervallic structure. Moreover, it does not indicate register in any way. In other words, it can be used for music involving radically different-sounding pitch collections.

In the example above, and others throughout the book,

A horizontal line over two notes, such as $\overline{55}$, indicates eighth notes where the downbeat comes on the first of the pair.

A number without any horizontal line above, such as 5, indicates a quarter note.

A double horizontal line over two notes, such as $\overline{\overline{55}}$, indicates sixteenth notes.

An "o" indicates a rest.

An "x" indicates a percussive strike.

In the text, I sometimes refer readers to a specific passage in the accompanying online audiovisual material (available through links at the web page http://www.ohioswallow.com/book/Gongs+and+Pop+Songs). For instance, 00.57 would mean the specific passage starts at fifty-seven seconds.

Chapter 1

ETHNICITY, GONGS, AND POP SONGS

On a Thursday afternoon in October, I found myself in the relative luxury of an air-conditioned taxi for forty-five minutes, enduring Jakarta's notoriously congested roadways in order to attend the opening ceremony of the 2003 Dazzling Exhibition of Indonesian Tourism. The advertisement in *Kompas,* Indonesia's largest national newspaper, had promised the event would be "celebrated with various regional *kesenian* [I, arts]." A call to the event's organizers revealed that the group selected to perform at the opening ceremony—attended and officiated by Indonesia's tourism minister—was from the province of West Sumatra. It seemed a perfect event for my research project on the celebration of ethnicity through music.

Walking into the exhibition hall, I passed rows of booths where government offices and private businesses from around the archipelago were advertising eco-, maritime, religious, or cultural tourism. They competed for the attention of domestic tourists, potential investors, and tourist agencies. In 2003 the central government of Indonesia was promoting the stimulation of the tourism sector—particularly domestic tourism—as a way to overcome the impact of the 1998 Asian economic crisis. To the obvious disappointment of booth operators, I walked straight past them, heading for the end of the hall, where I heard a musical group warming up. The eight young men playing were part of a performance troupe called Lansano Entertaint, which was representing the Office for Tourism and Culture in Padang, the capital of West Sumatra. The program they presented fused music, dance, and cultural practices together, including one piece incorporating a ritualistic welcome where three women dressed in elaborate ceremonial clothes offered the attending dignitaries betel leaves. I was particularly interested in the music because my research was focused on the sonic representations of the Minangkabau, one of the hundreds of recognized ethnic groups in Indonesia and the dominant one in West Sumatra.

The physical, visual, and sonic focus of the ensemble was clearly the *talempong* (M, small bronze or brass kettle gongs approximately seven inches in diameter). The sixty gongs were arranged on three racks that stood waist high. One musician played melodies on the central rack of thirty tuned gongs arranged in three rows, while the two musicians flanking him accompanied the melody on sets of fifteen gongs each. The sets of gongs were tuned chromatically, a system that accommodates both major and minor scales, the occasional modulation within a tune, and harmonic accompaniment of the melody using basic chord progressions derived from "Western"[1] tonal theory. A fourth musician enhanced the melodic line, alternating between different Minangkabau wind instruments—depending on the tune and section of the piece—including the *saluang* (M, an oblique bamboo flute), the *bansi* (M, a small end-blown bamboo block flute), and the *sarunai* (M, single-reed bamboo pipe). The lineup also included bass guitar and percussion, including local drums, djembe (an instrument now made in Indonesia), and tambourine. In addition to accompanying choreographed dances, the group played instrumental arrangements of nostalgic *pop Minang* (I, pop songs in the Minangkabau language) (video 1.1). The compositions, designed to align with the dance movements, were careful arrangements highlighting textural and timbral contrasts between sections. This style of music was *talempong kreasi baru* (I, new-creation talempong), more commonly called simply *talempong kreasi*. Over the next fourteen months, I ran into talempong kreasi ensembles playing in contexts ranging from tourist shows, arts festivals, theme parks, and government functions to cultural missions abroad and elite weddings. Talempong kreasi is the musical and talempong style that most frequently represented and continues to represent the Minangkabau. But how did a style of talempong that has its origins in the late 1960s come to do this, and what has happened to the older talempong practices in the meantime?

The Scope of the Project

Gongs and Pop Songs tells a story about the transformation of music in West Sumatra since the 1960s through different musical styles involving the same medium, talempong. The book is particularly concerned with the transformation of talempong from a musical practice that expresses and sustains identities of tight-knit, small communities where people know each other on a face-to-face basis (the criterion I use to define community in this text) into one that also became capable of articulating an ethnic identity where members rarely know each other so closely. The book asks how the sounds and meanings of this Minangkabau musical practice were shaped and reshaped in response to specific social, political, and economic forces, including a regional rebellion that failed (1958–61); the institutionalization of the arts, starting in 1965; the related professionalization of the artistic workforce; and the pressures of a free-market economy. Note that when I invoke the phrase *the arts* I use it as a gloss for the Indonesian terms *seni* or *kesenian,* both of which refer to the performing, literary, and plastic arts. It is significant that this terminology is Indonesian, not Minangkabau, as the project of institutionalizing the arts is very much a national one. These terms, moreover, have been adopted widely in Minangkabau contexts, replacing indigenous concepts.[2]

In short, the book presents a history of talempong styles that seeks to make sense of the various Minangkabau combinations of gongs and pop songs found in Indonesia in the twenty-first century. The journey moves from the villages of West Sumatra to metropolitan Jakarta as I explore talempong played in contexts ranging from classrooms to weddings and tourist performances. In each context, I ask how people understand themselves as Minangkabau in the world through their engagements with talempong or how these musical practices help people sound Minangkabau.

Gongs and Pop Songs provides a study of how expressive arts—in this case musical practices—can function as expressions of ethnicity. I take a cognitive approach to ethnicity in the book, asking how musical practices help create, produce, and represent ethnic sensibilities. The book also investigates how social, economic, and political processes help facilitate the constitution of ethnicities and artistic practices linked with them. I suggest, for example, that the emergence of the style called *orkes talempong* (I, talempong orchestra) is very much connected with the politics and cultural politics of the time in which it emerged, including a shift in national government and, as a handful of interlocutors strongly asserted, the failure of a regional rebellion, the Pemerintah Revolusioner Republik Indonesia ([PRRI] I, the Revolutionary Government of the Republic of Indonesia). According to this perspective, this musical practice helped Minangkabau intellectuals and artists negotiate a place in the new political order. The changes to talempong that I chronicle here are also set against a diversifying economy and the increasing entrenchment of middle-class values manifest in the processes of institutionalization and the subsequent professionalization of music where academic credentials are necessary for access to many performance opportunities, processes that were happening in West Sumatra, as they were elsewhere in Indonesia.

The founding of an educational institution dedicated to Minangkabau arts in 1965 contributed to unequivocal and irrevocable transformations in the contours of the Minangkabau musical landscape. When the institution was first established, there was a secondary division and a tertiary one; both were initially called KOKAR (I, Konservatori Karawitan, which will be glossed for now as Conservatory of Traditional Music). However, both divisions have gone through subsequent name changes. The tertiary division became ASKI (I, Akademi Seni Karawitan Indonesia, Academy of Indonesian Traditional Music) in 1966, STSI (I, Sekolah Tinggi Seni Indonesia, Higher Institute of Indonesian Arts) in 1999, and ISI (I, Institut Seni Indonesia,

Institute of Indonesian Arts) in 2010, the title it currently holds. The secondary division changed to SMKI (I, Sekolah Menengah Karawitan Indonesia, High School of Indonesian Traditional Music) in 1982, when it also moved its campus to Padang, and to SMKN 7 Padang (I, Sekolah Menengah Kejuruan Negeri 7, State Vocational High School no. 7 in Padang) in the 1990s. In chapter 3, I unpack these nomenclatural politics. In the text that follows, if the events I am discussing are located in a specific year that correlates to a particular title for either the secondary- or tertiary-level institution, I will use that name. If the time referent is vague or broad, I will use *institution* for the period when the secondary and tertiary divisions shared a campus, *institute* for the tertiary level, and *high school* for the secondary level.

Two shifts resulting from the institutionalization of the arts key in this book include the creation and bolstering of new styles of talempong and the production of hundreds of graduates, a cadre of academically trained artists who seek full-time employment in fields related to the arts. The emergence of this kind of artist is significant because their academic training sets them apart from artists in indigenous contexts, even in the rare cases in which the students enter the institute with extensive exposure to indigenous styles. These graduates, who operate as bureaucrats, composers, musicians, and troupe directors, engage with and promote the new talempong styles; that is, they are directly involved with the performance of ethnicity. The pressures of a free-market economy have encouraged further developments in talempong style as graduates look for work and respond to demands for the popularization of talempong and other musical practices. Consumers of the newest talempong style, *talempong goyang* (I, a mix of talempong with rock instruments), considered it a more authentic Minangkabau music than other forms of Minangkabau popular music, including pop Minang played on a synthesizer. Thus, the book traces the way talempong has been shaped and reshaped as an expression of Minangkabau ethnicity and the involvement of the arts institutions and people affiliated with them in that process.

Collectively these social, political, and economic changes over the last sixty years have transformed the practice of music in West

Sumatra: they have resulted in a qualitative difference in the way Minangkabau musics are produced, aesthetically shaped, ideologically framed, circulated, and ultimately consumed. In short, they have caused a paradigm shift within the Minangkabau musical world. But, this shift has not entailed the complete replacement of the old paradigm with the new one. Rather, there has been an expansion and diversification of practices leading to more paths through which to negotiate one's place in the world as Minangkabau. The story told here does not just detail the expansion of talempong styles but also the diversification of the kinds of musicians who operate in West Sumatra today, including the difference between skilled musicians who have accumulated their musical knowledge in villages and those who are trained at formalized educational institutions for the arts. In short, the book seeks to understand how there are different ways of thinking about, playing, and valuing music in contexts where most of the people involved think of themselves as Minangkabau at some level. People's engagements with ethnicity, however, are not uniform. The cognitive view of ethnicity provides analytical tools to make sense of this diversity.

The Cognitive View of Ethnicity

The Minangkabau are commonly recognized as one of the hundreds of ethnic groups in Indonesia. But what *is* ethnicity? What does it *mean* to be Minangkabau? Many people—lay persons and scholars alike—take ethnicity for granted, as Timothy Rice insists, "as a category of social life and of social analysis" (2007, 20; 2010): they assume ethnic identities are solid, bounded, concrete things in the world, rather than asking how and why people come to identify with a particular ethnic category and how those identifications might diverge. Until recently the study of ethnicity has largely been approached from one of two perspectives (Levine 1999). The first of these is the primordialist view that "situates ethnicity in the psyche so deeply that society and culture are bent to its will." The second, the instrumentalist or situationalist view, argues that ethnicity is entirely constructed but fails to show "how particular ethnic categories arise and become salient in social action." One alternative to this polarized argument has been a reactionary postmodern stance arguing for the "demolition of ethnicity" altogether (Levine 1999, 166–67), yet this approach fails to account for the way my collaborators and interlocutors in the field have become invested in their expressions of it.

A more productive alternative to emerge in the last decade or so—and the one I use in this book—has been the "cognitive turn" that shifts the emphasis onto how and when an ethnic-based category such as Minangkabau is created and invoked (Brubaker 2002, 2009; Brubaker and Cooper 2000; Brubaker, Loveman, and Stamatov 2004). This approach emphasizes that ethnicity is "not a thing *in* the world, but a perspective *on*" it (Brubaker, Loveman, and Stamatov 2004, 33; cf. Brubaker 2002). The cognitive approach urges an exploration of the "culturally specific ways in which persons, institutions, organizations, and discourses make sense of experience and interpret the social world." In other words, I am interested in the variety of mechanisms—discourses, institutional forms, private interactions, and so on—through and in which Minangkabau ethnicity works (Brubaker 2009, 32, 20), along with the variety of ways people engage with and experience the category of Minangkabau. Not all people are equally invested.

In Indonesia, claiming an ethnic identity is often—but not necessarily always—tied up with language. One way that some people engage with the category of Minangkabau, asserting and claiming Minangkabau ethnicity, is through language choice. Many people who identify as Minangkabau understand and speak a language known as Minangkabau. For example, some individuals I met used a phrase in the Minangkabau language *urang awak* (M, one of my/our people) in personal interactions to determine ethnic belonging. In other words, they were using a language-based category to ally themselves with those people who understand the term and differentiate themselves from other individuals who did not. However, there is considerable debate about what constitutes the language, or rather which particular regional variant is taken as the standard. For example, there are differences in vowel sounds or in word choices between the regional dialects that mark a speaker as from Pariaman, Sawahlunto, or Bukittinggi. Despite these differences, these variants share grammatical and lexical similarities that structure and categorize experiences in and perspectives on the world that may differ from the way a Batak or Javanese speaker might categorize her experiences, in this respect bolstering the relevance of the Minangkabau language to Minangkabau ethnicity.

However, it is important to note that there are also people who identify as Minangkabau even though Minangkabau is not their primary language and some who speak very little, if any, of the language. In the 2010 census, of the people who identified their ethnicity as Minangkabau, only 71.19 percent claimed Minangkabau was the primary language they spoke at home; 23.87 percent claimed they spoke Indonesian primarily; and the remaining 4.94 percent claimed another primary language (Ananta et al. 2013, 25).[3] While most of the respondents speak both Minangkabau and Indonesian, there is no data on what percentage speak both daily at home.

In my experience, Minangkabau is the predominant language in village contexts. I have encountered some people who do not speak Indonesian at all: they are generally older and have little formal education. Younger people in the villages tend to have more Indonesian because they have attended school longer. I also found that people who had migrated elsewhere in the archipelago and moved back had greater fluency in Indonesian. In the cities, the opposite is often true: people had greater fluency in Indonesian, and for some, the use of Indonesian equals or even dominates Minangkabau in their daily lives. The choice to speak primarily Indonesian has to do with educational and social capital, including an individual or familial sense of cosmopolitan identity. As Aris Ananta and colleagues state, Indonesian is both "the language of national identity and the language of education, literacy, modernization and social mobility" (2013, 23). For example, the primary language used in the household of my host family, which strongly identified as ethnically Minangkabau, was Indonesian. My host mother once explained that she wanted her children to be able to converse with cousins who identified as Minangkabau but lived in the multiethnic and multilingual environments of cities in Java, such as Jakarta and Bandung. She expected her children would pick up Minangkabau language from peers at school. Minangkabau people who live outside West Sumatra often prioritize Indonesian or the language of the region where they live. In families with mixed cultural backgrounds, people are likely to speak Indonesian and both parents' regional languages. Therefore, while language can be important as a way of articulating ethnicity and for many people is a strong marker, one's primary language alone does not necessarily determine ethnic affiliation. There are people who might identify as Minangkabau but for whom it is not the primary language and there are people for whom it is a language used daily at home but who do not identify as ethnically Minangkabau.

The cognitive view of ethnicity also takes into account both contemporary and historical factors. For example, the category of Minangkabau is invoked in the *tambo,* the mythic history of the Minangkabau that traces the origins of the Minangkabau back to Iskandar Zulkarnin (Alexander the Great) and claims the etymology of the name Minangkabau lies in a legendary water buffalo fight (Kahin 1999). Historian Leonard Andaya (2008) suggests that in the precolonial period Minangkabau ethnicity was an artifact of politics and economic power: for example, in the late fifteenth century individuals and communities became interested in the economic advantages and protection that membership in the "group" afforded. In the twentieth and twenty-first centuries, as will become apparent later in the book, a sense of Minangkabau is invoked through performances for tourists and state-regulated celebrations of regional diversity.

In this book, the investigation into the cognitive view is primarily concerned with the different ways people engage with and experience the same category, the political moments that animate identification along ethnic lines, the way ethnicity is tied up and encoded in music, and the contexts in which performative expressions of Minangkabau ethnicity occur—for example, at the tourism expo in the opening vignette. I investigate how the selection of particular talempong styles, ensembles, and repertoire—selections that exclude other possibilities—at the institutions, weddings, tourist performances, and government functions is tied up with individual and collective engagements of what it means to be Minangkabau. In chapter 4, for example, I show how orkes talempong was crafted in the late 1960s to sonically represent an emergent sense of Minangkabau ethnicity, combining references to local instruments and songs with diatonic tuning and functional harmony. Derived from the Greek for "two tones," *diatonic* refers to scales and systems of tuning based on a series of whole- and half-step intervals. Major and minor scales, for example, are diatonic. A chromatic scale is not, as it incorporates only half steps. In other words, in a diatonic scale, the space between any two notes—an interval—is one of two sizes. A listener will notice that there are larger and smaller intervals, thus it sounds uneven or gapped. In a chromatic scale, the space between any two notes is precisely the same. When hearing the notes in sequence, it sounds even. In West Sumatra, people at the institutions often used the word *diatonis* (I, diatonic) to refer to both diatonic and chromatic scales as a shorthand for differentiating these tunings from indigenous preferences, where interval sizes are not standard and rarely adhere to whole and half steps. More often than not, the particular sequence of intervals that results in a major scale was implied. *Functional harmony* means chord progressions based on harmonic function, where the tonic (I), subdominant (IV), and dominant (V) chords are central.

It is important to recognize, however, that the musical practices I discuss here do not just passively reflect ethnic identity but can also help actively foster and create ethnic sensibilities. The capacity of music and other forms of expressive culture to function in this way has been largely overlooked in the work on the cognitive view of ethnicity. This study is an effort to remedy that.

Who Understand Themselves to Be Minangkabau?

People identifying themselves as Minangkabau populate the contemporary Indonesian province of West Sumatra and are found in immigrant communities throughout the archipelago, Malaysia, Australia, and further afield. In a country that boasts the fourth largest, and one of the most culturally diverse, populations in the world, the people who identify as Minangkabau in Indonesia are neither a majority population nor entirely peripheral. Minangkabau people are known throughout the archipelago for their Islamic piety, matrilineal kinship system, astute trading abilities, proclivity to migrate, democratic practices, and spicy food.

The 2000 census was the first since Indonesian independence in 1945 that took into account ethnicity. Until then, discussing ethnicity in Indonesia was taboo, as it was considered to threaten national stability. Three scholars, variously from political science, social statistics, and population economics, crunched the 2000 census numbers and presented their analyses in a seminal work on the statistics of ethnicity in Indonesia (Suryadinata, Arifin, and Ananta 2003). Their analysis took into account ethnicity in Indonesia as a whole but also within each province. The next census was conducted in 2010 and analyses by demographers are just starting to emerge (Ananta et al. 2013). The data below comes from a combination of these demographic analyses.

On the 2000 census, respondents were able to identify their own ethnicity, though those individuals from mixed marriages were forced to choose or have a primary ethnicity selected for them. More than 5.47 million people selected Minangkabau as their ethnicity, making Minangkabau the sixth-largest category out of "1,072 ethnic and subethnic groups" listed by the Badan Pusat Statistik (BPS, Central Board of Statistics). Minangkabau was one of fifteen ethnic categories that had more than a million people. Yet with the population of Indonesia estimated as 205.8 million in 2000, this category constituted only 2.72 percent of the total. In comparison, the two largest ethnic groups—the Javanese and Sundanese—accounted for nearly 58 percent of Indonesia's total population. The third-largest group—Malay—in comparison had just 3.4 percent (Suryadinata, Arifin, and Ananta 2003, 6–10). In other words, the distribution of ethnic groups in Indonesia is unequal: in the 2010 census, almost 85 percent of the population belong to the fifteen largest groups while more than six hundred groups and

Ethnicity, Gongs, and Pop Songs

subgroups constitute the remaining 15 percent or so. On the 2010 census the Minangkabau dropped from the sixth-largest group to seventh, though their numbers had increased from 5.47 million to 6.46 million, 2.73 percent of a total 236.7 million (Ananta et al. 2013, 14–16).

In 2000, 68.44 percent of Indonesia's 5.4 million people who identified as Minangkabau lived in the province of West Sumatra (Suryadinata, Arifin, and Ananta 2003, 52–54), which is located midway along Sumatra's southern side (see map 1.1; webmap 1.1). The boundaries of the current province encapsulate the historical Minangkabau homeland located in the highlands. Minangkabau people constituted 88.35 percent of the province's population. The remainder of the province's population includes the indigenous peoples of the Mentawai island chain, along with migrant groups in larger towns and cities, including Batak, Javanese, Malay, and Chinese (Suryadinata, Arifin, and Ananta 2003, 16). Despite this cultural diversity, dominant representations of the province associate West Sumatra almost exclusively with the Minangkabau.

The boundaries of what is conventionally defined as the Alam Minangkabau (M, Minangkabau World) include the current province of West Sumatra and spill beyond it. Historically, the Alam Minangkabau was divided into the *darek* (M, cultural heartland) and the *rantau* (M, areas of migration outside the darek). The Barisan mountain range, with its towering volcanoes and jagged mountain ridges, splits the mainland of the province into a narrow coastal plain and a highland region with a series of fertile valleys and crater lakes. Three of these valley systems define the boundaries of the darek: the current regencies of Agam, Limapuluh Kota, and Tanah Datar. Historically, the rantau consisted only of the areas that now constitute the other regencies of West Sumatra, along with the areas outside but adjacent to the boundaries of the current province. However, the conceptualizations of these boundaries have expanded with increased rates of permanent migration; many people consider the province to now constitute the homeland and the rantau to encompass all areas in which people identifying as Minangkabau reside.

In 2000, 31.56 percent of people claiming Minangkabau ethnicity lived outside West Sumatra. They lived in neighboring Sumatran

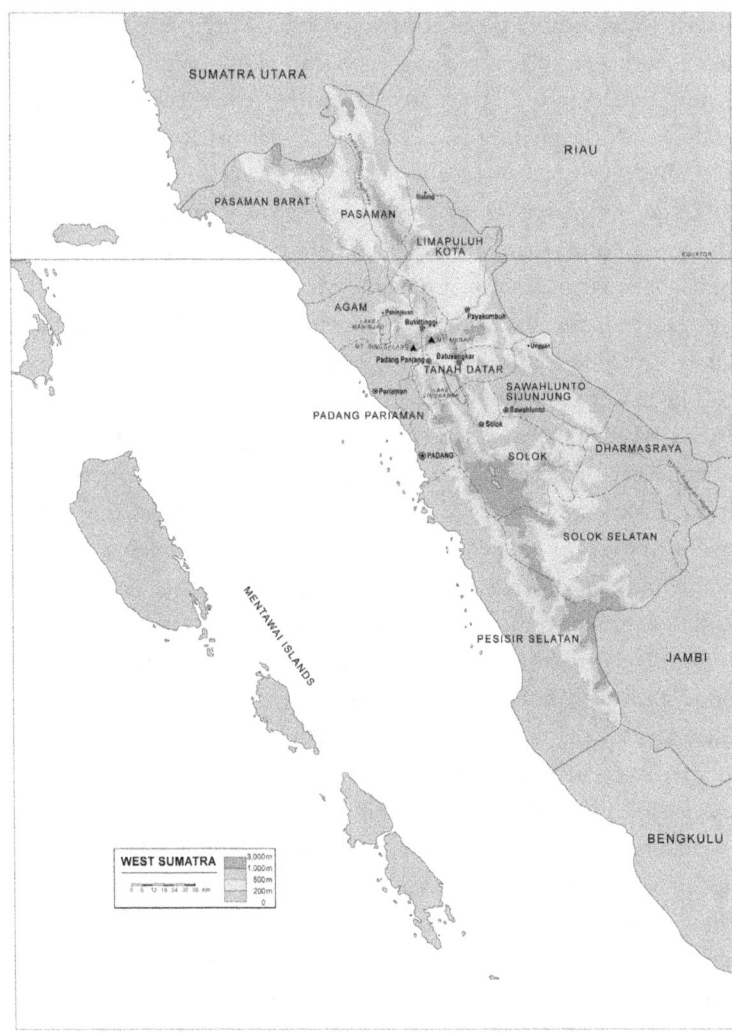

MAP 1.1. West Sumatra. *Source: Jack Thomas. Used with permission.*

provinces, such as Riau (9.77 percent) and North Sumatra (5.06 percent) and major cities such as Jakarta (4.83 percent). The remainder were scattered throughout the archipelago (Suryadinata, Arifin, and Ananta 2003, 54–55). The practice of migration is a cultural institution among Minangkabau people. As Mochtar Naim (1973) explains, the historical practice—known as *marantau* (M, to go to the outlying areas)—was voluntary and temporary, at least in intent. Young men left their home villages seeking experience, knowledge, and fortune before returning to settle down. Migration patterns, however, have shifted since the publication of Naim's seminal text. Today, many people—both men and women—migrate for purposes of employment, education, or marriage; the distances they travel have increased; and the move is often more permanent. There are now generations of Minangkabau people, as Ismet Fanany (2003, 179) points out, who have never lived in the homeland, a circumstance that has helped structure alternative views on being Minangkabau.

For most of the people I work with—regardless of whether they live in West Sumatra or in the rantau—Minangkabau is just one part of how they understand and position themselves in the world, and it is not always the primary aspect. They also identify in relation to the nation, the village or town where they reside, or their ancestral village. Sometimes they invoke a regional or provincial identity. As I explain in the next chapter, they also identify in relation to clans. At other moments people might identify in terms of socioeconomic class, religious or political affiliation, gender, age, or cultural outlook, though not all these identities are cause for collective action and expression.

Moreover, identifying with a particular category does not mean that people understand it in the same way. My host father, Arzul Jamaan, observed that people were quick to identify as Minangkabau but, if you asked them "what that means, what are the particular characteristics of being Minangkabau?" most people would be unable to specify them (pers. comm., 26 July 2010). Or at least they were not able to articulate these characteristics according to his standards, which stemmed from his position as a leader and local authority on *adat* (I, a term typically translated as custom or tradition, but in the Minangkabau case is thought of as a social code). He felt that most people were no longer intimate with this code—really, codes—of behavior that encapsulate the values that Minangkabau men and women should maintain in their daily lives.

To illustrate the point, people often jokingly identified me as an urang awak, one of their own, because I liked to eat *jengkel* (I, a pungent nut), though it is not specifically Minangkabau and is found in other regional cuisines, or because of my attempts to dress according to local standards of modesty. This application of the phrase illustrates the kinds of markers that can be and were used by some people to make assertions of Minangkabau ethnicity. To Arzul Jamaan, dress and food choices are not enough to mark one as Minangkabau: it is the standards of behavior—the values that one holds—that are critical. The point here is that while people's self-understandings as Minangkabau are strong, the habits that underpin and encapsulate what it means to be Minangkabau in the twenty-first century have shifted and diversified (Fraser 2011). Most people simply do not use the same criteria as Arzul Jamaan.

Multiple Minangkabaus

The category of Minangkabau has never been consistent across time. Historically the Alam Minangkabau was quite heterogeneous; there were differences in adat, dialect, architecture, music, dance, costume, and cuisine. The diversity of perspectives and practices speaks to the problem of subscribing to unitary and bounded notions of identity, whether they pertain to ethnicity, class, or gender. Factors shaping the contemporary cultural habits of people identifying themselves as Minangkabau include the place to which an individual traces her ancestral heritage and the place where she resides, along with her gender, generation, socioeconomic class, migration history, educational history, and practice of piety. There are predictable differences in some habits based on place of residence: for example, between a second-generation migrant living in Jakarta; someone who moved from the highlands to the capital, Padang, to work; and someone who was born and continues to live in the village where her family has resided for generations. But it is also important to find a way to discuss the habits they share that transcend locality.

Thomas Turino's (2008) model of "culture" and "identity" that focuses on habits of thought and practice allows analysts to move beyond bounded notions of homogenous practices to get at the points of convergence and divergence in individual lives. I find it useful to think about each aspect of identity as a continuum with a range of possible habits, to accept that an individual's habits can shift over the course of a lifetime, and to acknowledge that the different continua converge in specific—and sometimes unpredictable—ways at different moments in individual lives. These convergences in an individual's life shape her particular worldview and how she understands herself as Minangkabau.

Let me illustrate with a few examples. There is no neat correspondence between piety and economic orientation. I met impoverished people in villages who had practices of piety as strong as those of wealthy people I knew in cities. I know people across the socioeconomic spectrum who are lax about the implementation of the five pillars of Islam. Likewise, not everyone who aligns with a particular socioeconomic class acts in the same way. While the concept of class—defined by relative amounts of income, wealth, education, and political power—might frame experience and delimit habits broadly, this model is too totalizing: alone it does not explain the fluidity of practice, or how habits motivated by socioeconomic factors are inflected by other concerns. For example, a family hosting a wedding in the village of Paninjauan and a family in the town of Padang Panjang who have the same economic resources will not necessarily choose the same kind of musical ensemble. Moreover, while residence in a village versus an urban area strongly influences cultural habits, it would be inaccurate to think of a rigid rural-urban dichotomy. It is possible that someone who resides in Padang has cultural values more akin to those of village residents or that someone in a village has more in common with urban residents because of his economic status. I also find the rural-urban divide problematic because some communities straddle it. For example, Padang Alai is technically a neighborhood of Payakumbuh, a large highland town, but it also feels like a close-knit rural community with life structured around agricultural activity, including rice farming.

One model that helps provoke thinking beyond the rigidity of the rural-urban dichotomy is the concept of cosmopolitanism as outlined by Turino (2000; 2003). Here one's habits are influenced at least as much by orientation to cosmopolitan or indigenous frames as they are by place of residence. This theory—developed as an alternative to globalism, as a way to refer to similarities in cultural habits of thought and practice among particular populations in different countries—offers a constructive heuristic to understand the competing aesthetic, fiscal, and political concerns that shape musical practices. Accounting for habits that undergird individual and collective social action in daily life, the theory allows for individuals and communities with distinct cultural outlooks to coexist within the same society.

The model is concept driven rather than content specific; what constitutes cosmopolitanism in any specific place is constantly evolving. While some habits and practices are shared, they are shaped by the lives of people and cultural contexts they encounter, so that in the end a cosmopolitan formation in one place may not look identical to one in another country (Turino 2000). In this book I use the term *cosmopolitan* to refer to cultural practices that began among political and social elites as the adoption of foreign ideas but have since come to be internalized as their own. Although these practices accrue local markers in the process, they remain firmly within the framework of cosmopolitan ethics and aesthetics. In the Minangkabau case, most of these ideas stem from a modernist-capitalist cultural formation informing modes of economic production in which virtually all Minangkabau are engaged today, along with modes of musical production. I use the term *indigenous* not to suggest the purity of practices predating cosmopolitan influence but as a gloss for practices and lifeways that have roots in, and are primarily anchored to, village life and that people generally identify as older traditions.

These distinctions, moreover, are not rigid categories but frames guiding an individual's way of viewing—and being in—the world. Many Minangkabau individuals incorporate elements of both frames today depending on the situation. For instance, in July 2010 I was at the house of a seventy-year-old talempong musician in Paninjauan. Her son had just come home from Jakarta, where he resided most of the time, because he was seriously ill. He had undergone all kinds of allopathic diagnostic tests (blood work, x-rays, etc.) in Jakarta but as they revealed nothing wrong, he had come home for traditional medicine. The family was making preparations for a divination ritual where a chicken would be sliced open to reveal its internal organs. A *dukun* (I, healer) would then read the organs to diagnose what was wrong with the patient, making a direct correlation between disease in the chicken's organs and disease in the man's. Once the diagnosis was complete, the man would consume the innards and be cured. While I did not get to witness the ritual nor hear of the outcome, what is important here is the fluidity with which he moved between worldviews.

No single factor, then, determines all of one's cultural practices and outlooks. It is the intersection of these continua at particular moments in time that shape—and simultaneously limit—the habits and cultural realities of individual and communal lives. The seemingly myriad ways in which these factors intersect, along with divergent economic, political, and religious histories of the darek and rantau regions, help explain how there are multiple—and sometimes competing—interpretations of the ideas and behaviors that count as Minangkabau values and practices. When people claim identity as Minangkabau they are invoking these ideas and behaviors, but they are not always invoking the same version. One advantage of the cognitive view of ethnicity is that it allows space for multiple ways of understanding oneself, and being understood, as Minangkabau today. My goal here is to understand how that articulation is possible through the engagement with different musical practices.

Minangkabau Commonalities

If there is such diversity of habits and values, what, if any, factors do people who claim to be Minangkabau share? In spite of all the differences, anthropologist Evelyn Blackwood (2000, 25) identifies four areas that are key to defining oneself and being accepted as Minangkabau: 1) matrilineal descent and inheritance practices where one's lineage, and the land and property attached to it, is traced through the mother's line; 2) subscription to the tambo, the mythical origin story of the Minangkabau; 3) the profession of Islam as one's faith; and 4) and the concept of adat. But there are variations within their application, especially the last two.

Virtually all people who identify as Minangkabau profess Islam as their faith, though there are a few exceptions.[4] However, how people engage with that faith can differ radically. I know some people who strictly follow the five pillars of Islam, including prayer five times a day and fasting during Ramadan; I know others who rarely pray and do not fast. Some people drink and gamble while others do not. Individual lives can contain a lively mixture of orthodox, mystical, and pre-Islamic beliefs, such as belief in black magic, the protective powers of amulets, or the use of mantras before chopping down a tree. However, the large majority of Minangkabau are moderate Sunni Muslims whose incorporation of Islam into their daily lives is evidenced through visual, sonic, and other behavioral means, such as the call to prayer resounding across the landscape, women wearing headscarves, and many attending Friday prayers.

The discourse of adat,[5] disseminated and propagated through policies of the colonial and postcolonial state, has been influential in positing conceptualizations of the Minangkabau as unitary, despite the flexibility of the system and diverse interpretations across the Minangkabau region. Isolating groups through the codification of adat law, colonial administration helped establish differentiation on the basis of ethnicity (Tsing 1993, 42; cf. Kahin 1999, 85). Today, people identifying themselves as Minangkabau often invoke adat in their explanations of what it means to be Minangkabau. While *adat* is typically translated as custom or tradition in most Indonesian contexts, in the Minangkabau case *adat* takes on different meanings and is more integral to the value system, as it "refers to a whole body of standards and rules used by the Minangkabau to guide their lives, to structure social groups and social relations, to determine the rights and obligations of individuals and of groups, to select meaningful words to be used in speaking, and to face foreign ideologies" (Manan 1984, 4). Thus, adat can be considered a social code shaping Minangkabau lives.

However, there are variations throughout the region in part because change is not inimical to, but rather a fundamental part of, the system. There are four categories of adat, ranging from the most immutable to the most mutable. Seventy-year-old adat leader Taufik

Dt. Mangkuto Rajo explained that the first two—the laws of nature and of Islam—provide the fundamental basis of the system and are therefore universal throughout the Minangkabau region; the second two are malleable and adaptable to the times (interview 2010). Each *nagari* (M, village federation) shapes these practices according to their needs, leading to considerable diversity. Therefore, despite the malleability of some aspects of adat, the concept is something that all people identifying as Minangkabau share.

Mobilizing Ethnic Identifications

In the cognitive view of ethnicity, it is important to pay attention to *when* and *why* the sense of ethnicity—that is, when the category Minangkabau—is activated and becomes explicit for individuals and for which individuals. As discussed above, not all individuals engage with the category in the same way. For some people, their engagements are explicit. For others, as Rogers Brubaker and Frederick Cooper point out, self-understandings based on an ethnic category "may be tacit... and inform action, without themselves being discursively articulate" (2000, 18). Regardless, for many people I encountered, the label Minangkabau engendered what Brubaker and Cooper describe as an "emotionally laden sense of belonging to a distinctive, bounded group, involving both a felt solidarity or oneness with fellow group members and a felt difference from or even antipathy to specified outsiders" (2000, 19; cf. Barth 1969). In other words, if one affiliated herself with the category of Minangkabau then she was explicitly *not* something else, such as Javanese, Batak, Acehnese, Mentawaian, or Chinese. Two key processes that not only made ethnicity salient for people with whom I worked but motivated them to actively articulate it include their incorporation into the state and the experience of migration, where they encounter other groups.

The incorporation of the Minangkabau homeland into the state of Indonesia has definitively shaped what it has meant to be Minangkabau in the twentieth and twenty-first centuries. It also provides the backdrop against which this story of musical transformation unfolds. Although

West Sumatra is a relatively peripheral province from a geographic standpoint, the political history of people identifying as Minangkabau brings them much closer to the center. They played a key role in the struggle for independence and the initial formation of the new state in the first half of the twentieth century. Minangkabau freedom fighter Mohammad Hatta—better known as Bung Hatta—was initially appointed prime minister of the new state and later became vice president. But the relationship between Minangkabau people and the centralized government has changed since that time. These dynamics have helped shape the articulation of Minangkabau ethnicity.

After independence, Minangkabau people found themselves subject to strategies that increasingly resembled internal colonization by the Javanese (Kahin 1999; Ricklefs 1993). Minangkabau rebels joined other more marginal populations frustrated by this Javanese monopolization of power; the financial and political centralization ushered in partially by the transition from a federation to a unitary republic; and the subsequent undermining of regional political institutions and authority. As Indra Utama, a faculty member at the institute in Padang Panjang and son of its first director, explained to me, the objection of some Minangkabau people to the ways things were developing in the center was linked to their philosophy of egalitarianism (pers. comm., 11 June 2010). Tensions between the center and the regions escalated, with momentum for armed resistance mounting. The central government tried to quell the impending threat of rebellion, in part by manipulating provincial borders. When independence was first declared, the island of Sumatra was designated as a single province. By the middle of 1948, this had been divided into North, Central, and South Sumatra (Kahin 1999, 131). But in 1957 Central Sumatra was subdivided into West Sumatra, Riau, and Jambi, provincial designations that still exist, although some boundaries have since been modified with the establishment of new provinces. This maneuver was an attempt by the central government to undermine the unity of Minangkabau people (Kahin 1999, 184), but the effort to suppress hostilities failed.

A rebel government, the PRRI, was declared on February 15, 1958. The PRRI had headquarters in the Minangkabau highland town of

Bukittinggi, printed its own currency, and even received arms from the U.S. government. The demands of Minangkabau leaders, as Kahin claims, were not separatist in nature but were for equity between the center and the regions, and autonomy in some realms of government. But the rebellion had failed by 1961. At this point the rebels had no choice but to acquiesce to the center and West Sumatra became a region that had no more political clout or special status than Indonesia's many other regions. The failure, Kahin (1999, 229) argues, affected the psyche of Minangkabau people throughout the 1960s.

The rebellion is important for this story because of the political and emotional consequences on people who identified as Minangkabau (Kahin 1999; Ricklefs 1993). By 2003 and 2004, some intellectuals I worked with were adamant that the failure of the PRRI shaped how people expressed themselves as Minangkabau in the following decades. However, most Minangkabau people were inclined to ignore or actively deny this part of Minangkabau history, though the event was significant enough that I find it hard to believe one could have been alive at the time and unaware of it. It is the occasional voices of those people who claim it was significant, along with historical readings, that suggests there is another side of the story to tell. For those in support of this theory, there is a sense that Minangkabau people needed to recoup lost pride, political standing, and visibility within the state, and the arts became a dynamic avenue with which to negotiate a place. At the very least, the failure of the PRRI forms an important part of the historical background behind Minangkabau cultural developments in the 1960s, including the foundation of the institution (chapter 3) and the creation of new talempong styles (chapter 4), along with other political currents that redefined the political order, including the downfall of Sukarno's government, the genocide of suspected communists, and Suharto's seizure of power culminating in the official installation as president in 1967. Today, West Sumatra and people identifying as Minangkabau are fully integrated into the state and nationalist sentiments are strong. From the perspective of the state, Minangkabau people are merely one of Indonesia's constituent populations.

The other key factor activating a sense of ethnicity is the experience of migration. Whether migrating temporarily or permanently, migrants are forced to provisionally differentiate themselves from people they encounter who have different cultural habits and identify with a different ethnic category. As Arzul Jamaan suggested, some people begin to feel Minangkabau only when they move to the rantau. These contact zones activate migrants' interests in their cultural heritage, compelling them to explicitly invoke ethnicity in discursive and symbolic displays. In comparison, ethnicity is more tacit for those living in nagari, who rarely encounter people identifying with another ethnic category. They understand themselves to be Minangkabau, but they do not need to be as explicit in claiming that identity. While talempong in cosmopolitan contexts is often about saying "We are Minangkabau," in nagari contexts it is more about articulating community identity. But first it is useful to define *talempong* along with the pop songs with which it is sometimes combined.

Defining Talempong

Talempong is one of the most ubiquitous musical practices found among people who understand themselves to be Minangkabau. It is found virtually everywhere these people are: in the villages and urban centers of the Minangkabau homeland and as far beyond its borders as Australia and Singapore. Although there are similar gong practices among neighboring people in Sumatra, these traditions are not called *talempong;* for example, in South Sumatra the gong row tradition is called *kulintang* (Yampolsky 1996a). Yet despite talempong's ubiquity, its practice is pluralistic. Depending on the context, the term *talempong* refers to an instrument, ensemble, or style. The instrument most frequently encountered, typically connoted by the term, and the focus of this book is a small, bossed kettle gong made of bronze or, more commonly, a cheaper alloy such as brass that is approximately seven inches in diameter and three and a half inches deep. Individual

FIGURE 1.1. *Talempong,* 17 June 2010.

talempong are arranged into gong chimes: tuned sets of bossed kettle gongs that carry melodic function (see fig. 1.1; webfig. 1.1).

Other instruments referred to as talempong include *talempong batu* (M, stone talempong, a granite lithophone located in Talang Anau, although Uwe Pätzold [2001] suggests the relationship to talempong does not extend much beyond a figurative connection); *talempong kayu* (M, wooden talempong, or a xylophone with fixed or changeable keys and a variety of resonators) (see fig. 1.2; webfig. 1.2); *talempong batuang*

FIGURE 1.2. Nurlaili playing *talempong kayu*, 1 December 2003.

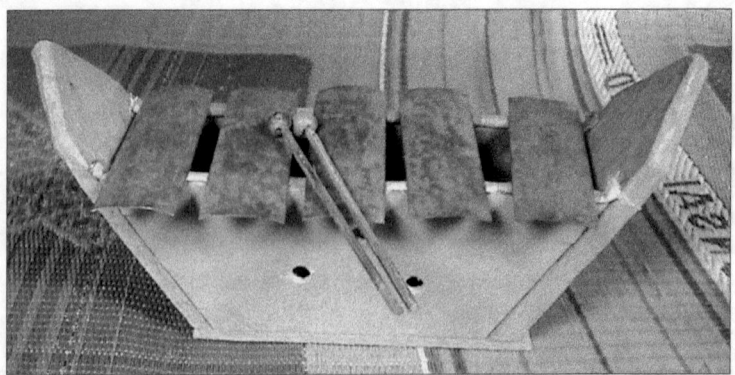

FIGURE 1.3. *Talempong jao*, 1 January 2004.

(M, bamboo xylophone); *talempong jao* (M, Javanese talempong, a metallophone resembling a Javanese instrument called the *saron*) (see fig. 1.3; webfig. 1.3; video 1.2); and *talempong sambilu* (M, a bamboo tube zither) (cf. Hanefi 1999). It is probable that some of these alternative instrument types predate the arrival of bronze culture in the region, but there is not enough evidence to establish an authoritative history. Certainly, the emergence of gong chimes followed the arrival of bronze culture in Sumatra, which Margaret Kartomi (2012, 147) suggests is around five hundred to one thousand years BCE.

During my fieldwork I found that talempong kayu and talempong jao were provisional substitutes for the kettle gongs in cases where the gongs were either not available or explicitly prohibited from being used. As the gong sets are not cheap, they are a relatively scarce resource, and not every musician has access to the instruments. In Paninjauan in 2014 the set resided with the group leader, Yusni, but in the past the group had to borrow the instruments. In Unggan, my teacher, Siti Aisah, either rented the set that was stored in her clan's *rumah gadang* (M, longhouse) for a nominal fee or one from a friend. In 2003 the cost was about Rp 20–25,000 (about US$2). These alternative talempong types were also prevalent in Unggan because of prohibitions against playing the metal gongs, which people there called *talempong gadang* (M, big talempong), along with the accompanying instruments, at certain times during the rice-growing cycle, including when it is first planted and the month or so before harvest. A nagari-wide prohibition was possible because rice is planted according to a calendar determined by the *niniak mamak* (M, male elders) rather than the schedule of individual landholders, as is more common elsewhere in West Sumatra. In Unggan people believed that the instruments were imbued with a sonic power attractive to supernatural creatures from the surrounding jungle. If such creatures were to visit, they would abscond with the yield, leaving nothing for the humans. The elders therefore determined when it was appropriate to play. For example, in September 2004 the provincial governor was planning to visit the village. Some people wanted to include talempong, something for which the nagari is famous, in the ceremonies, but the visit coincided with the prohibition period. People were debating about whether an exception should be made in this case, but the last I heard was that the elders would not permit it, suggesting that adherence to local adat practices prevailed over other interests.

In defining what talempong is today, the key differences are not instrumental but stylistic. Over the course of the book, I lay out the aesthetics—what I define as the system of musical procedures and stylistic characteristics that were permissible, desired, and ultimately ideal in performance (and the converse)—of the major musical styles involving talempong. I begin with styles with longer histories, including *talempong pacik* (M, hand-held talempong) and *talempong duduak* (M, seated talempong) (chapter 2). I then explore the newer styles dating back to the twentieth century, including the experiments of orkes talempong in the late 1960s (chapter 4) that morphed into talempong kreasi baru as it was practiced at the beginning of the twenty-first century. Finally, I consider the latest development, talempong goyang, which draws heavily on repertoire from several popular music genres (chapter 5). While the book traces the way talempong styles have been shaped and reshaped by political and economic forces, it is important to keep in mind that all these styles were actively practiced during the period of my research from 2003 to 2014, with the exception of orkes talempong. The newer styles have not fully replaced the older ones, nor are the older styles necessarily static; in some villages they are adapting to the times by incorporating tunes from local songs and pop songs. In other places, however, the indigenous styles have been lost or are in a state of decline.

The indigenous and newer talempong styles are guided not only by different aesthetics but also by divergent ideological and fiscal logics of participation, practice, and performance that suggest they operate in distinct musical spheres. Nonetheless, there is some conceptual and practical interaction between these spheres. In making choices, musicians and their audiences are complicit in actively excluding and denying other possibilities, though compromises are constantly being negotiated. For instance, at one wedding I attended on 18 March 2004, in Padang Alai, the hosts elected to have *orgen tunggal* (I, vocalists covering pop songs backed by synthesizer, all pumped through massive speaker systems; often and hereafter simply *orgen*) at the main daytime reception, while the local women's talempong pacik ensemble accompanied the processional moments (which overlapped at one moment with the orgen). *Dikia rabano* (M, an Islamic vocal genre accompanied by frame drums) entertained the (mostly male) guests during the evening.

Pop Songs

Pop Minang is arguably the most ubiquitous Minangkabau music today. A brief overview of the genre is necessary because pop songs are part of this story: today there is a range of talempong styles that incorporate pop songs or tunes into the repertoire. The term *pop Minang* has become a catchall for a variety of popular music styles in the Minangkabau language, some of which draw on and incorporate indigenous genres (see Barendregt 2002; Suryadi 2003). My account of the genre relies on the scholarship of others, who disagree over the roots of the genre. As Bart Barendregt (2002, 422) suggests, precise roots are difficult to establish, but the genre might stem from the influence of late-nineteenth-century cosmopolitan popular forms in the cities of West Sumatra, especially Padang, including *gamaik*, the

Minangkabau version of *orkes Melayu* (I, ensembles involving vocalists, violin, a lute called *gambus,* and drums performing harmonized songs). Others, such as prominent Minangkabau scholar A. A. Navis (1984), suggest that pop Minang emerged in the 1940s out of an interest in developing and extending *dendang,* a Minangkabau term used today as both a generic word for a song from any indigenous Minangkabau genre and a reference to a specific vocal repertoire from the darek, a genre called *saluang jo dendang* (M, flute with song). In either case, the term *dendang* is used to differentiate indigenous vocal music from popular forms, such as pop Minang, where a song is called a *lagu,* to use the Indonesian term. There is an implied aesthetic frame associated with dendang: songs are typically in a narrow range of a fifth (occasionally more) and accompanied by some kind of flute or fiddle. I deliberately leave that vague because there is considerable regional variation (see chapter 2). A particular dendang, moreover, is identified by its title and melody, not by the lyrics, which may vary from one performance to the next. In contrast, the pop songs I discuss here tend to have standardized lyrics.

Minangkabau scholar Yon Hendri (2005) lays out three phases of development for pop Minang: 1940s–60s, 1960s–90s, and 1990s–the present, each marked by general differences in style and media. The first period is the most significant for this story. Most scholars agree that as a genre pop Minang really began to crystallize in the 1950s, led by the Jakarta-based band Orkes Gumarang, established in 1953 and directed by Asbon Majid from 1955 to 1964. Philip Yampolsky's 1987 discography of Lokananta, the state-owned recording label, shows that Orkes Gumarang started recording at Radio Republik Indonesia (I, the Indonesian state radio station) in Jakarta in 1957, and songs were released on LP through the Lokananta label in 1959 and 1960. At this time, however, the band's music was not yet categorized as pop Minang. Rather, it was part of a genre invented by the state called *hiburan daerah* (I, regional entertainment), which involved small cocktail-lounge combos performing songs in regional languages within a Western idiom (Yampolsky 1987, 13, 160–61; cf. 1995, 706). Lokananta records, moreover, identified the music of Orkes Gumarang as

"Minang (modern)," in contrast to other Minangkabau recordings in their catalog labeled *klasik daerah* (I, regional classics), which include Orkes Minang Gantosari directed by *budayawan* (I, cultural authority) and author A. A. Navis, and Persatuan Talempong Muda Harapan. It is not clear, however, what these classics involved.

On the 1959 recording Lokananta ARI001, there are eight songs recorded in September 1958, all of which appear to have been previously released as 78s. In the late 1950s, as this recording illustrates, Orkes Gumarang had a definitive Latin sound, playing into the Latin-dance craze popular in cosmopolitan circuits around the world at that time. The band used Cuban rhythms, such as the rumba and the mambo, played on Latin percussion (Barendregt 2002, 424). Even though hiburan daerah used local practices as a source of inspiration, one would be hard pressed listening to the tracks on the 1959 album to identify any markers of indigenous Minangkabau practices other than language. The songs on the album variously feature a female soloist, male soloist, male and female soloists trading off, and same-sex duets in harmony. All but one of the tracks involves male backup vocalists singing in harmony. While Lokananta records list the names of the vocalists (Yampolsky 1987, 160–62), neither the names of the instrumentalists nor the instrumentation is listed. The 1959 recording, however, includes piano as main melodic lead, guitar, upright bass, and percussion, involving maracas, bell, and drums, as fitting with the feel of Latin percussion. A reprinted but undated photo I saw in a local newspaper in 2004 suggests that the percussion included congas and bongos at some point, along with a guiro and accordion, though the latter are not apparent on the 1959 recording I own.

During the next phase of pop Minang's development, from the 1960s through the 1980s, there were two significant shifts: a change of media and a change in stylistic orientation. The growth of the cassette industry in the 1970s shifted the medium from vinyl records to audiocassettes, but also opened up the market beyond the affluent people who could afford the phonograph machines and the discs played on them. Cassettes, in comparison, were cheap. More significantly, they were easily reproducible. According to well-known lyricist, Syahrul

Tarun Yusuf, beginning in the 1960s, pop Minang, like other regional pop musics, began to incorporate stronger references to local markers, including rhythmic, melodic, and poetic material that referenced dendang, along with the use of indigenous instruments, such as saluang (interview, 2010). Yon Hendri (2005, 138) links this stylistic move to the fact that many of the prominent artists of this phase were born and raised in West Sumatra, in contrast to the previous generation, who identified as Minangkabau but were based in Jakarta.

In the third phase, the 1990s through the present, there has been greater diversification of the genre in line with technological developments and music trends, indicated through the incorporation of disco or reggae beats. But as Hendri (2005, 140) points out, these songs have only temporary popularity on the market, constantly superseded by the latest trend. In comparison, the classic songs, what are now called *pop Minang standard,* enjoy ongoing popularity, with recording studios working to release new covers of old favorites. Pop Minang, Suryadi asserts, helps "rearticulate and redefine a sense of 'Minangness' among the members of Minangkabau society." It has done so in part because it has been one source helping solidify a regionally neutral variant of Minangkabau language, which helps people imagine their connections to each other (2003, 66–67). Pop Minang is one way some people make sense of what it means to be Minangkabau in the twenty-first century. This makes it a particularly effective resource for articulating Minangkabau ethnicity when it is combined with talempong.

The Combination of Gongs and Pop Songs

Music has the capacity to reflect on ways of being in the world and actively create new pathways. Particular combinations of tunes, instruments, and tunings are powerful because they can reference previous experiences, though people might experience the same thing in different ways. For example, to some people, the talempong practice from a given village engenders feelings of ownership and pride. For others who may have moved away, it generates feelings of nostalgia.

For yet another group of people hearing the practice as indicative of all things rural and backward, it might generate condescension. Meanwhile, new musical styles have the possibility of creating new ways of thinking and being to those who listen.

In this story, talempong, pop Minang, and dendang all have strong associations with people who understand themselves to be Minangkabau. Each of the gong styles I discuss here incorporated dendang and pop Minang in some way, though not all nagari incorporated these tunes into their local talempong practice. In the analysis that follows I explain the structural features of the music, including the particular ways gongs, pop songs, and dendang intersect in each of the styles. I argue that these intersections help articulate different ways of being Minangkabau in the twenty-first century. Different styles might use the same materials—talempong, dendang, and pop Minang—but the resultant sounds and meanings of the different combinations can vary. For example, even though the same tune is covered by different kinds of gong ensembles, their radically divergent aesthetic frames result in little sonic resemblance between the different renditions of the tune. Take, for example, the dendang "Singgalang ayak kapua" played on the talempong duduak ensemble at a wedding in the nagari of Unggan on 31 December 2003 (audio 1.1) and another version of it played on a talempong goyang ensemble at a wedding by the side of Lake Singkarak on 10 July 2004 (audio 1.2). More important, the distinct rendition of the same tune within different talempong styles creates distinct meanings. Each of these styles comes laden with values that speak to and resonate with different kinds of people. These different styles, as will become evident over the course of the book, have emerged in step with wider cultural, social, and economic shifts.

The Professionalization and Monetization of Minangkabau Music

In addition to the ways that talempong comes to articulate ethnicity, I am interested in how monetary value accrues to it and how it is caught up with processes of professionalization. I pick up on the work of neo-Marxist scholars in exploring the economic dimensions of musical practices (e.g., Qureshi 2002; Stokes 2002). While it is easy to view as commercialization the allocation of monetary value to artistic and cultural practices where none existed before, as communications scholar Joli Jensen (1998, 136) points out the term is not only laden with negative values but widely employed without agreement on its meanings. People often think of commercialized goods and services as being mass-produced, causing artists to sacrifice integrity and social relationships to be lost. *Commodification,* as Holly Wardlow's (2006) work on bridewealth in Papua New Guinea shows, is an equally problematic term. I therefore prefer to use *monetization* in the discussion that follows because I find it a more neutral term to talk about the allocation of monetary value to goods and services, such as music. It is important to consider what terms mean in light of the specific ethnographic context rather than uncritically assume the baggage that comes with the terms used in social analysis.

Historically, Minangkabau economic modes of existence were dependent on a mixture of subsistence agriculture within extended kin networks and small-scale industry (Kahn 1980, 1). These modes have shifted, however, due to an increasing, though by no means all-consuming, dependence on a capitalist economy. A larger part of the workforce than ever before is now engaged in wage labor and small-scale businesses in the interest of economic survival and, ideally, the accumulation of economic capital (cf. Sanday 2002, 64), though almost 50 percent of West Sumatra's workforce is still involved in the agricultural sector (BPSPSB 2009, 68). As a part of these economic shifts, some musical practices have come to acquire monetary value. For example, in chapter 2, I illustrate how talempong musicians in the nagari are paid for their services at weddings. However, because of the way these exchanges are framed, I argue that this is more akin to a gift economy, where people are socially bound through ongoing acts of reciprocity involving the exchange of labor and goods, than a market economy where the cash transaction is primary (Wegman 2005). The musicians and styles encountered in chapter 5, in contrast, are very much participating in a capitalist economy. Moreover, occupational opportunities to carve out an economic existence from this monetization of musical and cultural practices now exist where they did not a hundred years ago. But this process of professionalization requires sensitive ethnographic investigation.

The term *professional* peppers the ethnomusicology and historical musicology literature, but as Henry Spiller (2010, 102) points out there is no consensus on meanings. The treatment of the term remains surprisingly uncritical. Defining a professional as someone who gets paid for providing musical services, often as a primary source of income, in opposition to an amateur, whitewashes substantial differences in the way the term is applied to musicians across time and space (see Ames 1973; Baily 1988; Bauman 1991; Buchanan 1995, 2006; Neuman 1985; Noll 1991; Sargeant 2004; Turino 2000). It is not always *just* about the money received. Adopting the term *professional* in response to any amount of remuneration for a musical service is an oversimplification: it does a disservice to the nuances involved in the ways these musical practices are ideologically framed and the economic systems within which they are embedded (see chapter 2).

I build on the work of scholars who offer a more complex view by suggesting a continuum rather than a dichotomy between professionals and amateurs (Baily 1988; Buchanan 2006). In Marc Benamou's model the "dual criteria of skill and income can be used . . . to establish endpoints on a continuum" (2010, 31). In his study of Sundanese dance, Spiller (2010, 102, 187) provides a great example of why this definition must include both criteria: the professionals—the drummers and the female dancers—are engaged to create a performance environment in which men from the audience can participate. These male dancers may be highly skilled, but as they are paying for the privilege of participating, rather than being paid, they are not considered professionals in the local context, in part because they do not fill the dual criteria. Skill is also a useful marker when there is a range of people engaging in the same practice. Amin Sweeney (1974, 49), in his study of Malay storytellers, for example, argues that in a situation where almost everyone engages with oral literature to some degree, a professional performer must be able to offer a commodity distinct from those of lay practitioners. It is also possible to have skilled performers who do not make any money (see chapter 2).

Nonetheless, I believe the most decisive factor in whether a musician is considered a professional or not is the way the activity is conceptualized and framed within the specific ethnographic and historical context. For example, in his comparative study of two Nigerian groups, David Ames considers most musicians among the Hausa to be professionals not just because they earned money but because of the "extent of their commitment to this line of work." It was the way they thought about it. Their Igbo compatriots were happy to accept gifts, sometimes in the form of cash, but they did not think about the activity in the same way (1973, 258–59). In his study of Malay storytellers, Sweeney (1974, 56) suggests that intention to earn a living through performance is more significant than whether a performer actually does. Like Sweeney, I am interested in this element of intention. It is not just what musicians do, how much money they make, how much time they spend doing it, or even how they are trained that is critical, but rather how they *think* about musical and related cultural activities as a career path or a way to make a living, regardless of whether they can financially sustain themselves doing it. In West Sumatra today there are different kinds of musicians working in a range of genres who identify as and are recognized as professionals. In this book, I am primarily interested in the kind that emerges as a result of the institutionalization of the arts. For this kind of artist, professional status is concurred not so much by specialist skill in a particular art but by virtue of formal training and theoretical knowledge gained.

In summary, *Gongs and Pop Songs* is an ethnography of the vibrancy and complexity of lives as experienced, negotiated, and articulated through musical practices—making music, listening to it, or otherwise engaging with it—among people who understand themselves as Minangkabau at the beginning of the twenty-first century. It tells the story of how one musical medium—talempong—is shaped in different styles that come to articulate different understandings of

Minangkabau ethnicity. By tracing out different styles of talempong, I explore the continuation, evolution, and transformation of habits, logics, and aesthetics surrounding musical practices, helping explain the coexistence of talempong styles with competing aesthetic frames and just why people continue to invest in one style over another. In short, *Gongs and Pop Songs* offers a case study in the ways music expresses ethnic sentiments and the way that expression is shaped by social, political, economic, and cultural currents at the local, regional, and national level.

Chapter 2

TALEMPONG AND COMMUNITY

One Friday in July 2010, I traveled to Paninjauan, a nagari on the slopes surrounding Lake Maninjau, a crater lake, to attend a wedding. The journey from my home base in the town of Padang Panjang required a combination of two public buses and a motorcycle taxi. The views were spectacular as the second bus began the steep descent down to the lake through a series of forty-four hairpin turns (which are celebrated in a pop Minang song, "Kelok 44"), passing rice paddies and fields carved into the hillside (see webfig. 2.1). I got off the bus at the intersection leading into the nagari and took a motorcycle taxi up the hill. I had called Asma, a drum player and my host in the nagari,[1] on her cell phone ahead of my visit, but when I arrived at her house, it was locked up and she was not there. Neighbors who knew who was getting married in this small community of around two thousand people directed me down the hill to where preparations for the wedding were in progress and the musicians were already playing. The taxi driver used the sounds of gongs drifting across the rice paddies to direct us to our destination.

As we pulled up, I saw six women, most of whom were in their seventies, sitting on an old plastic tarp on the concrete porch of house, facing out into the dirt yard with a pile of rubble directly in front of them (see fig. 2.1; webfig. 2.2). A row of six talempong was center "stage." Two women sat behind it. Using four of the six kettle gongs, Mariani played the melody. Rosani accompanied her, playing

FIGURE 2.1. Women playing *talempong* at a wedding in Paninjauan, 9 July 2010. *Left to right:* Asma, Yusni, Mariani, Rosani, Samsinar, Mardiani.

a repetitive pattern on two gongs. They shared one gong between them, the parts they played interlocking so that they never struck the shared gong at the same time. This tune, unlike some others in the repertoire, required just five out of the six gongs. Asma supplemented the talempong parts, playing a double-headed drum, Yusni a frame drum, and Samsinar a tambourine with a plastic frame. Mardiani sat on the edge of the step, playing a large gong hanging from a crude metal frame. She used a young jackfruit wrapped in a plastic bag to strike the gong on the boss and held a fork in her left hand to tap out rhythms to the side of the boss. Each of these supplemental parts had its own repetitive pattern that changed little from one piece to the next. Another woman sitting on a plastic chair off to the side kept time playing a glass bottle with a fork. The six core members were dressed in matching outfits: *baju kuruang* (M, knee-length blouses over ankle-length skirts) and synthetic pull-on headscarves edged with diamanté and other decoration.

The group played from midafternoon on Friday until midnight, breaking at dusk for prayer and dinner. Throughout their performance, they did switch parts occasionally, but only Yusni and Mariani played the melody part, the most challenging one in the ensemble. That night the ensemble played to motivate the women who were cooking mounds of food in the indoor kitchen and makeshift stoves set up in the yard; to welcome the groom and his family, who had traveled from out of town; and as background for the evening's ritual activities, when male family and community members paid their respects and delivered ritual speeches. The next day they played again, playing until late in the evening, stopping at intervals to pray, eat, and rest a little. Over the course of two days, the musicians selected tunes from their repertoire of twenty or so, one rendition of a tune lasting anywhere from a few to fifteen minutes. There was little structural or timbral difference from one piece to the next, suggesting the music was less caught up with entertaining an audience and more concerned with providing a musical backdrop requisite for a festive atmosphere.

Talempong practices in the nagari of West Sumatra are examples of localized, indigenous musical traditions among people who understand themselves as Minangkabau. People's engagement with these gong traditions labeled *talempong*—and not one of Indonesia's many other gong traditions—marks them as Minangkabau, but the practice of talempong in the nagari, as this chapter explains, is less about articulating the broader category of ethnicity and more about engaging with the local community. In addition to discussing the musical style in several nagari, I analyze the social and economic values attached to these practices in order to introduce some of the ways people in the nagari move through their lives as Minangkabau. Later in the book I will discuss very different ways of being Minangkabau. This chapter draws on my ethnographic research in the nagari of Unggan, Paninjauan, and Padang Alai from 2003 to 2014,[2] and is supplemented with my experiences as a student at ASKI in 1998–99 and fieldwork at STSI in 2003–4, along with the scholarship of others, including Philip Yampolsky's (1996) recordings of talempong practices from Unggan and Padang Alai on *Gongs and Vocal Music from Sumatra* (vol. 12 in the Smithsonian Folkways Music of Indonesia series).

Although the talempong styles I discuss in this chapter are contemporaneous with the newer styles I discuss in chapter 5, including talempong kreasi and talempong goyang, they represent an older musical and cultural layer. In some areas, these indigenous styles have declined or become extinct. For example, when I traveled to Sialang in 2004 with my host father so that I could compare the version taught at the institute with the local practice, we found that all the talempong performers had passed on. We did meet the grandson of a man who was a resident artist at ASKI for a year, but he claimed the practice had not passed on to him. We were then directed to the nearby nagari of Durian Tinggi, where there was one surviving person who knew the melodies, but I did not have the correct permission from regional authorities to stay and do work. But in some communities, these older practices continue a vibrant existence. The kinds of people who choose to invest in these older styles over and above the newer ones have very different aesthetic preferences and social values than those who prefer the newer styles. I include discussion of these styles to illustrate the currency, vitality, and significance of these older practices and values for some communities in the twenty-first century. The old has not yet been entirely displaced or replaced by the new. Moreover, the examination of the aesthetic frames of these older styles here provides a basis of comparison that allows me in later chapters to explore how talempong was transformed in response to political and economic conditions over the last sixty years. Unlike the supralocal styles of talempong kreasi and talempong goyang that are about expressing an ethnic identity that transcends internal differences among people identifying as Minangkabau, these practices are deeply localized. They are about creating, articulating, and sustaining local communities established through life in the nagari.

Life in the Nagari

The concept of nagari (a word that refers to both the singular and the plural form) can be defined on a political, geographical, genealogical, and social level. The word's etymology is tied to the Sanskrit for *town* (Anwar 1999, 57). From a political perspective, nagari is the indigenous Minangkabau unit. Historically a nagari was an autonomous unit at the local government level. As Khaidir Anwar (1999, 57) points out, nagari was the highest polity recognized within adat and until the arrival of the Dutch it was arguably the most meaningful polity in Minangkabau life. While some scholars point out there were other polities during precolonial times with wider territorial scope (Young 1982; Drakard 1999), the nagari was usually the most relevant one in people's lives. Colonial rule reordered the political landscape, as did the independent state, undermining the nagari system. In 1979 a national law demanded that the Javanese concept of *desa* (village) became the standard unit across the country, thereby replacing the Minangkabau concept of nagari until the implementation of regional autonomy in 1999, when the nagari system was reintroduced. But there was one significant difference in the return to the nagari concept. In precolonial times nagari were completely autonomous political units; now, however, each nagari was embedded in larger political-geographical units of the *kecamatan* (I, district) and *kabupaten* (I, regency). Moreover, nagari were not necessarily established along preexisting lines. The head of Paninjauan nagari in 2014, Nofrizal Dt. Simarajo, explained to me that following regional autonomy, Paninjauan was combined with two other desa to become Koto Duo nagari. It was not until 2005 that Paninjauan seceded from the unit and was established as a nagari in its own right (interview, 2014). In 2009 there were 568 nagari listed in West Sumatra, a figure that excludes the subdivisions of the seven urban municipalities (BPSPSB 2009, 33).

Nagari are geographically bounded communities involving a thousand to a few thousand people. Residents know each other on a personal, face-to-face level. While it is tempting to translate the concept of nagari as a singular village, it is more accurate to translate it as a federation of villages because there are important internal geographical divisions organized around four or more *suku* (M, clans) (Hadler 2008, 65). These geographical divisions are called *jorong* (M, hamlets). The nagari of Paninjauan, for example, has four jorong: Paninjauan,

Cicawan, Pauah, and Data Simpang Dingin. In Unggan, there is a significant spatial difference between the jorong at the center of the nagari (see webfig. 2.3) and the outlying ones. In 2004 in the center, houses were laid out in a grid with a series of paved streets and cobbled lanes, whereas in the outlying area, houses were more spread out, lining a single arterial dirt road bordering wet-rice paddies (see webfig. 2.4). My hosts in the nagari in 2003–4, for example, were more than a mile walk from the center.

From a genealogical perspective, nagari are close-knit communities with complex kinship networks: as marriage used to be endogamous within a nagari, residents are often related to each other in some way through blood ties or alliances established through marriage. When explaining the interrelatedness of the community, the head of Paninjauan, Nofrizal, illustrated with an example of how he was connected through his wife to Jenni Aulia, a 1987 ASKI and 2011 ISI graduate,[3] who was helping me with interviews and therefore present at this one (2014). I constantly encountered such examples, struggling to keep all the connections straight. For example, two women in the talempong group playing at the 2010 wedding in Paninjauan I discussed above were closely related: even though they were just two years apart in age, Mardiani's grandfather and Asma's father were the same man; Mardiani's grandmother was his first wife, Asma's mother his second (he also had another three wives). Asma's son, Ediwar, now referred to in Paninjauan by his adat title, Dt. Kayo, and Jenni Aulia were also related: Ediwar's *mamak* (M, mother's brother) is Jenni Aulia's father. Therefore, as one inherits clan membership from one's mother they do not belong to the same clan.

People in Paninjauan are aware of both clan identity and their relative kinship to other individuals. Membership in a particular clan and lineage within it structures many elements of life for people in the nagari: it limits who you can marry (marriage is exogamous with respect to clan); the ensuing kinship relationships and social obligations to particular kinds of kin; which clan and lineage leader you can seek for advice; and participation in ceremonies, including invitations to attend or help out. In Paninjauan, each clan also met on a monthly basis. Dt. Parpatiah nan Sabatang, leader of the Caniago clan there, explained that these meetings, which have a religious and educational overtone, were also designed to "bring people closer to each other" (interview, 2014).

Life in the nagari is still based around agriculture. The head of Paninjauan, Nofrizal, estimated that 80 percent of the population were farmers, while the remaining 20 percent were civil servants or in private business (interview, 2014). Rice, as the staple of the diet, is the main crop; wet-rice paddies are laid out in the valleys or terraced into the hilly landscape (see webfig. 2.5). People also grow vegetables and tropical fruits and raise livestock (primarily chickens, goats, and cows). In some nagari, they harvest forest resources or grow cash crops, such as rubber, coconut, cinnamon, coffee, or cloves. Fishing is an important livelihood for those nagari along the coast or near crater lakes, though there also are cottage industry fish farms.

Some nagari are more isolated than others. For example, Paninjauan is just a one- to two-hour bus ride away from Bukittinggi, the second-largest town in the highlands. Unggan, in comparison, located on the border with the neighboring province, Riau, is at the end of a valley system, enclosed by mountains on three sides. In 2004 a small bus went once a day to the nearest small town, hours away via a dangerous mountain road (see webfig. 2.6). When I first visited Unggan in 2003, there was no piped water, electricity, or paved roads. Some people cooked with wood they felled themselves. Even though there was no electricity, the wealthier inhabitants invested in generators to power TVs, complete with satellite dishes. By the end of 2004, electricity and paved roads were on their way.

Historically, the nagari was a primary unit for social identity, as were the clan and lineage affiliations within them. Minangkabau as a social identity, Joel Kahn (1993, 186) suggests, was more significant with regard to claims of the royal family than in the lives of villagers. As John R. Bowen points out, while there have always been multiple ways people have identified connections to others, the concept of ethnicity is new: it "is a product of modern politics" (1996, 4). The following chapters illustrate how a sense of Minangkabau ethnicity was crafted through talempong practices in the second half of the twentieth century in response to such politics.

In contemporary times, if people reside and work in a nagari, their affiliation with the nagari is still a primary aspect of social identity, just as is jorong residence and clan membership. Social life is structured around these affiliations. However, this is not to say that nagari residents do not also think of themselves as Minangkabau. When conducting interviews in the nagari of Paninjauan and Gunung Rajo in February 2014, I asked people which affiliation was more important to them in terms of how they understood themselves: their nagari or Minangkabau? Their initial responses were telling. They often laughed; explaining that both were significant and that you could not necessarily disambiguate one from the other. To be from Gunung Rajo meant that you were Minangkabau. When I discussed adat in Paninjauan with people, we were discussing a part of what it meant to be Minangkabau. In short, all the individuals I worked with in the nagari understand themselves to be Minangkabau.

The relevant question to ask was not whether nagari residents understood themselves to be Minangkabau, but rather what activated a sense of ethnicity for them. Adat was definitely one mechanism. Encounters with non-Minangkabau another. For example, Rugusman from Gunung Rajo explained that how he identified was contingent on his geographical positioning. When he is in Gunung Rajo, there is no need for Rugusman to refer to himself as Minangkabau because everybody there is also Minangkabau. In the nearby town of Padang Panjang, he might label himself as someone from Gunung Rajo, but further away in the provincial capital city, Padang, he might need to say he is someone from Batipuh, a better-known nagari nearby. If he were in Jakarta or Banda Aceh, where most people he would encounter do not identify as Minangkabau, only then would he say he is Minangkabau. In that context, moreover, nagari affiliation is meaningless to most people he would meet. In the United States his identity would become Indonesian (interview, 2014).

There are three things to take away from this explanation: first, claiming any one of these self-understandings by no means excludes the others, but it momentarily becomes the primary or active one; second, identifications based on the nagari appear to function only in a limited radius; and third, a sense of being Minangkabau is activated when encountering people identifying with other ethnic groups. Such encounters, however, are rarely triggers for most people living in nagari where almost all the inhabitants understand themselves to be Minangkabau and, thus, in their daily lives, nagari residents rarely encounter non-Minangkabau. In other words, for people in the nagari their understanding of themselves as Minangkabau is more tacit: they do not need to activate ethnic sensibilities as frequently as people living in more ethnically mixed cosmopolitan contexts. Unlike people in cosmopolitan contexts, they have no need to make self-conscious declarations at their weddings that say, "This is Minangkabau adat, this is how we do things" or otherwise label their practices as Minangkabau. Likewise, they do not choose talempong to explicitly express their ethnicity. They choose it, as I will demonstrate through this chapter, as an investment in the nagari, its values, and its social bonds. Their expression of who they understand themselves to be in the world is not an explicit one about ethnicity but a more implicit one about local identity.

The Expression of Local Identity

The Alam Minangkabau historically contained considerable cultural diversity, including dialect, adat practices, kinds and types of ceremonies, ceremonial costumes, architectural style, and cuisine. Practices could differ from one nagari to the next or they could be more broadly based. There is still an extraordinary degree of diversity in indigenous musical practices throughout the province, one of the richest in Indonesia (Yampolsky and Hanefi 1994, 3). Cultural official and commentator Asnam Rasyid used the metaphor of bamboo to explain this variety: each stem stands separate but is equally important. The reason, he continued, there were so many options was because "we [Minangkabau people] are extremely democratic, everyone has their own [practice]. . . . We don't want this to become one" (interview, 2004).

In the Minangkabau context, some of the differences in musical practices occur at the regional level while others are tied to specific nagari. Musical styles that draw on indigenous or pan-Malay literary forms—respectively, *kaba* (M, epics) and *pantun* (I, a poetic form with rhyming couplets) (see Fraser 2013)—are prominent throughout the Alam Minangkabau. But there are considerable regional differences in performance style, including the accompanying instrument, repertoire, melodic characteristics, and textual factors, including dialect. For example, in *sijobang* (M, a genre found in the highland region around the town of Payakumbuh), kaba were historically relayed to the accompaniment of a matchbox shaken and tapped on the ground so as to create a percussive sound (Phillips [1981] 2009). Now, if it is performed at all, a *kacapi* (M, zither) accompaniment is more common. In the Pasisia, the southern coastal region, kaba are accompanied by the *rabab Pasisia* (M, a four-string fiddle shaped like a violin from that region) (Collins 2002, 2003). There are also regional variants on vocal forms accompanied by flutes. The most prominent live vocal genre today—saluang jo dendang—originated in the darek. The oblique flute used in this genre, just a length of bamboo with a beveled edge on one end, is called the *saluang darek* (M, darek flute). *Saluang,* the generic Minangkabau word used to refer to a range of flutes, is sometimes used to refer to this specific flute. Sometimes the *rabab darek* (M, darek fiddle) is used in this genre to accompany the vocals instead, but it is increasingly rare. Regions outside the darek have their own equivalents of this genre, using different kinds of flutes and textual structures, including the bansi in Solok, the *saluang panjang* (M, long saluang) from Muaro Labuah, and *dendang Pauah* (M, vocals accompanied by a block flute) in the Padang region. All these regional practices are under pressure from the popularity of saluang jo dendang, which now extends beyond its origins in the darek to other regions and has widespread coverage in the music industry.

The sense of place and identities tied to these regional practices are also conveyed through songs and their titles. In the current practice of saluang jo dendang, songs have affiliations with specific places, either originating there or connected through musical material (Yampolsky and Hanefi 1994, 8). When I tracked saluang jo dendang repertoire, I encountered many songs that were imports from localized musical practices, including songs from the genre of sijobang and a series of *suayan* (M, laments for the dead), both from the Payakumbuh region; the genre of *indang* (M, a vocal genre with Islamic associations that uses drumming and movement) from Pariaman; *sirompak* (M, a flute used in the Payakumbuh region for mystical purposes); and local dendang repertoires, such as those from Pasaman or Pesisir Selatan. In performance, singers try to reference a song's place associations through mentioning the place-name in an early verse or using words from the local dialect. Audience members request particular songs to assert a connection to a particular place and its people, related to their own experience, such as a song from their place of origin or their rantau experience (Yampolsky and Hanefi 1994, 8–9). I found songs and genres used in the corpus of recorded media following a devastating earthquake to reference affected areas (Fraser 2013). In other words, vocal genres and songs have the power to reference places and identities connected to them. I will illustrate how the same is true for instrumental styles such as talempong.

Talempong in the Nagari

In the nagari, two main styles of talempong are found. Talempong duduak, the style used at the Paninjauan wedding, is sedentary, as the term *duduak* (M, to sit) suggests. The style features melodies backed by the rhythmic ostinati of other parts that together provide a background groove. Talempong pacik, an entirely portable ensemble, as the term *pacik* (M, to hold) suggests, features a constantly changing rhythmic-melodic weave of parts. In Unggan, this style was also referred as *talempong bararak*, which alludes to its use in processions. Boestanoel Arifin Adam suggests that in the past talempong duduak was common throughout the darek: "Every rumah gadang owned a talempong duduak set, which young girls played to fill their free time" (1990, 54). By 2014 talempong duduak was rare compared to talempong pacik, which is often still key to wedding and other ceremonial processions throughout the province.

These indigenous talempong styles have long histories that predate the institutionalization of the arts, but there is little concrete archaeological or historical evidence to give an accurate history. Kartomi (1998, 600, 608) suggests talempong is among the genres that predate the arrival of Islam in Sumatra at the end of the thirteenth century. In the collective memory of a given community, practitioners and supporters alike claim the styles have passed on from the ancestors generation to generation. But when I have tried to establish how old a particular nagari or talempong practice was, I got vague answers at best. In my experience, most Minangkabau people, and especially those living in nagari, are not terribly interested in either written or oral histories. Time is measured in vague terms, at best. This attitude toward time makes it hard to track changes and developments that extend beyond the lifetime of my interlocutors and often even those changes that occurred within it.

However, in Unggan I encountered a legend that recounts the history of the talempong practice, even if there is no specific timeline to go with it. Over three visits in 2003–4, several people told me the story of how the ancestors brought the practice of talempong to the area, which was illustrated through the titles of twelve or so tunes. My teacher and head of nagari arts at that time, Siti Aisah, told me this story on my second day in Unggan (29 November 2003). In her version, two ancestors—Dt. Indo Puto and Dt. Paduko Alam—were credited with bringing the practice.[4] They set out in canoes from Pangkalan, a nagari near the border with Riau. They rowed downstream and then upstream ("Kancang dayuang mudiak") when they took a wrong turn ("Kancang dayuang ilia"). They came across a procession in Kuntu ("Pararakan Kuntu") and then walked through the forest, startling gibbons ("Siamang tagogau"), stepping on a sharp stick that penetrated someone's foot ("Batang tarunjam") and seeing squirrels twisting about ("Tupai bagaluik"). They kept walking until the nagari of Halaban, where they encountered kin and changed clothes ("Urang Halaban batimbang baju"). Then they walked to Unggan following the Singingi River ("Batang Singingi"), encountering old people looking for mangoes ("Urang tuo mancari pauah") and butterflies flying high ("Ramo-ramo tabang tinggi"). At the mouth of the river they were hot ("Muaro paneh") and then walked through the pass into the area where Unggan is now located ("Buka pintu"). During the course of documenting these accounts, I noticed tune titles and their order often changed with each raconteur. However, the veracity of these accounts is not as important as their telling, which claims a common past and assumes a sense of collective identity. That the raconteurs wanted me to have this knowledge also suggests the importance of the legend.

Talempong pacik and talempong duduak are broad stylistic categories that transcend differences in performance practice from one nagari to the next. The commonalities suggest an indigenous aesthetic that is supralocal, but few people in the nagari think about it in these terms. Mostly communities are engaged with their own talempong practice and have no need to think of stylistic commonalities with other nagari. The only exception to this I encountered was in feedback interviews in 2004, which were designed to elicit commentary on aesthetic preferences by playing a cassette with a range of talempong styles, including both indigenous and cosmopolitan practices. Some listeners remarked on commonalities with talempong practices in other nagari when asked to compare them to talempong kreasi and talempong goyang. For example, my teacher in Unggan, Siti Aisah, expressed a clear preference for the transparent textures of indigenous styles. For the cosmopolitan styles, she found the texture too dense to hear what was going on. This suggests there is a loosely defined indigenous aesthetic. The people quickest to recognize and celebrate the commonalities in indigenous practices are not those directly engaged with them, but outsiders, including people affiliated with the institutions and researchers. Like those before me, there is some value in recognizing the commonalities as a way to help distinguish indigenous practices from the cosmopolitan talempong practices I discuss later. I am very deliberate in my choice of terminology here: I use *indigenous* so as not to conflate these older talempong practices exclusively with rural areas. They can, and do, exist in more urban areas, such as the vibrant talempong pacik practice in Padang Alai, an area on the outskirts of the large highland town of Payakumbuh.

For my interlocutors in the nagari, the differences in how these styles are practiced in each nagari—undoubtedly stemming in part from the autonomy and relative isolation of them in the past—are more significant than the commonalities. The elements that can vary between places include instrumentation (e.g., Which instruments are used and what is their function?); playing techniques (Are the drums played with hands or a stick? Are the gongs hung on a stand or held in the lap? Are the gongs struck with a banana log, a rubber-covered mallet, or a young jackfruit and a fork?); terminology of the ensemble and the relationship of the parts; tuning of the talempong; and the tunes and the structure of pieces, including the melodic and rhythmic material and the tempi. The gendered associations of both these indigenous talempong styles also vary. Talempong groups in the nagari are either exclusively male or female. Talempong duduak is more likely to be performed by women, but there are exceptions, as in Sialang, where it was a male practice. In some nagari, such as Unggan, women play both duduak and pacik forms. In others, the forms are gendered: women play duduak, men play pacik. In Paninjauan, for example, the men play pacik as part of a drumming ensemble called *gandang tambua* during ceremonial processions (see fig. 2.2; webfigs. 2.7–2.10). Gandang tambua (M, a drum ensemble using a flat kettle drum, *tasa,* and a number of large double-headed drums, *dol*) is also found in other nagari around Lake Maninjau and in Pariaman, but in Paninjauan the ensemble also includes an instrument known locally as a *pupuik solo* (M, a rice stalk aerophone with a bell shaped from a coconut palm frond) (see webfig. 2.9).[5] The inclusion of the pupuik, as several people told me, is specific to Paninjauan. It becomes a marker of the local style in the same way that instrumentation in talempong ensembles helps distinguish different nagari. Below I isolate some of the broad stylistic characteristics of talempong duduak and talempong pacik while illustrating differences between specific practices, including instrumentation and tuning.

FIGURE 2.2. *Talempong pacik* as part of a *gandang tambua* ensemble with *pupuik solo* during a wedding procession, Paninjauan, 17 February 2014.

Talempong Duduak

The talempong duduak style features melodies on talempong backed by rhythmic ostinati. A set of five or six talempong is placed on a rack low to the ground to enable musicians to sit behind it. One person plays melodies on these gongs. The term for this melody part, the core of any talempong duduak ensemble, can vary from one nagari to the next. In Paninjauan the women used the verb *manggua* (M, to strike) when inviting me to take the melody part at a wedding in February 2014. In contrast, the women I worked with in Unggan used the term *talempong pambao* (M, bringer of talempong), which is used to mean the person who presents the melody. I also heard several verbs used to refer to the act of playing the talempong: *manggua, manokok* (M, to hit), or *mambuniin* (to make something sound—a verb that is an interesting combination of Minangkabau and Indonesian).

Sometimes in talempong duduak there is a second musician who also plays the talempong. This musician will use one or two gongs, depending on the tune, to play a pitched ostinato. If the part requires two gongs, one of those is usually shared with the melody part (see fig.

2.3; webfig. 2.11: Yusni, with two mallets, is playing the melody; Mariani to her right is playing the ostinato) and the melodies are structured in such a way that interlocking—rhythmic interpenetration—takes place. In Paninjauan, all the tunes I witnessed have this second part, as did the Sialang pieces I learned at the institute. In Unggan,

FIGURE 2.3. *Talempong duduak* in Paninjauan, 10 July 2010. *Left to right:* Asma, *gandang;* Mariani, *talempong paningkah* (first two gongs); Yusni, *talempong pambao* (last five gongs); Rosani, *giriang.*

only a couple of tunes incorporated it. The large majority required only one person playing talempong, including the two tunes you can hear on *Gongs and Vocal Music from Sumatra*, volume 12 (Yampolsky 1996). In all instances with which I am familiar, this second talempong part is called *talempong paningkah* (M, talempong that elevates).

Across the repertoire of the three talempong duduak practices that I know, a tune usually consists of three or more phrases. Most phrases are eight beats long, though there are exceptions, including the tune "Kaja-bakaja" from Sialang, which uses a series of even and odd phrases. In the piece "Tupai bagaluik" (M, Twisting squirrel) from Paninjauan,[6] the piece I will use in the remainder of this section to explain the structure of talempong duduak, there are three main phrases of eight beats each, which I have labeled *a, b,* and *c*. In a duduak tune, phrases are strung together in a particular sequence. Typically, a phrase is repeated at least once before moving on to the next phrase, and sometimes there is a slight variation in the melodic material to allow one phrase to bridge to the next. The sequence is then repeated, making the overall structure of the music cyclical. In "Tupai bagaluik," for example, the usual sequence of phrases in the piece is ‖: a b c b c :‖, though the number of repeats of each phrase is not always consistent. In a recording of the tune from July 2010 (video 2.1), where Yusni was the melody player, three of the first four cycles are structured differently, as you can see in table 2.1.

I prefer not to think of this variation in repetitions as errors, which presumes that there is a correct sequence in the first place. Rather, I think this variation is part of the practice, and the differences are not particularly significant in the context of the music. In Paninjauan, for example, nobody at performances—neither the musicians nor the audiences—keeps track. The larger cycle—the sequence of a b c b c—is repeated until the musicians stop playing the tune, sometimes with a brief ending pattern, sometimes just petering out.

The talempong melody part is combined with several accompanying parts, which together provide a groove. The accompanying parts may include the pitched ostinato of the talempong paningkah, in

TABLE 2.1
Structure of "Tupai bagaluik"

Cycle	Repeats
1st cycle	ax2 bx4 c bx2 c
2nd cycle	ax2 bx5 c bx3 c
3rd cycle	ax2 bx5 c bx4 c
4th cycle	ax2 bx5 c bx3 c
etc.	

FIGURE 2.4. Mardiani playing *aguang* with a young jackfruit, 9 July 2010.

addition to the different rhythmic ostinati or simple timekeeping patterns provided by unpitched percussion instruments. The ostinati are often syncopated, just four or eight beats long. In the Paninjauan ensemble, the *aguang* (M, larger hanging gong, see fig. 2.4; webfig. 2.12) player and the *gandang* (M, double-headed drum; see fig. 2.5; webfig. 2.13) player provide eight-beat ostinati. The *botol* (I, glass bottle; see fig. 2.6; webfig. 2.14)[7] player establishes a constant beat, as do the performers on the *giriang-giriang* (M, tambourine; see fig. 2.7; webfig. 2.15) and the *rabano* (M, frame drum) (see video 2.2). Music example 2.1 provides a reduction of the piece "Tupai bagaluik" (see video 2.1) with the melodic phrases, the paningkah part, and the ostinati and patterns established by the unpitched percussion.[8]

FIGURE 2.5. Asma playing *gandang*, 10 July 2010.

FIGURE 2.6. Samsinar playing *botol*, 10 July 2010.

FIGURE 2.7. Rosani playing *giriang*, 10 July 2010.

| Order of *talempong* on rack (L-R): | 2 4 5 3 1 6 |

PARTS

Aguang

‖: x o̅x̅ x x G o G o :‖

Botol & Giriang

‖: x o x o x o x o :‖

Gandang

‖: R L̅R̅ L R R L̅R̅ L R :‖

Talempong Paningkah

    a: ‖: 1 o 6 6 1 6̅6̅ o 6 :‖

    b:* ‖: 1 o 6 6 6 6̅6̅ o 6 :‖

Talempong Pambao

    a: ‖: 5̅4̅ 3̅5̅ 5̅5̅ 5̅5̅ 5̅5̅ 4̅3̅ 2 2̅3̅ :‖

    b: ‖: 3̅4̅ 3̅3̅ 3̅4̅ 3̅2̅ 3̅4̅ 3̅3̅ 2̅1̅ 2̅3̅ :‖

    c: ‖: 3̅4̅ 3̅3̅ 2 2 2 2̅1̅ 2 2̅3̅ :‖

aguang: x = fork struck on side of the gong, G = boss of the gong
botol/giriang: x = stroke
gandang: L = filler stroke on left-hand head with hand (these are unaccented), R = stroke on right-hand head (these are accented)
*: this *paningkah* pattern is played when the melody switches to phrase c
bold: numbers in bold may be dropped for variation

MUSICAL EXAMPLE 2.1. The "Tupai bagaluik" melody with *talempong pambao* and the supporting parts.

While this example illustrates how talempong duduak works in one nagari, it is important to remember the differences in tuning, melodies, instrumentation, playing technique, and gender associations between nagari. For example, ensembles in Paninjauan use five or six talempong depending on the piece, which are shared by the melody and talempong paningkah parts. The ensemble is supplemented with one gandang played with hands, a hanging gong played with a fork or spoon for striking the face of the gong, and often a young jackfruit for the boss, a tambourine, a frame drum, and a bottle. The musicians are all female. In Unggan, in comparison, where women also play, there are only five talempong. Some, but not all, of the pieces involve paningkah. A pair of gandang—there called *gondang*—is used and the two drummers use sticks in their right hands, executing patterns that interlock with each other. The parts are called *gondang pambao* (M, drum that bring the basic pattern) and *gondang paningkah* (M, drum that elevates that basic pattern), with the pambao pitched slightly lower than the paningkah. An aguang, there called an *ogung,* a third the size of the one in Paninjauan, is held on the lap and played with a piece of stem from a banana plant (see video 2.3). In December 2003, I heard that some talempong groups there had been experimenting for the last year with incorporating a tambourine and what they called, using the English term, a *piano*, by which I think they meant a small, battery-powered keyboard. One talempong player claimed it improved the practice, but I never actually witnessed this lineup. Talempong duduak in Sialang, in comparison, had been a male practice, the only male form of duduak I ever heard about. The tunes I know involved six talempong; there were always two interlocking talempong parts; two gandang were played with sticks in the right hand, the parts requiring interlocking; and there were two hanging gongs.

Another significant element distinguishing talempong practices from different nagari is the tuning of the gongs. There are no Minangkabau conceptual scale types that inform the tuning of instruments, such as the *slendro* and *pelog* concepts used in Java and Bali that set up a series of approximate interval sizes into smaller and larger ones, even if the realization of those interval sizes can vary considerably. Table 2.2 illustrates the diversity of tunings in talempong duduak practices of the three nagari I discuss above with regard to starting pitch and intervallic structures.

However, these tunings are from recordings made at a particular moment in time,[9] and in that respect should not be taken as the norm for that nagari from which other tunings deviate. In my experience, musicians in the nagari take a very informal approach to tuning, meaning that there is considerable variance in what they consider appropriate at any given moment (cf. Kartomi 2012). Musicians within the one group express different preferences, trading out one gong for another. Moreover, tunings sometimes changed between sets of

TABLE 2.2
Talempong duduak tunings from three *nagari* with absolute pitch

	Reference	f#	g	g#	a	a#	b	c'	c#	d'	d#	e'	f'	f#	g'	g'#
Unggan 2003	Cent offset							+3			−18	−11	−31		−78	
	Pitch							•			•	•	•		•	
	Interval size								248		106	180		240		
Paninjauan 2010	Cent offset						−21	+42		+37		−30	+4		−9	
	Pitch						•	•		•		•	•		•	
	Interval size							148	195		133	133		187		
Sialang	Cent offset	+50			−10		−70		−5	−10			+5			
	Pitch	•			•		•		•	•			•			
	Interval size		240			280		125		95		315				

instruments within a nagari or between visits. Table 2.3, illustrating intervallic structure, reveals some of these differences within a nagari. Note the differences, for example, between the four recordings from Unggan and also between the two from Paninjauan.

Table 2.3 also illustrates that none of these tunings is close to a diatonic scale,[10] where whole- and half-step intervals are measured in two-hundred- and one-hundred-cent units, respectively. This fact is particularly fascinating in the case of Unggan, as my teacher, Siti Aisah, used the solfège syllables do, re, mi, fa, and so to refer to the tuning of the talempong,[11] but the diatonicism suggested by this terminology is not borne out in the recordings. There are a number of factors, however, that suggest musicians in Unggan in 2003–4 were aspiring toward it: the use of solfège; the incorporation of instruments, such as the "piano," that offer diatonic possibilities; and the adoption of repertoire predicated on it, which I will discuss below. The relatively flexible approach to tuning and the distance from diatonicism is part of an indigenous aesthetic relating to talempong, differentiating these talempong duduak practices from the cosmopolitan styles predicated on diatonic and chromatic scales. For a nagari, its distinctive tuning system was one way of maintaining community identity through the talempong practice.

Talempong Pacik

Talempong pacik shares some aesthetic qualities with talempong duduak, such as tuning systems outside diatonicism, cyclical forms, interlocking parts, and nagari variation, but the structure of the music is different from that of talempong duduak. The set of five to seven talempong are divided among three (or four) performers, with each performer carrying one or two gongs in his or her hand (see fig. 2.8; webfig. 2.16). Each part features a distinctive, pitched rhythmic ostinato that in some cases may vary over the course of performance. In combination, the rhythms are aligned in such a way that the parts interlock.[12] Like talempong duduak, the names of the parts vary between

TABLE 2.3
Intervallic structure of *talempong duduak* tunings from three *nagari*, illustrating variation within a *nagari*

Size of intervals

	•	•	•	•	•	•	•	•
Diatonic Major	200	200	100	200	200	200	100	
Paninjauan '10	162	195	133	133	187			
Paninjauan '14	65	193	203	248	81			
Sialang	240	280	125	95	315			
Unggan '03	248	106	80	240				
Jao1	161	157	145	159				
Jao2	237	107	120	236				
Jao3	137	157	126	177				

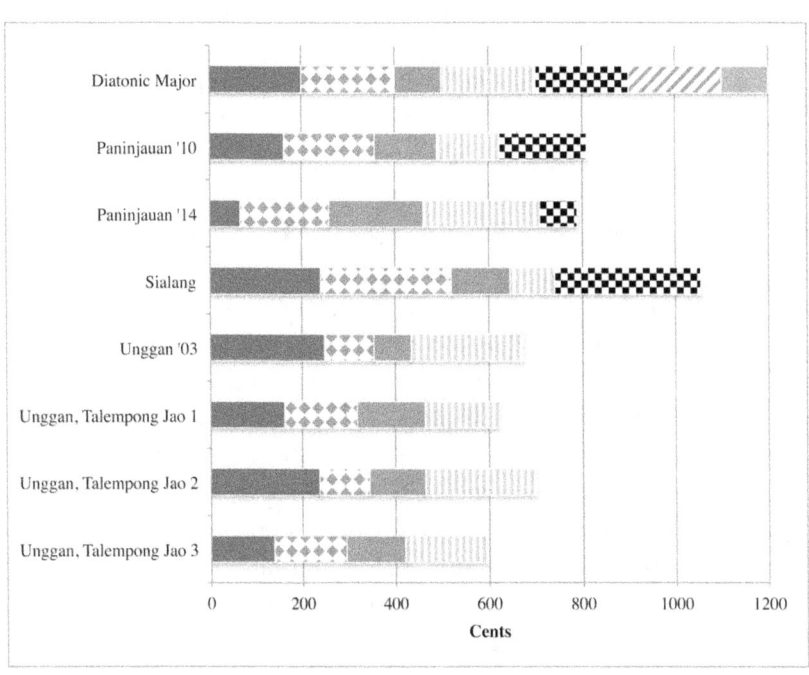

FIGURE 2.8. *Talempong pacik* in a wedding procession in Pesisir Selatan, 1999.

nagari. Depending on the nagari and the gender of the performers, the ensemble is augmented with other instruments.

In Padang Alai, where only women play talempong, the pacik ensemble includes six talempong divided among four players, a unique lineup, as pacik ensembles typically involve just three players. Two parts, the *polong* (M, channel) and *saua* (M, interlocking), involve two talempong, and two parts, the *tingkah* (M, elevator) and aguang, involve just one. The use of the term *aguang* suggests that this part might have been played on a different instrument in the past; however, it is unlikely to have been a large gong because of the challenges of carrying one in processional style, but rather a *tawak-tawak,* a smaller and lighter gong once used to announce the call to prayer in nagari life (pers. comm. with Gantiwarnis, director of the group; Wisma, artistic leader; and Hanefi, faculty member at ISI, 5 February 2014). The talempong ensemble is supplemented with a small double-headed drum. When the group plays for sedentary occasions or events outside the community, they also incorporate an instrument, the *sikatuntuang,* a wooden plank struck by poles that alludes to the mortar and pestle used for pounding rice (see video 2.4).

In Bungo Tanjueng, where men play, in contrast, the ensemble involves five or six talempong (depending on the piece) split into three parts. I have heard two different systems for naming the parts: 1) *jantan* (I, male), *batino* (M, female), and *panyaua* (M, the interlocker) (Hanefi et al. 2004) and 2) jantan and batino (referring respectively to higher and lower pitches of the part, just jantan if there is only one pitch used), paningkah, and panyaua, from Elizar, a faculty member who is from this nagari and taught this style at STSI in 2004. The talempong are supplemented by a rabano, a *rapa'i* (M, small frame drum with jingles), and a *pupuik batang padi* (M, rice stalk aerophone with a bell shaped from a coconut palm frond). The panyaua player is expected to vary his part throughout the piece.

The variations in the practice of talempong pacik and talempong duduak—that is, in the instrumentation, the tuning, the tunes, and so forth—from one nagari to the next are a way of marking and expressing localized identities, like differentiations in adat, dialect, or ceremonial costume. The use of five talempong tuned a certain way, playing "Tupai bagaluik," accompanied by two interlocking drums and a gong held on the lap is what it *sounds* like to be from Unggan, but not Paninjauan or Sialang. For Unggan residents, they have shared experiences hearing these sounds at previous weddings and other community events. To someone new to talempong or to cosmopolitans distanced from these practices, the differences between the style of one nagari and the next might seem inconsequential. But to the communities involved they are significant. This was evident in the feedback interviews in Unggan in 2004, where musicians and other community members were quick to point out stylistic differences between the nagari, suggesting the differences outweighed any parallels. Playing the same selections in Paninjauan, the women I was interviewing identified practices as *awak* (M, ours) or *indak awak* (M, not ours) and expressed a strong preference for their own talempong practice. For example, when listening to the talempong pacik practice from Padang Alai, they said it was boring: there was nothing interesting to which one could listen (interview with Asma, Jenni Aulia, Mardiani, and Yusni, 2004). One might surmise from these conversations that people invested in their community feel strongly about the ways it sounds to be from that place.

The Changing Repertoire

The ability of these practices to represent a nagari community, however, does not mean that are completely static. Musicians in some nagari choose to incorporate pop songs and dendang into the repertoire of both talempong pacik and talempong duduak ensembles. While the adaptation of these tunes to talempong might seemingly encourage a shift toward the diatonic tuning of the instruments (albeit within the span of a fifth or sixth), at least in the Unggan case, as illustrated above (see table 2.3), this does not happen in practice. Moreover, the structure of the music continues to emphasize an indigenous aesthetic with rhythmic ostinati, including interlocking, when appropriate to the nagari, maintained in the unpitched percussion parts.

When pop Minang songs or dendang are adapted to talempong pacik ensembles, the melodies are divided up between players in a hocketing fashion. Each performer still holds one or two gongs, but a performer will only play when the pitch he or she is holding is required in the melody (Hanefi et al. 2004, 37–42). The music is more melodic in character than typical talempong pacik pieces, which emphasize rhythm. The parts on the supporting instruments continue to involve ostinati that combined together supply an underlying rhythmic groove. In comparison, the incorporation of pop Minang and dendang tunes into talempong duduak entail a less drastic adjustment of playing technique, except, perhaps, for the arrangements of the gongs, which become more scalar (i.e., arranged from high to low pitch). While the melodic contour of a tune is explicit in these covers, the accompanying drums and gongs maintain consistent rhythmic patterns akin to other duduak pieces throughout, making the overall aesthetic frame sound decidedly indigenous. The instrumentation choices and rhythmic patterns used in these talempong adaptations of pop songs continue to mark locality while potentially contributing to a greater homogenization of repertoire as different ensembles cover the same tunes (Salisbury 2000, 203).

One of the nagari open to incorporating new tunes is Unggan. In addition to the twelve or so tunes labeled as *original*, the repertoire includes an expanding corpus of newer material. In 2003, Siti Aisah listed twenty-six new tunes, mostly a mix of well-known dendang and pop Minang songs. When I visited Unggan in 2010, she played me an example of a *dangdut* (I, a kind of Indonesian pop music) tune, "Kucing garong," adapted to talempong, suggesting that Unggan's repertoire of songs is constantly expanding. In 2003 she indicated that the incorporation of songs from pop and other genres dated back to the 1980s, when a government official asked for a cover of a particular song. The musicians in Paninjauan, in contrast to Unggan, do not incorporate any new material—either dendang or pop Minang—into the talempong repertoire. They did, however, play some familiar dendang and pop tunes when shifting to an alternate ensemble format to

FIGURE 2.9. Alternative ensemble in Paninjauan, 17 February 2014. *Left to right:* Samsinar, tambourine; Mardiani, gong; Asna, harmonica; Yusni, frame drum; Rosani, *botol;* Mariani, *botol;* two additional players, names unknown.

Talempong and Community

take a break from talempong at a ceremony. This alternative ensemble features a harmonica, what they call the *sarunai bibia* (M, lit., sarunai of the lips), in the place of talempong, which is backed by all the other instruments (see fig. 2.9; webfig. 2.17). For example, I heard them play the pop Minang song "Malam bainai" at a wedding in February 2014. They recorded that tune, along with some others, for me in 2010 (audio 2.1). So it is not that these women in Paninjauan were not interested in this pop repertoire but rather that they had no interest in incorporating it directly into the talempong ensemble, unlike the women in Unggan.

The incorporation of pop Minang material into indigenous talempong styles has led to heated opinions—often coming from people who are invested in notions of authenticity, rather than the practitioners themselves—about what material should count as traditional. Those people who favor endorsing older tunes, which are deemed more authentic than the newer ones incorporating material from pop Minang and dendang, include government officials from within the nagari; officials who work in departments dealing with some combination of tourism, arts, or culture; and academic musicians from the institutions. For example, Siti Aisah told me that when her group performed for the regent of Sawahlunto-Sijunjung on Independence Day, 17 August 2004, they were later instructed by officials from the local Department of Tourism, Arts, and Culture that in the future the group was forbidden from using the keyboard in the ensemble and playing dendang tunes. They should play only the original repertoire; the twelve tunes recounting the founding of the nagari. Ironically, as her husband, Jasril, told me, people from Unggan like the incorporation of the keyboard: they feel "it is more sophisticated, it elevates the art" (interview, 2004). They also like the dendang tunes. There is an interesting tension, then, between outsiders telling the community to preserve their traditions and the desire for change being generated internally. It has led to a bifurcated practice: in 2004 the women played the original tunes when playing outside the nagari and included the newer imports for ceremonies within the community. Regardless of the repertoire they incorporate, talempong ensembles in Unggan and Paninjauan continue to play at weddings and other community events. Weddings and the talempong ensembles engaged at them help engender and bolster feelings of community.

Celebrating Weddings in the Nagari

Weddings are a major rite of passage in Minangkabau life. They involve both rituals required by Islam, where the couple are married in a mosque in a ceremony witnessed only by close family and officials, and those required by adat, which can entail a complex series of events that vary across nagari (cf. Blackwood 2000; Sanday 2002). Minangkabau marriages do not just establish a partnership between two individuals but also alliances between their families. The series of adat rituals are designed to ratify the new alliances, reinforce old kinship relationships, and situate the couple within the community. Weddings, lasting anywhere from a day to several depending on financial resources,

FIGURE 2.10. Wedding procession in Paninjauan, 16 February 2014.

typically include a series of processions, ritual meals, and the *baralek* (M, main ceremonial reception).

During the peak wedding seasons, including the two months before Ramadan or after Lebaran (I, celebrations at the end of Ramadan), nagari are alive with the sights and sounds of ceremonial activity (see fig. 2.10; webfig. 2.18). In Unggan the wedding season follows communal harvest because that is when the prohibition against playing talempong, out of fear that the sounds will attract supernatural spirits, is lifted. My first visit to Unggan, in November 2003, occurred during a period of prohibition. Siti Aisah explained to me then that ceremonies are better with talempong, so families wait until after the harvest so they can have talempong at their weddings and other life-cycle ceremonies. I returned to Unggan a few weeks later, after the harvest, to witness this period. I attended a wedding for which Siti Aisah was engaged to direct the music and dance component of the procession and heard sonic evidence of several additional ceremonies in progress, the sounds of talempong drifting throughout the neighborhood.

Minangkabau weddings are occasions not to be missed: the closer the familial and friendship ties to the bride or groom and, equally (if not more) important, their parents, the more critical that one attends to fulfill ritual and social obligations. Guests attend to bear witness to the union, acknowledge the passage of the bride and groom from childhood into adulthood, and reaffirm their social relationship with the families hosting the wedding. Weddings mobilize large numbers of people: extensive kin relations, neighbors, and, if the couple or their parents have connections outside the nagari, friends and colleagues from that world. Close kin who have moved away from the nagari return if they have the economic resources to do so.

Minangkabau kinship networks are complex: distinctions are made between an individual's maternal and paternal relatives, and then between consanguinal relatives (people born into the family) and affinal relatives (people who married into the family). Weddings necessitate the involvement of extended kin, including the *bako* (M, the bride's paternal family); the bride's maternal female relatives (her sisters, mother, grandmother, aunts, and female cousins by birth);

her mamak; the wives of the mamak; the *sumando* (M, the men who married the sisters and mother of the bride and her mother); and the *sumandan* (M, wives of the bride's brothers and cousins). Who does or brings what differs according to the relative position of kinship (see Blackwood 2000; Klopfer 1999; Sanday 2002). For example, the bako are responsible for providing ceremonial clothing, while the bride's maternal family hosts the baralek. Historically, marriage was both exogamous with regard to clan and endogamous within the nagari, meaning that marriage alliances tightly knit the community together. But as people have moved for education or work, the range of potential partners has expanded. Alliances now stretch to neighboring or more distant nagari and even across lines of ethnic identification. For example, all three of the weddings I witnessed in Paninjauan in February 2014 involved spouses who were exogamous to the nagari. Two of those couples met in other Sumatran provinces.

Processions

Wedding processions are visual and sonic spectacles. At the wedding in Unggan on 31 December 2003, the couple was dressed in matching ceremonial outfits at the house of the groom's bako. Female kin from that side of the family gathered at the house, along with their children. Some kin were dressed as ceremonial attendants; the others in their finest dress. The processional route descended down a hill by a rough dirt track to pass through the center of the nagari—indicated by administrative offices, the market, and the mosque; across a rickety bridge with holey wooden slats; and ambled up and down the streets of the nagari, some paved, some dirt, before arriving at the groom's maternal home. You could hear other celebrations in progress in the background. Some women carried on their heads plastic or enamel tubs filled with wrapped gifts; others carried nylon parasols to shade themselves from the hot midday sun. The bridal couple was sheltered with parasols ceremonially decorated for the occasion. Three adolescent girls led the procession by performing an ambulatory version of *tari piriang* (M, the plate dance; I, *tari piring*). They held ceramic plates in each hand, performing a simple walking step and a series of patterns with their arms, variously lifting the plates up and down or twirling them around. They wore rings on each hand that they clicked against the side of the plates rhythmically. A talempong pacik ensemble was embedded in the middle of the group, with three women dividing the five talempong between them, followed by two women playing double-headed drums slung over one shoulder, using a stick to strike the head, and a sixth woman carrying the gong in the crook of her arm. The musicians were all kin of the groom. When the procession periodically halted over the course of the route, the talempong ensemble used these opportunities to change tunes (see video 2.5). Moving at a slow pace, the whole procession took more than half an hour.

Processions, predominantly a female activity, function to tie different kin groups together (e.g., the bride's paternal family with her maternal one, or her maternal family with the groom's family) through the exchange of food, words, and cloth when the processional group reaches its destination (Klopfer 1999). The number and nature of processions is dependent on the adat of the nagari, the participants in any given procession differing according to its function. For example, Siti Aisah and Jasril told me that in Unggan, when resources permit, weddings involve four processions spread out over two days. Each household that is the destination of a procession provides a ritual meal, often accompanied by the sounds of talempong duduak used to welcome the guests and energize the cooks. On day one, the bride is escorted by her bako to her maternal home, where the visitors are welcomed with a meal. There is a parallel procession and reception for the groom. On day two, there is a procession to pay homage to important kin on the bride's mother's side; then that evening the couple processes together for the first time to the bride's maternal home. If the resources are limited, as in the wedding I described above, activities are condensed into one day and there might be just one procession (interview, 2004).

In contrast, there were three processions in one day at a wedding I attended in Padang Alai in March 2004. Each procession was accompanied by the local talempong pacik ensemble, of which one of the bride's grandmothers was a member. The first procession, staged in the morning, was called the *bararak bako* (M, lit., to process with the bako) where the female bako delivered the bride (and the groom), after having dressed them in ceremonial clothing, to the bride's maternal home for the baralek (see video 2.6). The visitors were received by the maternal relatives and served a meal. The second procession, in the early afternoon, involved female relatives processing to the groom's house to collect uncooked rice. Held late at night, the third, called *manjapuik marapulai* (M, lit., to collect the groom), involved male and female relatives of the bride's maternal family processing to the groom's house to deliver ritual gifts. They were invited in to share a meal, after which they presented the gifts—including betel, money, cigarettes, and clothes—in exchange for the groom, an act negotiated through ritual speech. The visiting party then escorted the groom and his family to his new home at the bride's mother's house where they were welcomed in and shared a meal.[13] The following day there also were events at the groom's house, though I did not witness these.

Food plays a key role in processions through gifts conveyed by the visitors and shared meals offered by the receiving party (cf. Klopfer 1999). The content of the gifts and the method of displaying them are specific to the community. In Padang Alai, for example (see video 2.6), the female bako carried multitiered trays laden with brightly colored bundt cakes, sweets, fruit, and decorations, including plastic figurines of a Caucasian bride and groom, vases of plastic flowers, strings of electric lights that flashed when plugged in, and music boxes. A woman's offerings were on display for all to see, both during the procession and then at the baralek, where they were laid out on the floor. This is markedly different from Unggan (video 2.5), where women bought wrapped gifts in large plastic or enamel tubs. In yet other locations, such as Ombilin, a nagari by the side of Lake Singkarak, in July 2004, I saw offerings enclosed with elaborate ceremonial coverings and fabrics. The style of covering and conveying gifts is a marker of local identity.

As much as processions are visual spectacles, they are also sonic events: some kind of music is used to accompany the processional party on their travels. Talempong pacik is one of the most common styles used, but there are also communities that use local drum ensembles, such as gandang tambua in Paninjauan,[14] a brass band I saw once in Padang, or even electronic instruments plugged into a portable sound system carried in a wheelbarrow, as I have seen in photos by Edy Utama. The processional routes between one home and another are up to a mile long (motorized transportation is introduced for longer distances), the sounds dispersing throughout the processional route to publicize the ritual activity and draw the surrounding community into the celebration. But music is not just enhancing the ritual activity; it is also constitutive of the ritual itself and a marker of local identity. Processions in Unggan and Padang Alai, for instance, sounded different through the differences in instrumentation, tunes, and tuning in their talempong pacik ensembles, these ensembles sonically marking the boundaries of the communities.

The Baralek

The main purpose of the baralek is to formalize and celebrate the new union in front of guests, explained by a Minangkabau aphorism: *bagalanggang mato rang nan banyak* (M, to be witnessed in the eyes of many people). If there is just one wedding celebration, usually the bride's mother's house is the locus of the baralek, where the bride and groom sit on display and the invited guests—extended family, neighbors, and other friends—attend to recognize the union. When resources allow and especially when marriages extend beyond the nagari, there are two sets of celebrations: one at the bride's home and a parallel one at the groom's. These receptions can last a day or more. The home is specially prepared for the event: all the shared living spaces are stripped of furniture, walls knocked down in the most extreme cases, carpets or mats laid over the floor, and a *palaminan* (M, bridal alcove) installed in the front room of the house. The new union is formally displayed: the couple, attired in ceremonial dress, sits in state on the palaminan, receiving guests throughout the day. The simplest palaminan I ever witnessed was in Unggan: a covered mattress on the floor with velvet ceremonial hangings framing the cubicle. In the most common, a throne is flanked by decorative elements laden with symbolic meaning, including ceremonial umbrellas and miniature structures iconic of rice barns. The ceilings and walls are covered in brilliantly colored glossy fabrics.

Unlike weddings in the United States, the guests are not all there at the same time; they arrive sporadically throughout the day. In Paninjauan mostly women attend the baralek. In Unggan, I was told women attend during the day, men in the evening. The most common method of inviting guests in the nagari is an invitation by *siriah* (M, betel leaf), though occasionally *undangan* (I, invitations, typically printed) are also used. It is telling that Indonesian is the language used for the printed invitations: in both Paninjauan and Unggan, undangan are used when government officials or other people from outside the community are invited. This was the case in the second wedding I saw in Paninjauan, in February 2014, where the bride, a nurse who worked in the nearby town of Lubuk Basung, was marrying a man from there: her colleagues would have been invited with an undangan, while everyone in Paninjauan was invited by siriah.

When a woman goes to a baralek, she brings a gift, often involving foodstuffs. What constitutes the gift depends on the customs of the area but also serves to mark a woman's social proximity to the hosts and the method of invitation. Taking a gift helps maintain *silaturahmi* (I, from the Arabic; friendship, close relationship). The most common gift I witnessed at weddings in the various nagari was *beras* (I, uncooked rice), which was usually placed in a bowl and wrapped in cloth (see webfig. 2.19). Ernida, my host in Paninjauan in February 2014, shared a Minangkabau aphorism explaining the concept: "*bajalan babuah bati, malenggang babuah tangan*" which effectively means walking somewhere with hands swaying, which happens as women walk holding their gifts in their right hands by the knot in the cloth used to wrapped the bowls of rice (see webfig. 2.20). During that visit to Paninjauan, several people explained the gift system to me: when invited by siriah, the usual gift is uncooked rice; when invited by an undangan, the custom is to bring a wrapped gift or an envelope with money (see webfig. 2.21). There are some exceptions to these standards, however, for particular categories of kin. The in-laws should ideally give the couple two coconuts in their husks so that they can be planted and their fruit will help sustain the new family. The bako bring cloth, ready-made clothes, other wrapped gifts, or an envelope with money. As the head of Paninjauan, Nofrizal, explained, the bako are expected to bring more substantial gifts than ordinary guests at a wedding (interview, 2014).

Significantly, the gift is *dibalas* (I, paid back). Often the return gift is glutinous rice (for more details, see Klopfer 1999; Sanday 2002), but in Paninjauan cooked rice and *cubadak hitam* (M, a kind of jackfruit curry) was also common. At the 2004 Padang Alai wedding, the bako took home many of the cakes they had bought as gifts. I was deeply perplexed by this action until I realized it was a ritual exchange that cemented the connections between kin. Exchanges of foodstuffs such as these are at the core of a gift economy; the ongoing acts of reciprocity bind people together socially. As Nofrizal explained to me, illustrating with an exchange during Lebaran it was not so much about balancing the return gift with the effort put into the original gift, but about strengthening ties to particular kin (interview, 2014). At weddings, these exchanges of foodstuffs embody and strengthen social ties, but they also reference a particular community through the specific content.

Foodstuffs are also exchanged at weddings through meals. At a baralek, hosts honor the guests by serving them a meal. When I asked during an interview what would happen if there was no food, Yusni and Rosani laughed at the question, saying there was no such thing (interview, 2014). Each nagari has its particular ceremonial dishes; even if they are the same in name and basic concept, there are sometimes small differences in the method of preparation. For example, one nagari might use turmeric in the *rendang* (M, spicy beef curry) while another does not. These minute differences are an important part of community identity (Klopfer 1999). Some nagari also have ceremonial specialties, such as *bebek hijau* (M, a spicy green duck curry) in Koto Gadang, near Bukittinggi. At weddings in the nagari, people typically eat in the *bajamba* style (see webfigs. 2.22, 2.23), where big bowls of rice and dozens of plates filled with side dishes and sweets are laid out in the center of the room. Guests sit on the floor around the edges of the spread, segregated by gender if both men and women are present, helping themselves and eating with their hands. After eating, the guests congratulate the couple and take their leave, women picking up their bowl or tray that has been filled in return. For most guests, attending a wedding takes about an hour.

Like gifts, food and the labor required to cook and serve it is embedded within the gift economy, where reciprocity between close kin, neighbors, and friends occurs and ties are strengthened as a result. As Ediwar explained, in ceremonies such as weddings and *batagak pangulu* (M, the ceremony to install a lineage or clan leader; see webfig. 2.24), kin are obliged to help support events, both fiscally and through labor. To explain the concept he shared an aphorism in Indonesian:

Barat sama dipikul, ringan sama jinjing,
Ke bukit sama kita daki, ke lurah sama kita turuni,
Kalau ada sama kita makan, kalau tidak ada sama kita cari.

Something heavy will be carried together on our shoulders,
    something light in our hands,
Going to the hill we will climb together, going to the valley we
    will go down together,
If [food] is there, we will eat together; if it is not, we will look for
    it together.

(interview, 2014)

I heard the same aphorism in a shorter, Minangkabau version a couple of weeks later in Paninjauan when I asked Ernida and her husband, Gaspar, how they explained the concept of mutual help in the nagari: "*barek sapikua ringan sajinjiang.*" Essentially, this aphorism explains how people share both the good and the bad. Ernida and Gaspar also introduced another aphorism to explain the same concept: "*saciok bak ayam, sadanciang bak besi,*" which literally means birds chirping together and iron twanging together, but effectively means the same as the first saying. Applied to staging some kind of adat ceremony, such as a wedding, the burden is to be shared. Through the act of sharing, Ediwar explained, the feeling of togetherness rises, so that no one person has to bear the burden alone.

This sense of communal effort is very different from weddings in more cosmopolitan contexts. As my host mother said when I was interviewing her sisters-in-law, why do all the work of catering a wedding yourself when you can just call up a caterer and place an order for fifty, five hundred, or a thousand servings of rendang? It saves a whole week of work and the effort of organizing a team of cooks, buying the ingredients, commandeering or creating cooking spaces, providing sufficient crockery and silverware, serving guests, cleaning, and so on (interview, 2010). While ordering catering is undoubtedly an easier option, it demonstrates a different way of valuing one's labor (and leisure) time and thinking about the benefits of sociality created through communal labor. In the nagari, while some people can afford catering, there is no need for it. As Rosani said, "We have lots of neighbors; you just need to ask for their help" (interview, 2014). The feeling of community, nagari head Nofrizal asserted, "is *mendarah daging* [I, inculcated]" (interview, 2014).

Investing in Tradition: Music at the Baralek

Like food, music is an important part of baralek. Talempong duduak is just one of the possible options in the nagari. Other options include local styles, such as saluang jo dendang; *dikia rabano* (M, an Islamic vocal genre accompanied by frame drums); *salawat dulang* (I, two vocalists, using mostly Islamic texts, accompanied by brass serving trays); sijobang; or rabab Pasisia. If families can afford it, they might occasionally have a more cosmopolitan style, such as orgen or talempong goyang. When I asked the women in Paninjauan why talempong was so important, Mardiani commented that if there was no talempong, people might mistakenly think that there had been a death in the family hosting the wedding (interview, 2010). Yusni, in contrast, simply said a baralek was better—merrier—with talempong (interview, 2014). However, there are exceptions. For example, one of the weddings I witnessed in February 2014 did not include talempong because the groom's sister had recently passed away: talempong was considered to be too celebratory for the circumstances. In Paninjauan, when talempong is present, it is used to energize the labor force cooking late into the night the evening before the baralek and then the next day during the reception to convey *keramaian* (I, a festive atmosphere) while advertising the ceremony in progress to the surrounding community. When they are paid, the women play almost continuously, stopping only to eat and pray. When the group wants a break from talempong, they switch to the alternative ensemble featuring the harmonica.

While a talempong duduak ensemble provides the sonic requirements for the necessary keramaian, the music is not foregrounded, either visually or sonically. At the weddings I have seen in Paninjauan and Unggan, the ensemble is situated outside the main ritual space, often outside the house (see fig. 2.1; fig. 2.9). Moreover, the repertoire is not geared toward maintaining audience interest through variety but rather establishing a sonic backdrop that underpins the efficacy of the occasion. In Paninjauan, I have documented more than twenty tunes in the repertoire, but when I attended weddings or played with the group, it seemed the same few tunes were featured. Neither the hosts nor the guests appear to care about the repetitiousness. Most guests are only there for an hour or so and pay little attention to the music.

Just as weddings embody and define the social dimensions of the community, so the presence of talempong at a wedding becomes a sonic articulation of it. Wedding hosts choose the local talempong practice for a variety of reasons, including logistical concerns, morals, aesthetic preferences, and habit. For example, in Paninjauan, hosts often do not have the financial resources to engage what they consider the more modern musics, such as orgen or talempong goyang. Orgen, moreover, is problematic from a moral standpoint: it often entails inappropriate dress and behavior, such as tight clothing, consuming alcohol, and dancing between the opposite sexes. Mardiani related to me that older people would deliberately avoid weddings with orgen, but were willing to attend those with talempong (interview, 2010). Investing in a local group also is a more pragmatic choice: the musicians do not need transportation or accommodation.

Furthermore, if the group is local, the hosts personally know the musicians; their presence helps celebrate and deepen already established social relationships.

Perhaps the most cited explanation for the presence of the local talempong ensemble at a wedding, however, is the investment in tradition. For example, Jasril explained that if hosts in Unggan want orgen, they could not incorporate it unless talempong was used first because orgen's inclusion would "cause our traditions to be lost" (interview, 2004). Moreover, the presence of talempong is so critical to the success of events that in Unggan people schedule their weddings—and other adat ceremonies—around the prohibitions against playing talempong. When I mentioned that people in the cities often cite these talempong styles as backward, Asma's daughter, Eliagus, explained that people from Paninjauan would never say such a thing: they are invested in talempong because "it's the tradition of their own village." They do not want to lose their traditions (interview with Asma and Rosani, 2010). Related to these explanations of tradition were those in Paninjauan that suggest the talempong practice holds nostalgic value because it is something passed on through the generations: for the younger people, it brings to mind deceased grandparents; for the migrants who traveled back to the nagari for weddings, the presence of talempong made it sound like home. Mardiani, for example, said if "[migrants] say they miss the village, they want to listen to talempong so that they are content" (interview with Mardiani, Mariani, and Yusni, 2010). In other words, talempong sonically references their community—it plays on and recalls previous experiences and feelings of what life in Paninjauan sounded like when they lived or visited there. As Asma's granddaughter interjected into an interview, for people from the rantau, which includes herself, the local talempong practice is "*asyik* [I, cool]; it is unique" (interview with Asma and Rosani, 2010).

Moreover, most people in the nagari actively like the sound of these older talempong practices. Recall that when comparing styles in the feedback interviews, people in the nagari generally expressed a strong preference for the indigenous styles over and above the cosmopolitan ones. I heard even more compelling explanations during my 2014

Paninjauan visit. When I asked nagari head Nofrizal about the place of artistic practices introduced to the nagari from the outside, such as "Tari pasambahan"[15] (M, Welcome Dance), which I had seen with the Oberlin students in January, and talempong kreasi, Jenni Aulia responded. He explained the attitudes toward local traditions versus new influences: because the traditions are inherited from their ancestors, the traditions are inculcated. People feel ownership over them. They fit the conditions of the nagari. But because *kreasi baru* (I, new creations) practices involve change, the community does not really accept them (interview with Nofrizal, 2014). Later that night, I met with Jenni Aulia for a personal interview, where he reinforced this idea. He related how he tried to introduce kreasi baru into the performing arts of the nagari in order to "fit with the era." But because Paninjauan was a community with a deep commitment to traditional values and practices, his efforts were not well received. As he said, "the artists were influenced by the strength of the traditions within the nagari, they always maintain them." For example, he tried to introduce diatonic tuning into the talempong practice. But the women felt that the new tuning of talempong was "less than nice to play" and they requested he change the tuning back (interview, 2014).

When I asked Ediwar why it was important that performing arts are included in adat ceremonies, he explained that arts, such as talempong, strengthen the event and entertain the guests, but more important, they reinforce local adat practice and tradition. He called the arts *bungo adat* (M, flower of adat) and *penyemarak adat* (I, the thing that makes adat shine). When I asked if you could substitute orgen or talempong goyang for the local talempong practice, he responded that orgen was not appropriate, but you could have talempong goyang because it had "Minangkabau nuance." It was better, however, for the penyemarak adat to be "arts that were of the same color with the adat of the environment." The values of the local talempong practice, he maintained, uphold adat better than arts from outside the nagari (interview, 2014).

So although wedding hosts in Paninjauan often choose talempong out of habit, that habit is deeply meaningful. In the nagari, choosing the local talempong practice becomes an investment in the community and a tacit statement about what it means, sounds, and feels like to be from that place. The presence of local styles also deepens the feeling of social connectedness between participants from the community because not only is the music familiar to them but it also is unique to that community. Talempong does not sound like that anywhere else.

Other Contexts for Talempong Performance

Weddings are the most frequent occasions for talempong performance in nagari, though both talempong pacik and talempong duduak can be found in other adat ceremonies and communal events. These other contexts include a child's first ritual bath, a procession where the child is shown to her bako, circumcision ceremonies held for prepubescent boys, and batagak pangulu. In some nagari, for example, Paninjauan, talempong duduak is also used for communal work parties to harvest rice, the sound motivating the workers. In Unggan, a group plays for a communal feast outside the mosque at harvest time. It is telling that with the exception of Ediwar's batagak pangulu ceremony in January 2014, I have never witnessed one of these other events involving talempong. They are less common occasions than weddings.

Talempong groups also perform to represent the nagari: either by welcoming a group of visiting dignitaries or performing at sports events, festivals, and government functions outside of it. For example, in September 2004 a talempong group accompanied Unggan's soccer team to a match. The musicians joined the athletes standing in the bed of the truck, the drums strapped to the roof of the cab (see webfig. 2.25). In these cases, the sounds of talempong sonically represent that community to outsiders. But these opportunities also cause internal friction about who has the legitimate right to represent the nagari. While music was often an integrative practice for a community, at other times it could be divisive with jealousies raised over the opportunity to perform.

The Economics of Talempong

Analyzing the economics of talempong practices in nagari life provides insight into its value for the community. In 2010 the group in Paninjauan was earning just Rp 200,000 to Rp 300,000 per gig, the lower figure just above the monthly income that constituted the poverty line in the province at the time (BPSPSB 2009, 185). The fee was usually split among the musicians present. By 2014 the group was earning more, typically ranging from Rp 500,000 to Rp 800,000 per gig, but exceptions were made for hosts who could not afford the higher amounts or were socially closer to the musicians. In 2003–4 in Unggan, when musicians were paid, the amount was equally nominal—compensation for time lost at other income-generating activities. After costs were covered, such as renting the instruments (Rp 25,000), members of Siti Aisah's group received around Rp 10,000 (then a little over US$1) per person. To put these figures in perspective, in 2004 the most affluent villagers derived income from the timber trade; men hiked several hours into the jungle, felled a couple of trees, and hauled the logs back down river by hand, earning about Rp 75,000 per day. Few musicians that I know who play talempong in the nagari rely on the income generated by performance as their primary form of sustenance. In both Paninjauan and Unggan, most of the women are occupied as homemakers or farmers, though the older women no longer work in the fields and are instead supported by their children. However small, the impact the earnings from gigs make in these women's lives should not be minimalized.

The association of talempong with monetary value in the nagari, however, is relatively new, part of a broader shift toward the monetization of social and cultural practices in other contexts. In Paninjauan, the shift can be actively tracked: women who played talempong did not receive money for playing at events until after 2004, when a group was assembled and traveled to STSI for a three-day workshop in May. Before then, when a wedding was held, the hosts rented a set of instruments and any women who attended the wedding, as help or as guests, were free to play. A woman usually played for an hour or two and then went home, as there were plenty of women who could play back then. Those who did play were not paid anything: they got a meal and some foodstuffs to take home, much the same as all guests. Playing talempong at a wedding in the past was therefore more in the spirit of participating in the communal effort it takes to stage a wedding.

Within the year following the 2004 workshop, however, talempong in Paninjauan was formalized. A group, with Yusni as head, was formed. This group from the jorong of Paninjauan is the one I have worked with the most and the one referenced here unless otherwise specified. The group goes by the name Talempong Uaik-Uaik[16] and is by many accounts the best in the nagari and the one most frequently called to play at weddings. When I returned to Sumatra in 2010, after six years' absence, Hanefi and Ediwar told me about the rejuvenation of talempong in Paninjauan, something that Hanefi (2011) was writing about for his master's thesis. The rejuvenation was a result of interest and intervention from people affiliated with the institute and, subsequently, government officials. In the interim, other groups had formed in each jorong and were each given a set of instruments. Yusni's group now wore costumes, with matching outfits and headscarves (see fig. 2.3). More important, wedding hosts now had to pay for the group if they wanted talempong at their weddings. Hanefi noted in 2014 that the intervention of people affiliated with the institute, including Ediwar and himself, has changed the practice of talempong in Paninjauan from something that was very "inclusive," where any woman could play, to something that was "exclusive" (pers. comm., 5 February 2014, Padang Panjang; cf. Hanefi 2011).

I interviewed Ediwar and some of the women about the matter of payment in 2014, curious if they ever offer their services for free. Normally, the women explained to me, hosts are expected to pay and are willing to do so when they engage the group's services. A host will approach Yusni, as head of the group, negotiating a fee directly with her. There are occasions, however, when the group does not get paid: for example, if someone in the group is related to the wedding hosts. Sometimes wedding hosts also ask for the group's help, such as the second wedding I attended in February 2014. I interviewed Yusni and Rosani the afternoon before the baralek, a time when the group would normally be playing to entertain the women cooking. But this time Yusni's group was not officially engaged, as the bride's father had bako in the jorong of Pauah who played. Yusni's group, however, was asked if they could help out, as Yusni explained, to "find tunes that sound good." Their participation, she continued, was a way of making a contribution to the wedding. In response to my confusion that they would be asked to help but not get paid, my interviewees clarified the situation: they would not play for long, just a couple of hours. (This is very different from when they are paid: then they play for one night and one day). Yusni and Rosani explained that it is awkward to refuse such requests to help out, especially given that the host family in this case lived just around the corner and the community is so tightly knit. This happens quite regularly, as Yusni elaborated, because the performers have "lots of family" in the nagari (interview, 2014). It is important to note the subtle distinctions in language used by these women and others in the nagari to distinguish between requests for the different types of participation: *panggia* (M, called) is used when they will be paid and *minta tolong* (I, asked to help) when they will not.

When I attended the wedding the following day, the group was already playing, taking a break with the harmonica ensemble. Once I ate, I joined them, playing for an hour or so. As I was getting ready to leave, the bako showed up: I was surprised that there were only two of them, not a whole group, including one woman who had gone to STSI for the workshop in 2004. They took over the melody and talempong paningkah, with members of Yusni's group supporting them by filling out the rest of the parts. The combination of forces underscores the community spirit of the music. All together, their voluntary contribution probably lasted about four hours.

When the group is not paid for playing talempong at a wedding, such as this one, the transaction is clearly part of a gift economy dependent on the exchange of labor and goods for strengthening social bonds. But what happens when the group does get paid? Does the introduction of money into the transaction between wedding hosts and musicians necessarily make it a commercial one? Drawing on the work of other scholars, I suggest the answer is more complex than a simple yes or no.

In laying out his gift theory, musicologist Rob Wegman (2005, 426–28) suggests that the commercial transaction is an impersonal one with no previous relationship between the client and the service provider, which is definitely not the case in this context. Meanwhile, Sidney Kafsir (1999) suggests that viewing the transaction as a purely commercial one—the exchange of a commodity for money—denies the complexities of the ethnographic context. Anthropologist Holly Wardlow argues that the key element in exchanges is not "the nature of the transaction" so much as "the nature of the *relationships established through and after the transaction*" (2006, 125; my emphasis). Ethnomusicologist Martin Stokes, moreover, urges scholars to explore how "money and the commodity form enter into a dialectic and mutually constitutive relationship with local symbolic systems and spheres of exchange" (2002, 147). I join these scholars in taking a more nuanced approach: rather than focusing on the exchange of cash, it is important to think about the ethnographic context, including how the transactions between wedding hosts and musicians were conceptualized; the social politics bound up in the exchange; and the meanings of the money to those who give and receive it.

In Paninjauan, where the community is very closely knit and musicians perform for family, neighbors, and friends, the women are not just thinking about the cash they might earn but also about the social value of the music. Playing at a wedding, regardless of whether, or how much, they get paid, serves to cement social ties with people in the community. The women are compelled to participate as much by social ties as they are by the promise of some money. When I talked with Ediwar about the matter of payment, he claimed that in Paninjauan arts are genuine offerings from the heart, offered to reinforce the already high feelings of community spirit (pers. comm., 20 February 2014, Padang Panjang). In other words, the musicians are not participating primarily to profit. Playing music is part of the community effort it takes to celebrate a wedding, hence the challenge in declining to play at all. If there is no money, however, they might decline to play for longer periods.

The significant conceptualization of the monetary transaction in Paninjauan, therefore, is about time committed to the endeavor; the introduction of money does not lessen or flatten the social ties. For the hosts, paying for talempong guarantees more hours of music at the wedding and, thus, a more successful ceremony. When I asked Jenni Aulia if payment of the talempong performers threatens the feeling of social intimacy with the hosts, he answered in the negative, explaining that payment was actually a way of respecting the women and compensating them for the time they invested. Before, when they were not paid, they were at the back of the house, just entertaining the women cooking and serving. Now, they are up at the front and valued (interview, 2014). In short, talempong performers are now more integral to a wedding than ever.

Therefore, although there is monetary value attached to the performance of talempong, the nature and depth of the social connections made the exchange more like a gift than a commercial transaction. The use of money in these exchanges did not signal a new kind of transaction so much as an extension of older practices with a new way of calculating the exchange. But to illustrate there were no hard-and-fast rules about being paid, there are contexts in which talempong musicians in the nagari explicitly prioritize the monetary—not the social—value of the musical services they offer. The ideological framing of the exchange establishes a difference between performing for the community and performing for commercial gain: in the latter case, the music is offered in exchange first and foremost for money. In both Unggan and Paninjauan, musicians I work with angled to expand the market for their music beyond the immediate community. As Tomi Chandra Putra, Paninjauan's head of nagari in 2010, declared to me, he hoped the local talempong duduak groups would "go *internasional*" (interview, 2010). The talempong groups in the nagari were hiring themselves out for government, tourist, and other events in nearby regions. Likewise, in 2003 Siti Aisah and her husband were trying to carve out a living from artistic activities alone, but had to supplement that revenue by tapping rubber, making bricks, and performing agricultural work. My apprenticeship to Siti Aisah helped her efforts to turn professional. Even more key was her work supplementing performances at community weddings—where compensation was minimal—with other engagements, charging Rp 300,000 for the group at gigs in nearby areas and Rp 800,000 for those further afield. In 2004, her group performed for the wedding of the daughter of then vice-presidential candidate Yusuf Kalla. Although Yusuf was from Sulawesi, his wife was Minangkabau and from Lintau, a town near Unggan. The musicians were handsomely rewarded with Rp 2 million (then equivalent to a month's salary for senior university faculty, an astronomical sum for the Unggan community) (interview, 2004). The ways musicians and their audience frame these experiences are critical because thinking about performance in economic terms is still relatively new in indigenous contexts. Indra Utama (1999, 317), for example, tells the story of a man who was astounded that someone would pay him for dancing.

Finally, although these musicians in the nagari are fiscally compensated for their performance, they do not think about themselves—nor does anyone perceive them—as professional musicians. It is useful here to recall Sweeney's emphasis on intention. Most of the performers of indigenous talempong practices think about playing music as an avocational activity; with a few exceptions they do not think about or aspire to performance as a full-time occupation or career choice. The shift to thinking about music in that way is often linked with institutionalization, which is discussed in the next chapter.

Older talempong practices enjoy a certain currency, vigor, and importance for some communities in the twenty-first century, including Paninjauan, Unggan, and Padang Alai. They choose these styles over and above newer, contemporaneous ones, such as talempong kreasi and talempong goyang. By continuing to invest deeply in indigenous practices, people in these communities are making a statement about their aesthetic preferences and, more important, their social values. They are invested in a different—and generally older—set of values than those prevalent among people who also identify as Minangkabau but are living in cosmopolitan contexts. For example, people in the nagari are committed to strengthening and maintaining social ties within the community.

Part of the reason people in Unggan and Paninjauan are deeply invested in the local practice and ensuring its continuation is that talempong practices in nagari are about creating, articulating, and sustaining community. Groups are motivated to play for community events—weddings and other life-cycle events—as a form of social bonding and community engagement, even if they do get paid. With unique stylistic features, such as melodies, rhythms, tunes, and instrumentation, when groups perform for community events, the sounds are important markers: they remind the community of what it sounds and feels like to be from Unggan or Paninjauan. When a talempong group from one of these nagari performs for events outside its physical boundaries, the sounds come to represent that nagari to others. Even though these talempong musicians are usually paid for their services, the monetary reward is overridden with the social worth of the contribution.

However, these practices are vibrant only as long as there are people to perform them, and there is some evidence to suggest that may not always be the case. The head of Paninjauan, Nofrizal, suggested that changes in economic conditions have threatened the continuation of indigenous practices, including talempong. In the past, people planted a rice crop only once a year, leaving plenty of spare time to engage in the performing arts. Now there are two or three harvests a year, leaving less free time (interview, 2014). I often spoke to young and middle-aged women who were interested in learning talempong but they were too busy juggling the demands of education, career, and motherhood to invest the time in learning what they considered to be a challenging music. In the past, women did not have to worry about the first two as much. In contrast, in Unggan back in 2003, young girls were learning talempong, but at that point in time they were learning the new tunes, not the original repertoire. It is possible that while the practice will be maintained, the repertoire will morph as it has done in the past with the introduction of dendang and pop Minang tunes. When I visited Padang Alai in February 2014, the older women

I had worked with in 2004 had stepped back or passed on, and the following generation of women were now playing. Rather than let the practice die out, they had made an active choice to maintain it. The group still had engagements: they were going off later in the week to a play at a batagak pangulu ceremony in a nearby neighborhood of Payakumbuh.

But in Paninjauan, the future of the practice is a little more precarious: as long as this generation of women is able to perform, the practice is alive and well. But I have seen only three members of the group ever play the melody part; the majority of the repertoire knowledge lies with Yusni. While there have been efforts to document the practice through recordings and academic theses (Aulia 2011), it is likely the embodied, kinesthetic knowledge of many of those tunes will be lost once Yusni, who is in increasingly poorer health each visit, passes on. Practices will be on the verge of extinction if there is no one left who has the specialized knowledge of the melodies or how the parts fit together. Over the years, I have heard reasons why the younger women are not interested, ranging from lack of time, the practice being too antiquated, lack of access to the instruments, and the practice being too hard. There is, however, a glimmer of hope: when the group of Oberlin College students visited Paninjauan for a talempong workshop in January 2014, a group of teenage girls had started learning.

If talempong is all about community in tightly knit nagari life, both in the past and the present, the twentieth century has seen political and economic changes that engendered new styles of talempong that were about transcending those differences between nagari in order to articulate and actively construct a sense of ethnic identity. The book moves on to explore those talempong styles and processes, starting with the institutionalization of Minangkabau arts.

Chapter 3

INSTITUTIONALIZING MINANGKABAU ARTS

The founding of an educational institution for Minangkabau arts in 1965 introduced new ways of shaping, thinking about, framing, teaching, and disseminating Minangkabau music. Although it was founded under the auspices of the state, part of a national system of secondary and tertiary institutions dedicated to the arts, the initial impetus came not from Jakarta, but from prominent Minangkabau intellectuals; they believed the rich variety of indigenous Minangkabau practices needed to be rescued from decline and fostered. These practices were important because of their centrality to adat and encapsulation of key Minangkabau values (cf. Hanefi 1999, 297). The establishment of the institution, then known as KOKAR, signaled an ideological engagement with, and embodiment, of what it meant to be Minangkabau sonically and kinesthetically. Therefore, the institution—and its creative output—represents one mechanism through and in which Minangkabau ethnicity was shaped and realized. The project, however, did not involve or affect all people who understood themselves as Minangkabau in the same ways. The institutionalization of practices now labeled as the arts was an inherently cosmopolitan project. It was cosmopolitans involved with the institution—faculty, staff, and students—that claimed, packaged, and marked particular practices as Minangkabau. This is not to say that artists from the nagari, such as Unggan or Paninjauan, were not involved in the project, but the

FIGURE 3.1. The institute in Padang Panjang when it was known as STSI, 17 August 2004.

nature of their participation has been limited and circumscribed, as will become evident later in the chapter.

Established in 1965, the institution (see fig. 3.1; webfig. 3.1) was both caught up in and affected by the prevailing political currents at a critical juncture in Minangkabau and national history. Interest in a formal institution in West Sumatra began to build in the years following the declaration of independence, in 1945, and the formation of the new state. Significantly, it was founded—through support of the state—just four years after the failure of the PRRI rebellion spearheaded by Minangkabau that challenged the central government. Initially, the project to establish arts institutions was part of the state effort to celebrate and preserve the cultural practices—albeit a very selective sample—of the newly founded nation. Later, the cultural policies of Suharto's New Order regime (1967–98) emphasized the nominal celebration of Indonesia's regional diversity, which included the province of West Sumatra. Importantly for this story, the institution's foundation and the surrounding sociopolitical contexts had much to do with how talempong transitioned from an expression of localized community identity into a broader expression of ethnic identity. While the details of the aesthetic transformations will come later, this chapter lays the groundwork for understanding how localized arts, such as talempong, were shaped and reshaped in response to this process of institutionalization. Who was involved in the founding and initial development of the institution? How have their backgrounds, training, and politics shaped its pedagogical and aesthetic agendas? Which practices have been selected for preservation? How were indigenous Minangkabau performing arts taught and who taught them?

In short, institutional agenda and curricula have resulted in the production of a new class of artists: academically trained people who aspire to careers in music and related fields. I am not, however, the first scholar interested in the transformational effects of powerful institutions on musical practices in Indonesia; there is a considerable literature examining the contributions of comparable institutions in the archipelago (e.g., Benamou 2010; Brinner 1995; Heimarck 2003; Sutton 1986, 1991, 2002; Weintraub 1993; Zanten 1995). Brett Hough's 1999 article is a particularly excellent account of the consequences of institutionalization of the arts in Bali, while also providing a thorough overview of the national policies affecting all the institutions. While there are some similarities in institutional goals and pedagogical approaches between these institutions in difference places, the history and specifics of the Minangkabau institution have not been told before, aside from a cursory mention in Margaret Kartomi's 1979 article on the modernization of Minangkabau music.

The Founding of the Institution

Since the infancy of the state, the Indonesian government has demonstrated an active interest in certain cultural practices, including the performing arts. As Hough states, "In Indonesia, culture [narrowly defined] is ideologically and constitutionally held to be an appropriate domain of government intervention" (1999: 232; cf. Sutton 2002:21), though there have been some significant differences in the ways successive governments have intervened. Clause 32 of the 1945 constitution underpinning such intervention and cited in the short history of the institution included in every edition of the institution's *pedoman* (I, handbook) states, "The government shall advance the national culture of Indonesia." But there has been considerable debate on the question of what constitutes national culture: Does national culture include just those expressions that celebrate the new nation as a whole, or does it also involve the sum of its constituent parts? (For an incisive analysis of the debate, see Yampolsky 1995.)

Performing arts were key to the nationalist projects because they were considered to embody the cultural heritage—identity—of the nation. They were also envisioned as tools to help shape emergent senses of national identity and regional identities, as long as the latter were in service to the nationalist agenda. The constant tension between local and national demands in Indonesia was regulated by the state to ensure stability. The arts needed to be managed—selectively rediscovered, preserved, fostered, developed, and improved—in order to protect and serve the nation. During Sukarno's presidency (1945–65), cultural policies encouraged the construction of novel expressive practices that could help define the new nation, along with the selective reshaping of local practices to fit nationalist agendas (Murgiyanto 1991, 1993; Ramstedt 1992; Yampolsky 1995; Zurbuchen 1990). Institutions for the arts were considered key to the nation-building project because they could inculcate a sense of national identity and indoctrinate students in national values (Hough 1999; Sutton 1991, 2002).

The first institution to specifically deal with musical practices, Konservatori Karawitan Indonesia (I, KONSER, or KOKAR, for short), was opened in the court city of Surakarta (Solo), Central Java, on 27 August 1950 (Sutton 1991, 174). The use of *karawitan* in the title is curious for an institution intended to have national import, as the term suggests a regional focus: it is a Sanskrit-based Javanese word coined in the beginning of the twentieth century to refer to Javanese refined arts, especially court-style gamelan. The issue of a Javanese term being adopted to describe arts elsewhere in the archipelago, a kind of internal colonization, will be taken up later. The placement of *Indonesia* in the title is equally ambiguous, allowing for three possible interpretations: "Conservatory of Indonesian Karawitan," "Indonesian Conservatory of Karawitan," and "Karawitan Conservatory of Indonesia" (1991, 174–75). It was initially hoped that KOKAR would incorporate a number of regional practices so as to encourage experimentation with the creation of new, composite national forms. But the experiment did not work and the focus was ultimately on court-based gamelan practices (Murgiyanto 1991; Sutton 1991).

Institutions were later established in other regions: KOKAR Bali was established in 1959 (Ramstedt 1992, 68), and ASTI (I, Akademi Seni Tari Indonesia, Academy of Indonesian Dance) in Yogyakarta in 1963 (Murgiyanto 1991, 56). Therefore, when the West Sumatran institution was established, in 1965, the precedent had already been set for institutions of its kind in Indonesia. Table 3.1 lists all the secondary and tertiary institutions in this system and their dates of founding, along with updates in status and nomenclature. Eventually there were seven secondary institutions established (two of which appear to have provincial funding) and six tertiary ones.[1] The institution in West Sumatra was the fourth one to be established in the archipelago and the first one in the "outer" islands—not in Java and Bali. Importantly, it remains the only state-sponsored tertiary institution in the outer islands.[2]

The establishment of an educational institution for the Minangkabau arts in the highland town of Padang Panjang was formalized by a decree issued on 7 July 1965. It was formally opened on 15 September of that year. At that time the institution bore the title KOKAR, but it was amended with a subtitle: Jurusan Minangkabau (Minangkabau Department). As the subtitle suggests, in the beginning it was not an administrative body in its own right but a department of another institution, in this case, KOKAR Surakarta in Central Java. Initially, the Minangkabau institution involved both secondary and tertiary divisions under the same name. But the nomenclature changed not long afterward: on 16 April 1966 the tertiary division officially changed its name to ASKI. KOKAR and ASKI shared a campus until 1982, when

TABLE 3.1
List of state- and province-funded arts institutions in Indonesia

Surakarta (Central Java)	KOKAR	1950			SMKI	1976	STSI	1988	SMKN 1997	ISI 2006
Yogyakarta (Central Java)	KONRI	1961	ASKI	1964	SMKI	1977			SMKN 1997	ISI 1984
Denpasar (Bali)	KOKAR	1959	ASTI	1963	SMKI	1976	STSI	1988	SMKN ??	ISI 2003
Padang Panjang (West Sumatra)	KOKAR	1965	ASTI	1967	SMKI	1982	STSI	1999	SMKN prior to 2003	ISI 2010
Jakarta			ASKI	1965						
			IKJ	1968						
Bandung (West Java)	KOKAR	1963	ASTI	1970	SMKI	1975	STSI	1995	SMKN ??	
Surabaya (East Java)*	KOKAR	1973			SMKI	1977-8			SMKN 2012	
Banyumas (Central Java)*	Private				SMKI	1978				
South Sulawesi		1972	KONRI	1974	SMKI	1977-8				

Key

ASKI = Akademi Seni Karawitan Indonesia
ASTI = Akademi Seni Tari Indonesia
KOKAR = Konservatori Karawitan
KONRI = Konservatori Tari Indonesia
IKJ = Institut Kesenian Jakarta
ISI = Institut Seni Indonesia
SMKI = Sekolah Menengah Karawitan Indonesia
SMKN = Sekolah Menengah Kejuruan Indonesia
STSI = Sekolah Tinggi Seni Indonesia
* operated by provincial government, not state

the former relocated to Padang, the provincial capital, and changed its name to SMKI. It was then they became truly distinct institutions with separate administrative and curricular concerns. On 15 June 1999 the tertiary institution was upgraded to an STSI, though ASKI had started issuing four-year bachelor degrees, rather than just three-year diplomas, back in 1997. On 17 July 2010, STSI was upgraded to become an ISI and had the ability to offer master's degrees. Because of the shared location and history of the secondary and tertiary divisions in the early years, it is often difficult to disambiguate policies at one from the other; thus I continue to refer to it as the institution when necessary.

The Aftermath of the Failed Regional Rebellion

On the surface, it seems remarkable that the institution was founded just four years after the failure of the PRRI. Initially, I wondered why it was the only institution for the arts in a peripheral province and why the center would reward a rebellious province with an institution to maintain and preserve its cultural identity through the arts. Over the course of my research, however, I learned that the initiative for an arts institution came not from the center, but from prominent Minangkabau leaders, bureaucrats, budayawan, and artists concerned about the decline of indigenous arts and their prominence on the national stage, especially compared with more famed regions, such as Java and Bali.

It is nonetheless important to locate the institution's founding in the prevailing political climate of the time: the aftermath of PRRI failure. It was an event that all people identifying as Minangkabau would have known about, whether they were supporters of the reactionary government or not. Regardless of one's political affiliations and whether one was willing to talk about it with a foreign researcher more than fifty years later, it forms an important part of the historical backdrop to the events I am discussing here. Several historical accounts of the emotional and political climate during this period (Kahin 1999; Navis 1999; Ricklefs 1993), along with personal narratives, reference the political repercussions of the failure: many Minangkabau people were struggling to understand who they were and how they fit into the new political and social order that defined Indonesia in the 1960s, following the rebellion and the other pivotal political events affecting the stability of the state.

Indra Utama, for example, related stories to me that he learned from his rebel fighter father, Boestanoel Arifin Adam, who not so incidentally became the first director of ASKI. As Indra explained, the "defeat of the Minangkabau people in the PRRI insurgency was felt as extremely bitter" (e-mail interview, 15–16 August 2011). Many people identifying as Minangkabau moved away from the homeland, to other parts of Sumatra, the archipelago, and Malaysia. Many moved to Jakarta (Kahin 1999, 236; cf. Naim 1973). Confused why Minangkabau people wanted to move closer to the place that epitomized the root of the conflict (the centralization and Javanization of government), I asked Indra about it. For many people, it was a way to hide their identity as Minangkabau: by changing their names to Javanese ones, in Jakarta they could more easily blend in (e-mail interview, 15–16 August 2011). As essayist A. A. Navis (1999, 439) explains, hiding one's Minangkabau identity was intended to alleviate any prejudice—verbal and institutionalized—targeted at Minangkabau people for their role in the rebellion. But not everyone hid in fear of political repercussions. As Indra explained, "it wasn't like that for my father. He went directly to Jakarta. He would say to me: 'To defeat the tip of the weapon is to do it from its base.'" So Boestanoel took his wife and then only child, Indra, to Jakarta, where they stayed for seven years, to do his work from within the system (e-mail interview, 15–16 August 2011).

"Meanwhile," as Indra's narrative continues, "West Sumatra was changing." Harun Zain, a Jakarta-born Minangkabau and an economist trained at Berkeley, was inaugurated as governor of West Sumatra on 4 June 1966, the first Minangkabau governor after the PRRI (Kahin 1999, 299). As Indra explained to me, "Lots of people hung their hopes on this new governor, one of whom was my father" (e-mail interview, 15–16 August 2011). Kahin's account credits Zain as playing a key role in rebuilding the province and pride in claiming to be Minangkabau (1999). While the founding of the institution actually predates his appointment as governor by a year, it indicates a similar interest in reinvesting in things Minangkabau.

One of Zain's strategies was to reverse the brain drain by luring Minangkabau intellectuals, budayawan, and university graduates back to the homeland. "My father," Indra explained, "was called back to help develop the field of culture. So he returned and was asked to direct [ASKI], which was already established but was not advancing well." Zain, Indra clarified, was applying the philosophy of *mambangkik batang tarandam* (M, to revive logs that have been submerged) (cf. Navis 1999). This metaphor for revitalization draws on building practices for rumah gadang: the best trunks for building were not those freshly felled but those that had been soaking in water for sometime, as soaking gave them greater structural integrity. Translated to this context, the metaphor suggests that those individuals who left the homeland and had gained experience elsewhere soaked up knowledge that would help rebuild a stronger version of the province (pers. comm., 6 June 2010; 16 August 2011). Change, regardless of whether one considered the PRRI a factor or not, was afoot.

Celebrating Minangkabau within the Nation

In the years following the institution's founding, state cultural policies were shifting away from visions of crafting a culturally homogeneous nation to the celebration of Indonesia's regional diversity, a shift that is generally attributed by scholars to the change in presidency from Sukarno to Suharto (Ramstedt 1992; Sutton 1991, 176; Yampolsky 1995). In this formulation, *region* stands for the province, not for its ethnic diversity. As I discussed in chapter 1, the acknowledgment and discussion of ethnicity was considered threatening to national stability during this period. In the case of West Sumatra, however, the celebration of the region meant the celebration of Minangkabau practices. The perfect vehicle to celebrate regional identity was what Suharto's New Order regime identified as *kebudayaan* (I, culture), which did not refer to the widest range of cultural practices, but focused on elements that could be displayed, including performing arts, costumes, architecture, handicrafts, and food (Sutton 2002, 29; cf. Hough 1999).

During the New Order period of Suharto's presidency (1967–98), the nominal celebration of Indonesia's diversity took place within an imposed and circumscribed framework. Moreover, only certain regions were celebrated: for example, ASKI was the only tertiary institution for the arts established in the outer islands. With performing arts a key locus for the celebration of regional diversity, these educational institutions for the arts became salient sites where both the indoctrination of national values and the celebration of the regional—albeit always in service to the national—could be realized.

In the beginning, the concern to improve West Sumatra's position within the state was a driving force behind the establishment of an institution for the arts. The advocates of the institution aspired to achieve a position for Minangkabau arts commensurate with those of more famous regions, hoping the institutionalization of Minangkabau arts would engender the same level of cultivation from the state that Javanese, Balinese, and Sundanese arts received following the founding of comparable institutions in those regions. The demand for an institution can be seen as an active assertion of Minangkabau ethnicity, an attempt to demarcate the place of Minangkabau people within the state through artistic and cultural expressions.

The use of the term *karawitan* is one way commensuration was achieved, but it is a puzzling one: the general Minangkabau population at the time the institution was established did not know the word, but were familiar with the Minangkabau term for musical practices, *buni* (M, sounds). Discussions with people involved in the early history of the institution indicate that the word *karawitan* was imposed by the center to suggest uniformity between the performing arts institutions throughout Indonesia, regardless of the resulting incongruity for musical practices that were not identified as gamelan. While the initial use of the term reflects Javanese dominance within the state and the arts world, the term has accrued additional meanings; as Sutton (1991, 5) points out, it came to refer to other indigenous musics and performing arts in general, as institutions with *karawitan* in the title also teach dance and theatrical forms. By now this understanding of the term has been thoroughly socialized into the institutional discourse. Although the term was no longer in the title of the institute when it was upgraded to the next bureaucratic level, in 1999, it was retained as the title for the department dealing with indigenous musical practices, the Jurusan Karawitan. It has been a convenient rubric to distinguish this department from the one that teaches a very different kind of music, called Jurusan Musik (I, a term that is often shorthand for Western music). It continued to permeate course listings and discussions of musical theory through 2010, though it also generated divided opinions on its applicability.

Regardless of the meanings that have accrued to *karawitan,* at the time the institution was established, commensuration with Indonesia's more famed artistic regions was a clearly articulated goal; a normalizing label such as *karawitan* actively helped establish and demonstrate equivalence. The concern to maintain visibility within the state by achieving equality with more dominant, and thus visible, regions within Indonesia was a recurring theme in my interviews. Only a handful of people, however, directly connected this claim for visibility with the political environment following the failure of the PRRI, in 1961, and the subsequent need to recover Minangkabau pride. Some people, moreover, suggested the arts were a nonconfrontational way to get cosmopolitan Minangkabau reinvested in their cultural heritage and assert their rightful place within the nation but yet others, especially those who would have been of age in the 1960s, declined to acknowledge a connection. I wonder how much they have been socialized to not politicize this traumatic event that affected people on all sides of the fight. Regardless of the motivations looking back, the intellectual, political, and artistic elite considered an institution for the arts to be a positive thing for the province in the 1960s.

Goals for the Institution

The primary impetus in founding an arts institution in the 1960s was the preservation and development of indigenous Minangkabau arts. But the interest in arts education and the development of indigenous arts actually predated its establishment. For example, the Indonesisch Nederlandesche School (otherwise known as INS Kayutanam), founded in 1926 by Mohammad Sjafei, a fervent nationalist and influential educator, had a nationalist agenda where the arts were central to the curriculum. The emphasis was not on indigenous practices so much, but cosmopolitan ones, such as guitar, flute, and violin (Martamin et al. 1997, 136), along with some experimental blends bringing indigenous practices into cosmopolitan frames (Navis 1999). The INS socialized generations of pupils into these cosmopolitan practices originally identified with the colonialists, but increasingly internalized as their own cultural practices. It is important to mention this school, moreover, because the most influential Minangkabau artists in the mid-twentieth century—and several people involved in the founding and early development of the institution—have connections to the INS and related cosmopolitan art circles.

Significantly for this story, these personages include Indra Utama's father, Boestanoel Arifin Adam (1923–1993), and his uncle Irsjad Adam (b. 1929). Both men trained as violinists at a Belgian conservatory from 1952 to 1956. Boestanoel had a strong nationalist streak: he fought for freedom during the Indonesian independence struggle and was a partisan rebel during the PRRI. In addition to Irsjad, Boestanoel had two other siblings involved in the arts world, all trained in a blend of traditional, modernist, and Islamic traditions (Murgiyanto 1991, 260): famed choreographer Hoeriah Adam (1936–1971) and composer Achiar Adam (d. 2003). All three siblings also became faculty at the institution. The training and background of individuals is significant to this story because it helps explain why Minangkabau arts were shaped in very particular ways, including the use of diatonicism, which is relevant to the development of talempong at the institution.

The impetus for establishing an institution was partially preservationist: to save threatened cultural and artistic practices that were, as the rhetoric goes, on the brink of extinction. But, like its institutional counterparts in other parts of Indonesia, the preservation of indigenous arts at the institution also entailed their development. As Taslimuddin Dt. Nan Tungga, a former teacher, declared in his speech at the inaugural alumni convention, the original objective "was to *manggali baliak* [M, discover, unearth again] Minang culture and *mangambangkannyo* [M, develop it] in accordance with the changes and conditions of the era" (23 December 2003). The rhetoric is very telling: according to this perspective, indigenous arts were lost but also needed updating. What is implied, but not explicitly stated, here was that the people who had lost touch with Minang cultural practices were cosmopolitans. These sentiments of recovery and development can be linked with modernist attitudes regarding the reform of indigenous practices (Turino 2000). It is important to note that the people driving the project to recover and save indigenous arts were cosmopolitans trained in European art musics, not the practitioners of indigenous arts themselves. Historical narratives about the foundation of the institution reinforce the notion that the ideal beneficiaries of its activities were cosmopolitan. Murad, simultaneously an employee and student during the early years, claimed an institution was necessary because it was no longer clear "who we were as Minangkabau people" (interview, 2004), a sentiment frequently alluded to in post-PRRI rhetoric. Irsjad, Boestanoel's brother, clarified this explanation, asserting that there was a loss of knowledge about indigenous Minangkabau arts among urban populations. The only Minang music they knew was Orkes Gumarang, therefore the institution was necessary to stimulate the interest of these urban Minangkabau in their cultural roots (interview, 2004). In the years following the institution's founding, efforts to develop—and thereby "improve"—indigenous arts (Yampolsky 1995; cf. Buchanan 1995) were ultimately about repackaging them for cosmopolitan tastes.

By 1985,[3] the mission of ASKI was formulated as "*menggali* [I, to discover], *mengembangkan* [I, to develop], and *membina* [I, to cultivate] Minangkabau traditional arts in the framework of enriching and preserving elements of National Indonesian culture" (ASKI 1985–86, 19). The nationalistic rhetoric is significant: as a state-funded body, ASKI was subject to the ideologies and guidelines of the Indonesian state, including its centralized educational policies. The institution was in service to the nation. This was clear in the goal to craft model citizens.

For many years students were required to take classes in civics, Pancasila (the five principles that are the foundation of state ideology), religion (interpreted at the institute only as Islam),[4] and Indonesian language, ensuring the education of model citizens who would contribute to building, furthering, and maintaining the nation and the ideologies of the state. This nationalistic emphasis had lessened slightly by the time of my fieldwork in 2003–4, in accordance with the new values of the *Reformasi* (I, Reformation) era, the period following Suharto's downfall, in 1998.

Another way the institute served the goals of the state was through the production of professional artists who could apply their knowledge, skills, and creativity toward the betterment of society. The discourse of the professional—which uses the term *profésional,* the Indonesian adaptation of the English term—has been explicit in institutional literature since at least 1985. One of the specific goals stated in the institute's handbook that year, and repeated since, was "to educate a labor force of *seniman* who are creative and skilled in the field of traditional arts [and] that have professional capability within that field" (ASKI 1985–86, 19) This goal, however, needs some unpacking. What is a seniman and what does it mean to have professional capability in the field of traditional arts in West Sumatra?

The Indonesian term *seniman* means artist in a broad sense, but in institutional contexts it has come to mean a very specific kind of artist: only one with formal, academic training. In this context, "professional capability" is conferred by virtue of formal training and theoretical knowledge. Artists without formal training were lexically distinguished from those with training by the use of the marked terms *seniman alam* (I, natural artist) or *seniman tradisi* (I, traditional artist) (Hough 1999; also see Noszlopy 2007; Weiss 1993). However, in contexts outside the institutional realm, Minangkabau artists did not use these terms that had been projected onto them but rather indigenous ones. These indigenous terms reference function, including a performer's instrumental or vocal specialization: for example, *padendang* (M, vocalist in saluang jo dendang), talempong pambao, *tukang saluang* (M, player of saluang), or *tukang sijobang* (M, performer of sijobang). These indigenous terms do not make any presumptions about the possibility of earning an income, degree of specialization, or the kind of training the artists had. Some arts, like sijobang or saluang jo dendang, require highly specialized skills. In the latter, vocalists and flute players have to be familiar with hundreds of tunes, while vocalists also have to be adept at poetry. Both these arts promised some income if one was skilled enough, but only sijobang involved formal training in the form of an apprenticeship (Phillips [1981] 2009, 14).

The kinds of seniman produced by the institutional system, on the other hand, did come with assumptions about the kinds of training received and at least the aspiration to, if not the realization of, a full-time career related to the arts. The institute is engaged in training a very particular kind of professional musician: the set of skills students acquire for their tool kit include theoretical, academic training and a little practical experience in a wide range of genres. This is a very different skill set from those of other Minangkabau musicians to whom the word *professional* might apply: these musicians specialize in one genre, such as saluang jo dendang, rabab Pasisia, or salawat dulang, and those skilled enough have the capacity to earn some income, even if it is not their sole source. Thus, these musicians comfortably fit Benamou's (2010) model of a professional musician that requires both specialist skill and earning capacity. The institutional model of a professional artist arguably does not, and certainly not in the same way.

The institute's Department of Traditional Music imagines a number of possible careers for the students it is training, many of which are new career paths. It trains students to become performers, composers, and researchers, and to a lesser extent to find work as civil servants in cultural offices or in the tourist industry, with little regard for the actual job opportunities. The word *professional* is attached to this training in part because there was the *intention,* to borrow Sweeney's (1974) word, that graduates would make their living through fields related to kesenian and kebudayaan. Regardless of whether they could or not, students and graduates *aspired* to do so, which is a very different way of thinking about the arts than the way women in Paninjauan thought about their talempong contributions;

while they might have received money for performance, they were more motivated to participate by other factors, such as community spirit. The way the activity is framed is key, and in this case formal training alone is considered to confer professional status, regardless of employment opportunities or actual skill level. Later in the chapter I return to the disconnect between the careers that were imagined and the reality of work after graduation.

As graduates were set apart from those without academic training, a driving question of the chapter is how this academic training compares with the kinds of training that artists receive outside institutional contexts. In other words, what does institutional training provide graduates that musicians without that training, including those who perform talempong in nagari contexts, do not get? To understand some of the effects of institutionalization and subsequent transformations within the Minangkabau musical world, it is therefore important to understand what students at the institute were taught and how. I will focus on courses in the Department of Traditional Music.

First, however, it is important to recognize the kinds of people who enrolled in the department as students. Aptitude and previous experience were not necessarily prerequisites for enrollment. From 2000 to 2004, the acceptance rate in the department, advertised on the whiteboard in the department, ranged from 70 to 80 percent. While I do not have hard data, in my experience the gender balance of an enrolled class ranged from a relatively equal mix of men and women to a two-to-one ratio respectively. Some of these students had very little musical experience, while others had some experience, participating in a school or local performance group, such as a *randai* (M, a Minangkabau theater form) or gandang tambua troupe. Experience in an indigenous style of talempong was rare, and very few students had extensive exposure to one of the vocal genres that had the capability to generate income, such as saluang jo dendang or salawat dulang, before coming to the institute. My sense is that, unlike students enrolling at peer institutions in Java and Bali, those enrolling at the institute in West Sumatra have less previous exposure to or foundational experience in the genres taught on campus, which Benamou found to be a significant indicator of professional success in Solo (2010, 9). Thus, students in West Sumatra were not trying to confer legitimacy on artistic expertise they already possessed, helping assure access to certain professional worlds (Hough 1999; Hughes-Freeland 2001; Noszlopy 2007). Most students simply did not have a foot in both worlds. If students did not come in with much prior knowledge, what skills and knowledge did they take with them when they graduated? I turn to an analysis of the curriculum to understand that.

Curricular Concerns

Over the course of the institution's history, a number of interests—sometimes competing and always fluctuating in magnitude—have driven the construction of the curriculum, including national requirements versus regional interests, a preservationist versus developmentalist agenda, and practical versus theoretical training. The kinds of musical styles taught have also shifted over the years. These issues are important to consider because they have shaped generations of graduates and thereby contributed to the general transformation—or diversification—of Minangkabau music as graduates dispersed throughout the province and beyond, taking these skills, knowledge, and experiences with them. Given the strong interest in ensuring the preservation and continuity of indigenous practices claimed at the time of the institution's founding, I am particularly interested in the place of indigenous arts—and especially talempong, as an important expression of Minangkabau identity—in different versions of the curriculum. The selection of specific styles for inclusion in it not only served to legitimate certain practices over others but also reveals the differential attention to preservationist and development approaches to indigenous arts over the years. What place did talempong have in the curriculum and how did indigenous styles fare compared to newer, cosmopolitan styles developed at the institution?

By emphasizing indigenous practices and related cultural knowledge, such as adat and *pasambahan* (M, ritual speech), the curricular emphasis in the beginning was on the preservation of Minangkabau cultural practices. Until 1979 there were no departments and just one curriculum. All students were required to take classes in music, dance, theater, and culture. My conversations with faculty and students from the early years suggest that the musical content covered several of the best-known indigenous Minangkabau instruments and genres, including saluang darek, talempong (both processional and seated styles), dendang, gandang, sarunai, and bansi. When I asked Zuryati Zoebir—one of two graduates in the first graduating class (1971) and a teacher in the dance department at SMKN—about curricula changes, like many of the first generation of students, she lamented some of the transformations that had occurred. Back then the curriculum was comprehensive regarding Minangkabau adat and related cultural practices: "We studied lots about Minangkabau [culture], not just about music and dance, but also about *pepatah-petitih* (M, aphorisms), pasambahan, *silek* (M, self-defense arts), and theater." They also learned about manners, etiquette, and customs. But in 1979 things changed: separate departments of dance, traditional music, and Western music were established and the curriculum became more specialized. This meant that many of the subjects in the broader introduction to the Minangkabau cultural realm were jettisoned. From Zuryati's perspective, the consequences are dire: students no longer know their culture (interview, 2004).

The curriculum has changed multiple times since 1979. Rather than rehearse all those changes, I want to focus on the kinds of skills and knowledge that were developed. Three broad trends worth noting are the expansion of the focus on Minangkabau arts; increasing specialization, with the establishment of composition versus research tracks; and the emphasis on theoretical subjects over practical ones. The analysis of curricular structure that follows draws on personal accounts for the years before 1985, the first year I was able to access archival records, and data presented in institutional handbooks or personally collected since, including data from 1985–86, 1991–92, 1994–99, and 2003–5. The numerical and statistical calculations are a result of my own computations based on this data.

When the institute was upgraded from ASKI to STSI, in 1999, the focus on Minangkabau arts was expanded to include Melayu arts. Defining what constitutes Melayu or Melayu arts, however, is difficult. Yampolsky suggests that the term *Melayu* is problematic as there are "many senses—ethnic, historical, racial, political, linguistic, and cultural—of that complicated and contested word" (1996b, 3). The institute's definition of *Melayu* limits the scope of Melayu cultural influence to Sumatra, where Minangkabau are subsumed within the broader category of Melayu. This focal shift garnered mixed reactions, partially because of the problems defining *Melayu:* support from those who view Minangkabau practices as a cultural subset of broader Melayu ones, dismay from those who believe the broader perspective will marginalize Minangkabau arts, and bewilderment from those who question the ontology and validity of Melayu as a meaningful category. The shift was palpable, with students having to take from 12 to 18 units out of 149 in Melayu subjects by 1999, whereas before that, as suggested by the 1994–97 curriculum, there were no classes with a Melayu focus. Some of these new classes were theoretical and were required of all students, including the Study of Melayu Culture, Aesthetics of Melayu Arts, and Language of Melayu Literature. Others were practical, which will be discussed below.

When the institute switched from offering three-year diploma programs to four-year degrees, listed in printed curricula as early as 1997 (two years before the institution was officially upgraded to STSI), students had to choose a specialization in either composition or research. The focus of training shifted to teaching students theoretical and practical skills related to their track. The composition track, for instance, comprised 16 units of composition out of the total 149, while the research track included transcription and analysis, along with field research methods. In 2003 there was a clear preference for the composition track among the student body; of the second years, there were fifteen students specializing in composition and just one in research; of the third years, sixteen and four respectively; and of the fourth years, nine and one. Students are generally encouraged to take the research track if their performance skills are not strong. In

2004, when the curriculum shifted again to the new one set by the Department of National Education, these specializations were further emphasized, though there was a third track for performance, which was based on a model of gamelan where students specialize in one instrument within the ensemble for the duration of their studies. This track was not offered on the West Sumatran campus, partially because the model—where one becomes a professional performer on that instrument—does not, according to some faculty, translate to the Minangkabau case. In other words, there were no practical applications, though arguably the institution could have trained students for one of the professionalized vocal genres, like saluang jo dendang, rabab Pasisia, or salawat dulang. While the composition track offers few significant career possibilities, there were even fewer—that is, none—related to arts research.

Although not stated explicitly, there are classes in the curriculum that suggest training students to work in the tourism industry was an institutional objective. For example, the 1997 handbook states the aim of the arts management course was to teach students to "understand the management and presentation of arts [with regard to] appreciation, *show bisnis,* and tourist packets" (ASKI 1997–98: 142). However, compared to Bali, the explicit attention to arts in relation to the tourism industry was relatively downplayed, though it perceptibly increased following the implementation of regional autonomy, in 1999, and the subsequent interest of regions within West Sumatra in the possible revenue from tourism. During the periods of my study and research at the institute, the marketability of skills and musical styles was only minimally addressed in the discourse and curriculum, such as the arts management class. The concern, however, seems manifest in the prioritization of cosmopolitan styles of music and dance—the ones adopted by *sanggar* (I, glossed for now as performance troupes) who perform at government and tourist events—in the selection of material for practical classes.

By 2004 the curriculum featured more emphasis on academic, theoretical subjects and less on practical training in specific musical traditions. For example, in 1985 practical training in Minangkabau and related arts constituted 62 units out of a total 115 required for the three-year diploma. By 2004 the students in the composition track of the four-year degree were completing 52 units in practical classes out of a total 148 (the increase in total reflecting the addition of a year for the bachelor's degree), while the students on the research track were doing just 30.

More important, the early interest in giving students a holistic view of Minangkabau performing arts in their cultural context disappeared in preference for training what faculty considered well-rounded, professional musicians. For example, students took just one semester of Traditional Music Theory but seven semesters of classes pertaining to what was understood locally as Western music theory, including piano, solfège, learning to write staff notation, and basic functional harmony. The particular nature of these subjects reveals the biases of the department, which deemed these skills necessary for understanding, interpreting, and practicing indigenous Minangkabau musics. When I was taking classes in 1998–99, vocal technique was part of our training in dendang (defined in this context as indigenous vocal musics). Taught by a faculty member from the Department of Western Music trained in operatic technique, the skills learned in the class were incongruous with the techniques employed in indigenous vocal music. Nonetheless, as Zahara Kamal pointed out, these kinds of subjects were useful for teaching music in public schools, a career path followed by many graduates (interview, 2004). The inclusion of these kinds of subjects, moreover, reveals the academic-scientific approach, which placed indigenous musics in new epistemological, analytical, and performative frames, a methodological bias that has deepened over time. This was a particularly institutional way of approaching the issue of preservation. This discussion also helps clarify that the kind of professionalization of music through institutional training has entailed the application of formalized, so-called scientific approaches, which are markedly different, as I will illustrate shortly, from indigenous ones, both in the ways arts were taught and understood. But, first, what did the students learn in these practical classes?

The genres and musical styles that students learned at the institute are connected to those they disseminate after they graduate. In the 2003 curriculum, a wide range of practical classes was offered. Unless otherwise marked, all the classes are two-unit courses. Some classes were compulsory for all students, including dendang darek, dendang from other regions (4 units), salawat dulang (4), traditional dance, *tari kreasi* (I, newly created dances), coastal dance, traditional theater (10), randai, and instrument technique. All students had the choice of 8 units of electives choosing from the following two-unit classes: indang; *barzanji* (I, a pan-Indonesian Islamic vocal genre with texts recounting the Prophet Muhammad's life); dikia rabano; salawat dulang; talempong pacik/pupuik gadang; talempong from Sialang; talempong from Unggan; talempong from Pariaman; talempong kreasi; saluang/rabab darek; saluang panjang, *sampelong* (M, an end-blown bamboo flute from the Limapuluh Kota region that has mystical associations), sirompak; *saluang Pauah* (M, an end-blown flute from the region around Padang used to accompany *dendang Pauah*), rabab Pasisia, *rabab Pariaman* (M, a coconut shell fiddle from Pariaman), sijobang, *Melayu Deli* (I, a genre that involved violin, accordion, vocals, and frame drum when I took the class in 1998–99), *gambus Melayu* (I, strummed lute, distinguished from the oud that is played in Indonesia and sometimes also labeled *gambus*), gandang tambua, and *gandang sarunai* (M, a drumming practice from Muaro Labuah). In the composition track, students had to take two classes in Melayu dance styles and they had to specialize in eight units of one of the following: salawat dulang, talempong kreasi, saluang/rabab darek, saluang Pauah, rabab Pasisia, rabab Pariaman, or sijobang. In the research track, the students had to take talempong kreasi, talempong from Sialang, gambus Melayu/*gambus Riau* (I, gambus music from the province of Riau), gandang tambua, Batak music (which when I took the class in 1999 involved learning an ensemble music called *gondang sabangunan* [Byl 2014] and was taught by I Dewo Nyoman Supenida, a Balinese member of the faculty), and Sundanese, Balinese, and Javanese gamelan. In other words, students in the research track had the greatest exposure to musics from other parts of the archipelago.

While a wide range of genres was listed in the curriculum, a much narrower selection was actually taught based on faculty availability and student demand. For example, in the first semester of 2003–4, there were just three specialization classes for second-year composition students with disproportionate enrollments, the numbers indicated in parentheses: talempong kreasi (11), salawat dulang (2), and sijobang (1). Third-years also had an uneven split: talempong kreasi (9) and saluang/rabab darek (1). Based on these numbers, it is clear most students took talempong kreasi for their eight-unit specialization that stretched over four semesters. The two-unit elective classes also showed particular trends: *indang Pariaman* (11), gambus Riau (5), dikia rabano (5), gandang sarunai (6) and talempong pacik (2). It should be noted that no students opted to take any of the talempong duduak classes and only two were interested in talempong pacik. Talempong kreasi, the cosmopolitan style, was clearly preferred over the indigenous styles by the students. Although this data is specific to one semester, it indicates general trends: students opted to take classes that were popular and their friends were taking. As several faculty members commented to me, students also deliberately chose classes that were not too challenging—for example, talempong kreasi is much easier than indigenous styles. Likewise, most students shied away from challenging vocal and instrumental styles, like saluang jo dendang or rabab Pasisia. The situation changed, however, with the new curriculum introduced in 2004, when students no longer had any electives from which to choose. Some faculty preferred this approach, because it mitigated student preferences for easy options and it was easier to schedule compulsory classes than electives dependent on enrollment.

So what happened to the indigenous practices the institution was ostensibly interested in preserving, such as saluang and talempong? The exposure to vocal practices, such as dendang and kaba styles, was scaled back in favor of exposure to a greater diversity of styles, including Islamic genres that were Minangkabau, such as dikia rabano or salawat dulang, or pan-Indonesian, such as barzanji or *nasyid* (I, an a capella genre). The story is similar with the instrumental styles used to accompany the vocals; by 1999 rabab Pasisia, saluang darek, and rabab darek had been reduced to minor electives and specializations for composition majors, but few students chose them. Indigenous talempong styles have suffered a similar fate. The focus has shifted away from them to the diatonic, cosmopolitan style developed at the institution. In 1998, when I was a student, the only compulsory class in indigenous-style talempong was for students in the research track. In 2004 a two-unit class, out of a total 148 units, in indigenous-style talempong was required of all first-year students. From 1998 through 2004, a number of electives in talempong traditions from specific nagari were offered, but these classes generally did not generate enough student interest to be held. In comparison, from 1998 to 2004 all students learned talempong kreasi during a two-unit class on how to accompany kreasi dances. From 1999 to 2003 the students could also fulfill their eight-unit instrument specialization requirement with talempong kreasi, and many chose to do so because it was easy and was useful experience if they were thinking about a career related to sanggar and tourist performance or working in the public-education system. To summarize, in the 2003–4 academic year, students were taking just two units of indigenous styles[5] while often taking ten units of talempong kreasi. In conclusion, the curricular structure indicates institutional bias toward talempong kreasi. This is an important part of the story, given the investment in indigenous practices when the institution was founded. More important, this kind of selectivity is significant because the graduates go on to disseminate the skills and styles learned at the institution that puts these styles and aesthetic frames out into the world.

The inclusion of indigenous arts in the curriculum is only one aspect of how those arts were engaged in the institutional setting. Because ensuring the continuity of indigenous arts has remained a key goal of the institute, it is critical to also think about who taught those arts, the background of those individuals, and their teaching methods. This examination will further clarify some of the effects of institutionalization and the transformation of musical practice in West Sumatra.

The Pedagogy of Indigenous Arts

At the outset, the faculty body of the institution was formed primarily through a combination of visiting lecturers—prominent intellectuals and faculty from IKIP (I, Institut Keguruan Ilmu Pendidikan, the Teacher Training Institute in Padang)—and indigenous artists of various traditions. By the time of Boestanoel's appointment as director, in 1967, there were only six permanent faculty members, but none of them were practitioners of the indigenous arts that the institution hoped to preserve. Why were indigenous artists not just appointed to the faculty body? Edy Utama—a strong critic of the institutional system—got to the crux of the issue: even though the indigenous practitioners were highly skilled performers, "because they didn't have a degree, [it is] said they were not capable of teaching" (interview, 2004; cf. Hough 1999). Zuryati, who ironically bemoans the decreasing involvement of indigenous artists, clarified the matter: they simply did not possess the requisite *ilmu* (I, scientific framework) to manage and teach the content in the institutional setting. In other words, a lack of formal training meant a lack theoretical knowledge. Sutton (2002, 170) found a similar privileging of formal training in operation when an institution in Sulawesi was converted from a private one to become part of the state system in 1974: the less competent musicians with formal training replaced the experts (with regard to Bali, cf. Hough 1999). At the KOKAR in Surabaya, hiring people with academic qualifications meant hiring teachers with greater familiarity with the Central Javanese style of gamelan than the East Javanese ones ostensibly the focus there (Sutton 1991, 179)

Although virtually nobody had formal training in indigenous arts in West Sumatra at the time of the institution's founding, in 1965, the concept was still privileged. The institution immediately set about training a cadre of qualified candidates it could hire back. Djaruddin Amar, an early employee, explained how Boestanoel, the first director, had a desire to "mold from the inside" and develop "permanent faculty to teach these arts," rather than constantly bringing in "instructors from the outside." To get the ball rolling, for the first decade or so indigenous artists were brought to campus for residencies lasting up to several months. Gradually the faculty members took over responsibility for the subject material themselves (interview, 2004).

Administrative staff and promising students were cultivated to fill the desperate need for teaching staff. Both Zuryati and Sulastri Andras became assistant teachers at the institution before they had even graduated, both going on to teach at SMKI when it moved to Padang. While Murad was initially hired to work in administration in 1965, he was simultaneously enrolled as a student and taught music in both the secondary and tertiary divisions. Although trained as a classical violinist with no previous exposure to indigenous musics, Murad was charged with finding material from practices labeled *traditional* to incorporate into the curriculum (interview, 2004). Like other cosmopolitans hired by the institution, he retooled himself to fit the demands of the job. Not only did he teach indigenous forms until his retirement from SMKN, he changed the shape of Minangkabau music radically: he was the individual who created the prototype for what would become talempong kreasi. That story, however, will come in the next chapter.

In other words, the first generation who held the responsibility for teaching indigenous arts were cosmopolitans and often had a background in cosmopolitan musical styles. The paradox is that people newly acquainted with indigenous practices taught them because formal training was privileged over musicianship and repertoire. Subsequent generations of teachers learned indigenous arts primarily within the institutional framework. The institutional system eventually became self-perpetuating, although by the mid-1990s the system was no longer able to absorb even its most talented students, many of whom had gone off to complete a bachelor's degree at another arts institution in the system that offered them, including Solo, Yogyakarta, Bandung, and Bali. A handful went to USU (I, Universitas Sumatera Utara, University of North Sumatra), where there was a thriving ethnomusicology program in the 1980s. Each time the institution was upgraded, the faculty were encouraged to seek a degree higher than the one granted on campus, meaning they had to seek out other institutions for their education and thereby lend credibility to their home institution.

In 1991 the total number of faculty in three departments (traditional music, Western music, and dance) had expanded to 113 (ASKI 1991). By 2003, after the addition of two departments, there were 143 faculty members, 42 of whom held a master's degree and another 31 of whom were in the process of acquiring one (speech by Zulkifli, 24 December 2003). When I returned in 2010, many faculty were pursuing a PhD. The expanding ceiling of academic credentials helped create an increasingly larger disparity between those artists with and those without formalized training: indigenous artists operated outside the institutional system, where artistic capital as a performer was construed in a very different way, and not by conferral of an academic degree or title, which in Java and Bali pushed artists to enroll for the academic credentials offered. But in West Sumatra this was rarely the case: graduates were generally not using the degree to legitimate previously acquired specialist skills. Another interesting element in the constitution of the faculty body is gender balance. In the Department of Traditional Music in 2004, the gender ratio was 3:1 men to women, which indicates the bias in opportunities within the institutional system, although there was more gender parity in student enrollment.

How did the first generation of cosmopolitans acquire knowledge about indigenous practices? The first generations of faculty and students (including those who would go on to be faculty) had comparatively extensive involvement with practitioners of the indigenous arts, including artist residencies of several months on campus and students living and studying with artists in their home communities as a form of required community service.[6] By the 1980s extensive artist residencies were a thing of the past, replaced by the strategy of sending faculty on research expeditions to purportedly discover indigenous practices that they could then bring back to the institution and incorporate into their teaching material. Such expeditions also contributed to the project of knowing and inventorying Minangkabau musical practices. The trips, sometimes involving arduous travel into the province's interior, often lasted just two or three days. Sometimes performers were also invited back to campus for a residency but were there for only a few days. This brief exposure is not remotely long enough for anyone to master a practice, but sometimes it still resulted in a faculty member introducing that particular practice into the curriculum. When such fleeting exposure to the aesthetic frame of a style becomes the basis for teaching and presentation it should raise concern, all the more so because the heft of the institute as an artistic authority automatically confers legitimacy on the standards it and its graduates come to disseminate.

By 1998–99, when I was an exchange student at ASKI, there was very little engagement with indigenous artists on campus. The *krisis moneter* (I, monetary crisis; *krismon* for short) and political turmoil of the new Reformation era were partially responsible for this state of affairs. By the time of my research in 2003, the economy was more stable. STSI was awarded a grant from 2001 to 2006 that was designed to improve the quality of undergraduate education. Administered by the Director General of Higher Education, the grant was named and structured after a World Bank initiative called Development for Undergraduate Education (DUE) (http://dikti.org/duelike/duelike.htm, accessed 10 March 2007). This grant enabled more students to work with indigenous arts and artists, including brief campus visits and additional funding for research. Still, compared with the 1970s and 1980s, the opportunities to interact with indigenous practitioners in 2003–4 were limited.

The shift in practice, and especially attitude, can be correlated with the increasing conviction of many faculty that there was no longer a need for indigenous artists in institutional contexts, as they could represent indigenous practices better than the indigenous artists themselves. Faculty member Herawati, for example, supported the dissolution of involvement from indigenous artists, arguing that faculty "already possess skills at the same level with traditional artists" (interview, 2004). To support her argument, she gave the example of Halim, who was accepted as a professional saluang performer in the performing circuit outside the institute, but he was one of the very few faculty members for whom this was true.

But there was some debate about the role indigenous artists should play. On the other side of the argument to those saying indigenous artists were no longer needed were people bemoaning the loss of their involvement. Zuryati, for instance, thought that it was necessary to directly study with practitioners from a given region because otherwise, as evidenced by the contemporary generation of students, "one does not fully comprehend" a given practice and thereby "does not infuse it with spirit" (interview, 2004; cf. Sutton 2002). She promoted the return to month-long immersion experiences for the students. Edy Utama also criticized the two- to three-day immersion model as a source to teach those practices.

Closely related to the matter of who taught indigenous arts at the institute is the matter of how those arts were taught. From the outset, the instruction of indigenous practices was approached from the standpoint of Western music theory, including solfège. So although the focus was on indigenous musics, they were interpreted in a distinctly cosmopolitan frame that undoubtedly stemmed from the training and background of the director, Boestanoel Arifin Adam, and other teaching faculty, including Murad and his brother, Irsjad.

The institutionalization of indigenous arts therefore brings these practices not only into new contexts but also prompts new intellectual methods of framing and approaching them. In the cosmopolitan world of the institute these practices became something different altogether. The institutionalization of indigenous arts creates what I call a paradox of preservation: a disconnect between what the institute is aiming to do (save endangered practices from extinction) and what it does do (change them in the process). The formalized systems of learning in place at the institute engender the creation of entirely new practices that are parallel to, but ultimately distinct from, indigenous experiences. In other words, there are two systems in operation: while there might be some resemblance in content, the differences in epistemological and pedagogical approach are substantial enough to produce distinct entities. The preservationist discourse underpinning the institute nonetheless is predicated on and works to elide any difference. In his study of musical competence in Java, Benjamin Brinner (1995, 10) explores some of the ways educational institutions have altered it. In his study of gamelan, Marc Perlman makes a distinction between explicit knowledge that is verbalized, or learned through "explicit tuition," and implicit, nonverbalized knowledge absorbed "through watching and imitating" (2004, 22). Inspired by their work, the remainder of this chapter examines the alteration or, more accurately, the diversification of kinds of competence and musical knowledge in West Sumatra.

In West Sumatra, the institute has played the leading role in the formation of explicit knowledge about musical practices. The pedagogical approaches adopted at the institute involve new, explicit models for apprehending musical structure, including notation, analysis, and the formulation of a new lexicon to talk about the music (cf. Benamou 2010). While these methods of approaching music were cosmopolitan in origin, they were adapted to fit the needs of the institute and were gradually internalized by the faculty as their own practices. "Often motivated by desires for rationalization and standardization," Brinner argues, the transformation of pedagogical approach at institutions "may drastically alter the structure and content of musicians' competence" (1995, 110). But in the Minangkabau context it is not so much an alteration of competence (students rarely enter with skills in the indigenous practices taught) as it is producing individuals trained in a different system with a set of new competencies. Individuals in West Sumatra are rarely exposed to both systems of learning, but learn and operate in one or the other. Below I conduct a comparative study of the transmission practices relating to indigenous-style talempong in a nagari context and then at the institute to illustrate how knowing the same music in different ways leads to distinct renderings of ostensibly the same thing, the institutional version often a more anemic version of the original.

Transmitting Talempong in the Nagari

A key part of learning talempong in nagari is the continued exposure to the music. In these contexts, most children grow up accompanying their mothers to ceremonies—weddings, circumcisions, and the like—where talempong is performed. Critical in creating the necessary keramaian, talempong is performed for hours and, historically, days on end. Regardless of whether their mothers attended ceremonies as musicians, helpers, or guests, many of the women I interviewed grew up surrounded by the sounds of talempong, exposed to the constant iteration of the same tunes. In the talempong duduak form one tune can be repeated indefinitely (see chapter 2). In performance, a tune lasts anywhere from five to twenty minutes. The cyclical nature of the music undoubtedly facilitates its internalization, especially for the supporting parts, which vary less and are often common between pieces, such as the supporting talempong part (the talempong paningkah), the gong part, and the drum parts. These musicians therefore often have a strong acoustical and experiential grounding in the style before they begin the process of transferring this implicit knowledge into instrumental competence.

Some of these women in Unggan, including Siti Aisah, my teacher, and her friends Asnamawarti and Hendrilisna, started playing when they were five or six years old, barely large enough to reach across a rack of talempong. These aspiring musicians would watch and listen, later trying to imitate the pieces on their own. Walking home from the ceremonies she had attended with her musician mother, Siti Aisah related how she would try out the tunes on a homemade rubber *genggong* (I, Jew's harp). Hendrilisna described a similar infatuation; after hearing tunes at a ceremony, she would try them out as soon as she got home. These girls took advantage of every opportunity to practice. When the performers at ceremonies were taking a break to eat, Siti Aisah tried playing the talempong, thereby allowing knowledge absorbed through listening to be realized in practice. When she was fourteen she started playing with a group of older women, including her mother. Taking turns to play all the parts in the ensemble, she learned how the parts went together. This learning process allowed the girls to intuit and gradually absorb the parameters of musical style. Once initiative and interest in learning was established, observation was often, but not necessarily, supplemented by guidance, usually from a relative or more rarely through tutelage by someone outside the family.

When the children were learning to play talempong, they learned on instruments that were accessible. Like most women in Unggan, Siti Aisah learned on talempong kayu before transferring these skills to the gongs. Generally reserved for ceremonial purposes, these gongs were also beyond the economic reach of individual musicians. During my research in 2003–4 some girls in Unggan still learned on talempong kayu, but talempong jao was more common. Siti Aisah's husband, Jasril, made these instruments by fashioning keys from old oil drums. When the ideal instruments, the gongs and drums, were not accessible, musicians took a pragmatic approach and used whatever materials were at hand. I heard stories of practicing the gong part on a cake tin or bucket and the drum part on an old can. I witnessed the use of plastic cookie containers, plastic washtubs, and powdered-milk tins (video 1.2). In Unggan the use of alternative materials was not only expedient and cheaper but also engendered by prohibitions against playing at certain times during the rice cycle.

When the talempong duduak style from Unggan was incorporated into the curriculum at the institute, the aesthetics were very different from those in the nagari, according to Erianto, a graduate who was from there. According to him, the professors who taught the class had not been involved in either workshops or research expeditions but relied on notation—simplified and at times erroneous—that was developed by their colleagues. During class, the instructors never played through the tunes themselves but expected the students to learn directly from notation and replicate it precisely without any kind of aural guide to the style. Students were therefore not exposed to the indigenous aesthetic frame at all, a habit that largely paralleled my experiences as a student at the institute. The reliance on notation jeopardized the aesthetic complexities of the style, including ornamentation and personal variation considered critical. Erianto, who had studied with his mother in Unggan, perfectly summarized the consequences: "I did not get the *roh* [I, spirit] of *talempong Unggan* [talempong from Unggan] when studying at ASKI" (interview, 2004; cf. Sutton 2002).

I turn now to an empirical examination of pedagogical method at the institute, focusing on the only class in indigenous-style talempong taught during my primary period of fieldwork, in 2003–4. Some of the issues raised in Erianto's narrative recur in this account.

Indigenous-Style Talempong at the Institute

The talempong class was split into two halves, recognizing both indigenous styles. The first half of the class, my focus here, was devoted to talempong pacik from Bungo Tanjueng, a nagari not far from the institute itself. The second half was devoted to talempong duduak from Sialang, a nagari rather remote from Padang Panjang. The Sialang style—perhaps because it was considered comparatively easy by both faculty and students—has remained in the curriculum for a number of years, providing students' primary exposure to talempong duduak. When I took the Traditional Talempong class in 1998–99, this was the style I learned.

In the talempong pacik component of the class, Elizar taught the style from the nagari where he was born and raised, Bungo Tanjueng (see chapter 2). However, as an alumnus and faculty member of the institute, his training in the institutional system overshadowed and obscured any experience he might have had with indigenous approaches to learning. Like their counterparts in performing arts schools in Java, faculty at the institute "have developed" what Brinner calls "rationalized, analytical approaches to imparting knowledge" (1995, 157). One of those approaches included the fragmentation of more complex pieces and melodies into component parts, phrases, and motifs.

The most consequential departure, however, from indigenous methods was the use of notation. I have never see anyone in an indigenous context use notation, except maybe for some lyrics. But at the institute, notation was primary, part of the rational approach to knowing these musics. Tunes were not only considered to be captured by notation, but the practice allowed for closer analysis. More important, it is likely the institute was driven to keep up with comparable institutions, to show Minangkabau practices were worth notating, like Banyumas gamelan (see Sutton 1986). It was a concrete way to evidence the modernity of the institute. Faculty members found it a practical pedagogical tool. Endorsing the use of notation in her talempong teaching manual, Herawati comments, "If material is given by an oral method only or is limited to imitation alone, the time used for mastering a tune is rather long. In comparison, after a tune is fragmented into phrases and those phrases are practiced separately, the mastering of a tune requires a relatively short time" (2003, 141). Notation, in other words, simplified and expedited the learning process, giving the students a tool they could use to practice the melodies on their own. Notation was the cornerstone of the so-called scientific method of approaching indigenous musics. But the use of notation had its own costs. Who needed an indigenous practitioner when the practice was neatly encapsulated within notation? Providing a rigid model to imitate, notation exerted an ossifying effect, encouraging precise repetition. Notation was also overly reductive, missing many subtleties of an aesthetic system, including variation.

In teaching talempong pacik, however, Elizar tried to reconcile indigenous preferences with learning in an institutional setting by taking a systematic approach to learning how to vary the parts. He began the semester with a maneuver I had never witnessed in any other classes I attended at the institute: he played recordings of the indigenous version of the style. In this style, the five to six talempong are divided among three parts: what Elizar calls *jantan-batino, paningkah,* and *panyaua* (see chapter 2). In the classes that followed, he provided the students not only with the notation of each piece but also examples of how to vary it.

Rather than use the cipher notation typical at the institute, Elizar first introduced the students to notation generated by a computer program, Fruity Loops (FL Studio) (see fig. 3.2). A series of boxes on the horizontal axis represented the pulse, the lowest subdivision of the beat, while pitch was represented on the vertical axis. Each line in the notation represents the pitch of one gong, each pitch marked on the left-hand side. A box was shaded lighter when that pitch should be sounded. The result is conceptually related to the Time Unit Box System (TUBS), which is commonly attributed to ethnomusicologist James Koetting. In this particular piece each part requires two pitches:

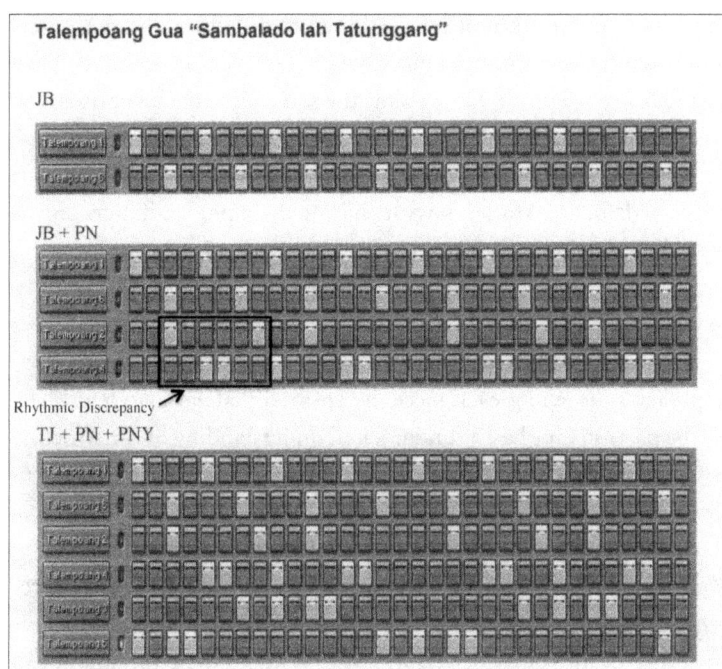

FIGURE 3.2. Computer-generated notation for the piece "Sambalado lah tatunggang."

on the notation in figure 3.2, JB is jantan-batino, PN is paningkah, and PNY panyaua. In this model, Elizar had added the parts one by one to visually demonstrate the concept of interlocking.

From an analytical perspective the notation was visually very effective. As a prescriptive model for performance, the computer-generated notation was problematic: for example, the pulse was so rapid it was difficult to read while playing. More important, the students did not understand it. Because the students were bewildered by this style of notation, Elizar gave them a homework assignment to translate it into the cipher system. But the students were unable to complete the task: they were in their second semester of studies and had little experience with notation of any kind. In a subsequent class, Elizar spent time explaining the computer-generated notation and helping the students transfer it to the cipher system. Throughout the talempong pacik unit he continued to distribute the computer-generated notation for each piece, writing out the cipher equivalents on the board. Figure 3.3 represents the same piece in cipher notation. In this piece there was rhythmic discrepancy (marked on the figures) between the computer-generated notation (fig. 3.2) and the part he played for the students with that of the cipher notation on the whiteboard, where the second "2" is a sixteenth note earlier than it is meant to be. A subtle difference, perhaps, but one that was integral to the syncopation of the style.

After providing the students with notation, Elizar took a systematized approach to teaching each piece: he ensured that each student knew all the parts so they had a fundamental understanding of the structure before he moved on to teaching the principles of variation. When students struggled with the rhythm, Elizar demonstrated it on the side of the talempong, urging them to play along at the same time.

It is typical in talempong pacik that one or two parts out of three will vary both melodic and rhythmic material of the so-called basic pattern over the course of performance. Without these variations, Elizar told his students, the music would be boring. When he introduced the first piece of the semester, "Gua cak din din," he handed out the computer-generated notation, which included both the basic parts and a series of variations for the panyaua, the part that gets to vary, while reminding the students that people do not use notation in the nagari. Music example 3.1 presents the basic parts in cipher notation, while music example 3.2 presents the series of notated variations, or what he

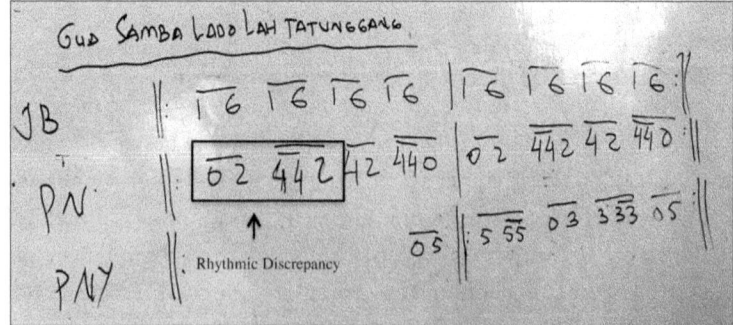

FIGURE 3.3. Cipher notation for "Sambalado lah tatunggang."

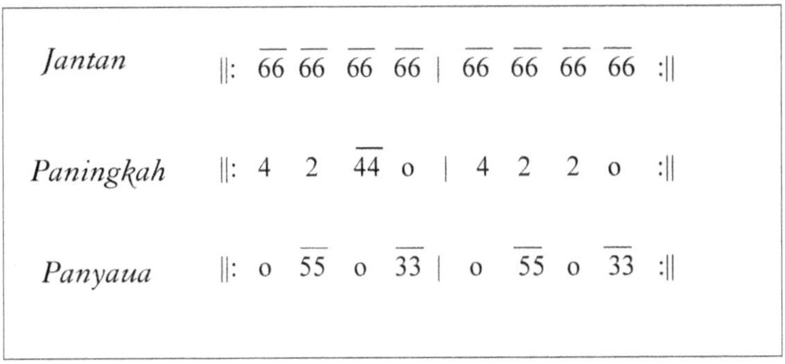

Jantan	‖: 6̄6̄ 6̄6̄ 6̄6̄ 6̄6̄ | 6̄6̄ 6̄6̄ 6̄6̄ 6̄6̄ :‖
Paningkah	‖: 4 2 4̄4̄ 0 | 4 2 2 0 :‖
Panyaua	‖: 0 5̄5̄ 0 3̄3̄ | 0 5̄5̄ 0 3̄3̄ :‖

MUSICAL EXAMPLE 3.1. "Gua cak din din" with basic parts.

also called *pengembangan* (I, developments) or *improvisasi* (I, improvisations), terms of a cosmopolitan rather than indigenous derivation. Talking the students through these variations, Elizar synthesized and demonstrated the basic principles. The students were not expected to replicate these variations precisely but to use the principles to develop their own. They should begin by mastering the basic pattern, and then, by playing around with it, the ability to improvise would eventually come.

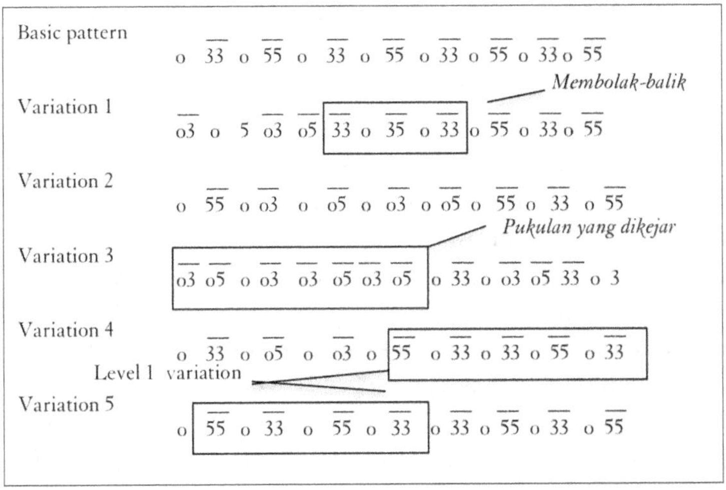

MUSICAL EXAMPLE 3.2. Notated variations for the *panyaua* in "Gua cak din din."

Institutionalizing Minangkabau Arts

Elizar's explication of the process of improvisation is worth going into at some length because it provides insight into institutional epistemologies, or rather the way analysis helped faculty and students come to know the music. Elizar explained that when performing, the basic pattern should be firmly established before any variation is launched. Then he explained that there were several different levels to which one could take variation. The first level of variation involved keeping the same rhythm by sustaining it on one pitch for an extra beat rather than returning directly to the other pitch (video 3.1). The second level also involved keeping the same rhythm, but employed *membolak-balik* (I, switching back and forth) more frequently between the pitches (video 3.2). The following level of variation involved *pukulan yang dikejar* (I, strokes that are chased), referring to the more immediate alternation between pitches. "The principle" of this kind of variation, Elizar explained, "is always to try to cause the rhythm of the part to be present on . . . the upbeat," an English term he borrowed to explain the syncopation (video 3.3). These techniques have been marked on music example 3.2. The final aspect to consider, Elizar informed his students, was the speed necessary for the character of a piece; "Gua cak din din" should be fast (video 3.4). To approximate the aesthetic frames of the indigenous version Elizar encouraged the students to practice playing "Gua cak din din" up to speed and with variations.

While Elizar provided a thorough explication of the principles of variation, it is unlikely that in the nagari the musicians are able, or need, to articulate the different variation techniques as thoroughly as he did. Learning through imitation and by practice, they just do it. In other words, what is an implicit form of knowledge in indigenous contexts becomes an explicit form in institutional ones, including a vocabulary to reference different strategies of variation. The terms Elizar used, often derived from English or Dutch, stemmed from his academic training in analysis.

Throughout the semester Elizar made a more concerted effort to present the indigenous aesthetic frame than was typical in other pedagogical contexts I witnessed at the institute. Not only did he teach his students the principles of variation, he also referenced indigenous preferences regarding tuning and technique—for example, he encouraged them to use the plain wooden handle of the mallet, which produces a more strident sound than the cotton-wrapped end, and mimics the plain wooden sticks often used in indigenous contexts. Although he encouraged the students to use the principles of variation to develop their own, the students had little opportunity to explore and internalize these subtleties. In the seven weeks devoted to this style, they learned four different tunes. Many of the students struggled to grasp even the basic parts provided in notation before they moved on to a new piece. Recall that in the 2003–4 curriculum, this was a student's only exposure to indigenous talempong.

Regardless of Elizar's attempts to school the students in the specifics of aesthetics, it was curious that the students never had any interaction with the nagari musicians or the style in its entirety, even though Bungo Tanjueng was a mere six miles away. Furthermore, the class focused only on the talempong parts within the ensemble and did not include the other instruments critical to its overall aesthetic frame, including pupuik gadang, rapa'i, and *tambua* (M, a large double-headed drum played with a stick) (Hanefi et al. 2004). Although Elizar was the son of a talempong performer from the nagari and brought more of the local aesthetic frame than was usual in a class at the institute, this exposure was not the same as hearing the music in its local context. When discussing the limitations of the institutional approach, Brinner suggests drummers produced at the comparable institution in Central Java glean tips from listening to drummers outside that institution (1995, 158). In the West Sumatran case, this comparative perspective—learning outside the institute—was often absent.

Life after Graduation

Many students attended the institute for the vocational training offered, aspiring to build a career that would provide a living income. But the supply of graduates far outweighs the demand for their skills and services. The graduating class across the institute has grown from 2 in the first class in 1971, to 231 in 1985 (twenty years after its founding), to a staggering 1,463 by 1998. I do not have access to data since then but the numbers can only have exponentially increased with the addition of more departments and levels of degrees. While KOKAR-ASKI was initially able to absorb its own graduates as faculty, the system could not keep up with the number of graduates. Faculty positions, along with relatively lucrative civil service positions in offices managing culture, art, and tourism or at Taman Budaya (I, Culture Park),[7] became increasingly scarce and coveted (Noszlopy 2007, 143). Graduates in the last couple of decades were forced to look for work elsewhere. Some were simply better, in the words of Stokes, at the "mechanics of turning music into money" (2002, 143).

In February 2014, I chatted with Hanefi about postgraduation career paths. In his estimation, more than 50 percent of all graduates are K–12 teachers, working in a variety of public, private, and religious institutions. According to him, this work was readily available: local government offices were frequently making requests of schools for performances, so schools need someone to train and prepare students for them (pers. comm., 5 February 2014). However, my host father, Arzul Jamaan, who is a faculty member in theater but was completing his PhD in education, pointed out that recently graduates even had problems getting teaching jobs, as they lack the certification now necessary (pers. comm., February 2014).

The increasingly specialized and competitive job market forces graduates without civil service or teaching placements to creatively think about avenues through which they can support themselves. For example, some graduates found freelance work in the private sector as composers, arrangers, choreographers, recording artists, gigging musicians, and sanggar directors, avenues that I will touch on in chapter 5. But the numbers in these fields are relatively small. Moreover, only a handful have gone on to careers as performers specializing in one of the professionalized vocal genres, such as saluang jo dendang, rabab Pasisia, or salawat dulang. The training in these genres at the institute was not specialized or extensive enough to allow students to enter this path. The graduates who do break through are not only talented but have extensive experience and exposure to the genre outside the institutional setting. Furthermore, Hanefi thought perhaps a total of twenty to thirty graduates are working in Jakarta as seniman, primarily as composers and performers. They are able to eke out a living there because the performance opportunities are more frequent and varied. In comparison, those graduates who belong to sanggar in West Sumatra have no chance of making a living from that activity alone: payment for a gig is often just a packet of rice with side dishes. Moreover, most of these people freelancing usually do not specialize in just one musical practice but patch together a living from diverse activities, styles, and genres, often with competing aesthetic and ideological frames. This is one way in which the exposure to a number of diverse styles rather than specialization during studies is actually a benefit. Moreover, very few graduates have the luxury of participating in just those practices they consider artistically worthwhile.

There are also many graduates who cannot find work in the arts. Hanefi estimated that 15 to 20 percent of graduates are in this category. Some of these have no work at all, but he had met former students who were working as *tukang ojek* (I, motorcycle-taxi drivers) and even one who worked as a laborer collecting sand from riverbeds. Felicia Hughes-Freeland found a similar situation in Java, where some graduates of the peer institutions were forced to work as parking attendants, laundresses, or prostitutes. The institutionalization of the arts, she asserts, offers "false expectations" (2001).

Therefore, there is a disconnect between what the institute focuses on training its graduates to do—perform, compose, and research—and the kinds of work they can get. Some faculty acknowledged that the institute is preparing its students for imaginary career paths. Very few graduates are engaged with indigenous arts, and those students who came from nagari to study at the institute rarely return after their studies. In part, this is because the opportunities to make a living from the arts are virtually nonexistent there. But it is also true that the institute changed these students, pulling them into a cosmopolitan world and leaving them with middle-class dreams (cf. Hughes-Freeland 2001).

As alumni disperse throughout the province of West Sumatra and neighboring provinces, into Jakarta, Medan, and other large cities with vibrant artistic scenes and communities, they bring with them the styles, aesthetic frames, and discourses internalized during their studies (cf. Becker 1980), including indigenous arts that are altered through new pedagogical methods or developed into something new. As Zulkifli, then head of STSI, declared at the opening of the inaugural alumni reunion, in 2003, "Alumni are the face of STSI. The sounds of alumni are the roars of STSI. The skills of alumni represent the skills of STSI" (speech, 23 December 2003). Importantly for this story, alumni have affected the way people think about, practice, and engage with talempong.

The founding of the institution was tied up with Minangkabau people negotiating a place within the nation following the failure of the PRRI and in the new political milieu of New Order Indonesia, with a cultural politics focused on the nominal celebration of ethnic diversity. Institutional projects, including the purported preservation and development of Minangkabau arts, help make sense of the social world in ethnic terms (Brubaker 2009, 32, 20): the institution helped, and continues to help, shape what it sounds like to be Minangkabau by selecting which arts get incorporated into the curriculum, as I have discussed in this chapter, and those that are shared with the outside world through performance, as I will discuss in the next. The institutionalization of the arts was, however, an inherently cosmopolitan project from the outset. Indigenous practitioners were barely involved, and increasingly less so over the years. Cosmopolitans shaped these experiences of sonically interpreting the world in Minangkabau terms.

An element of selectivity in building the curriculum was inevitable (cf. Sutton 1991, 180): it is not possible to cover the diverse musical practices of West Sumatra. Some of the reasons are pragmatic, but sometimes the choice is about which arts epitomize and best represent what it means to be Minangkabau, including talempong, dendang, saluang, and salawat dulang. Those practices that make it into the curriculum at the institutions, however, do so at the expense of others.

The consistency of those choices with the authority that the institutions carry has helped shape a canon of Minangkabau arts.

Putting indigenous arts into a conservatory context also entails, for the most part, abstracting them entirely from their original contexts. They are no longer transmitted in the same way, they do not involve the same kinds of people teaching or performing them, they are not performed in the same contexts, nor do they serve the same function. They loose their embeddedness within local communities and the related ethos (cf. Sutton 1991). Equally important, the aesthetic consequences are often great: a fraction of a repertoire is covered, students do not always learn to improvise or vary within the parameters of the style, learning is compartmentalized, and instrumentation is not always complete. Students in a dendang class, for example, did not learn to sing with the saluang, they did not learn to create texts, and they learned ornamentation by rote. Teaching through notation and minimizing variation are homogenizing and decontextualizing processes.

If the talempong practices examined in the previous chapter are taken as an example, at the institute these practices are no longer learned through intensive immersion where aspiring players have heard and seen the tunes performed over and over again at ceremonies before they try their hands at playing. Instead, students at the institute learn through formalized pedagogical approaches that involve designated authorities; take place in classrooms and usually in large groups, as opposed to an individual endeavor; and entail notation and precise memorization of the notated form. In one semester, the students learn only a handful of tunes and usually not any of the accompanying instrumentation. Moreover, whereas talempong is gendered exclusively male or female in the nagari, at the institute the practices become either mixed gender or sometimes even opposite gender (e.g., men exclusively playing talempong from Unggan or Paninjauan). Performances are not for communal work parties, weddings, other life-cycle ceremonies, or community celebrations, but for entirely different contexts, such as festivals, bureaucratic events, or end-of-semester staged performances.

Talempong in the institutional context is not about creating and articulating localized community identities, as it is in indigenous contexts. Instead, indigenous talempong styles in the institutional context are abstracted, generalized representations of a broader Minangkabau identity. Rather than specializing in a particular tradition, as often happens in indigenous contexts, the curriculum involved learning a variety of Minangkabau traditions so that graduates of the institute who become professional musicians have tokenistic amounts of a variety of traditions at their fingertips. Viewed as the authoritative body on Minangkabau arts, the institute—or really particular individuals affiliated with it—gets to select which arts best represent Minangkabau people, and that representation includes talempong. The next chapter asks how talempong has intersected with ethnicity, why talempong was central to the project, and how talempong has been transformed from its indigenous forms discussed in chapter 2 to represent Minangkabau ethnicity.

Chapter 4

REFORMING TALEMPONG

> *ASKI, or STSI, takes on the task of preserving and developing traditional arts. . . . After students graduate . . . they will be returned to society as an extension of the institute's arm . . . so they can revive traditional arts, which are in the community because they know traditional arts have to be revived, have to be restored. What is the method of preserving and reviving [them]? They have to be developed with the method and system that fits the present era. Without changes and development, traditional arts will definitely be left behind by a society that is always changing and developing. (Zulkifli, speech, 22 May 2004)*

The institution was founded to preserve and develop indigenous Minangkabau arts. The focus of the last chapter was on the institutional engagement with indigenous practices and practitioners, including the incorporation of indigenous-style talempong into the curriculum, who taught it, and how. This chapter looks at a different consequence of institutionalization: the purported preservation of Minangkabau practices through their development, a clearly articulated goal of the institution in general and the traditional music department specifically, as attested by Zulkifli in his speech. The development of indigenous practices, which implies modernizing and improving them to be in accordance with the times, raises questions about the tensions between the preservation of a tradition and demands for innovation. The style of talempong I discuss here encapsulates and thus helps explicate what is at stake as the chapter shifts the focus on to some of the ways local talempong practices were aesthetically and functionally altered in order to not just articulate, but also actively create, a broad sense of Minangkabau identity that transcended any local affiliations. In this transformation, talempong was expanded from a musical practice that had the ability to represent the identity of a given nagari, such as in Unggan or Paninjauan, to an expression that disregarded local markers and was intended to represent Minangkabau ethnicity.

The chapter details the emergence of this new talempong idiom at the institution, then KOKAR-ASKI, in the late 1960s and early 1970s. Like the timing behind the emergence of the institution itself, the time frame in which this new talempong idiom emerged is critical: it followed closely on the heels of the founding of the institution and took place in the political milieu following the failure of the PRRI where some Minangkabau were busy negotiating a place within the new political order of Indonesia. Like other modernist experiments in Indonesia, the new talempong form is very much a product of its political times. This idiom departed radically from indigenous forms by using diatonic tuning and functional harmony, two characteristics seen in West Sumatra then—and now—as Western imports, although by now they are as natural to a certain segment of the population as they are to people who listen to pop music in the United States. Why was the idiom first created? Who were the individuals involved in shaping the form? Why and how did it come to encapsulate and convey a sense of Minangkabau ethnicity? For which kinds of Minangkabau people was this expression of ethnicity activated?

In the cognitive view of ethnicity, this talempong idiom becomes a vehicle for Minangkabau ethnicity to be realized and articulated through musical practice. It offered one way of sounding Minangkabau. It is important to recognize that the arts do not just passively reflect ethnicity, but they can also help actively foster and create ethnic sensibilities. By reforming an indigenous practice to appeal to cosmopolitan tastes, the style's architects helped forged a new way of musically being Minangkabau in the world, a way that was distinctively Minangkabau yet also modern. To transform talempong from an expression of local identity to a form that transcended these local affiliations to become pan-Minangkabau required aesthetic modifications. The institution, moreover, was key in the creation of the new form (cf. the creation of pan-East Javanese blends at KOKAR Surabaya, Sutton 1991, 181).

Despite the pervasiveness of the diatonic talempong idiom and therefore its importance to the history of Minangkabau music, it has garnered very little scholarly attention. There is a body of work recognizing the contributions of early dance innovators, including Boestanoel's sister, Hoeriah Adam (Murgiyanto 1991; Navis 1999; Nor 2011) but virtually nothing on the parallel music scene. The English-language scholarly literature that references talempong has almost exclusively focused on the indigenous styles (Kartomi 1980, 1990, 1998; Salisbury 2000, 2009; Yampolsky 1996a). The Indonesian-language literature, including institutional research reports and teaching manuals, has not done much better (Adam 1990; Hanefi et al. 2004). An important exception is Margaret Kartomi's (1979) article on the modernization of Minangkabau music, where orkes talempong, as the diatonic idiom was known in the early 1970s, receives a few paragraphs and a partial transcription. Although offering an invaluable historical snapshot of the style, the overview is necessarily cursory in a broader discussion of musical change. That Kartomi never returned to examine it closely, however, is telling. In contrast, I hope to demonstrate the importance of sustained engagement with the musical idioms that many scholars dismiss as aesthetically distasteful and not traditional enough (cf. Weintraub's [2010] defense of studying dangdut), not only because they are meaningful for their audiences but also because they tell an important story.

Drawing on ethnographic interviews with inventors, performers, arrangers, and bureaucrats involved in the diatonic talempong idiom in its formative years, along with rare archival recordings and photographs generously provided by Kartomi that yield rich details about an otherwise lost style history, I examine the conception and development of the idiom at the institution. The materialization of the diatonic talempong idiom, according to some people, is rooted within the political events of the decade preceding its conception, and its particular aesthetic shape is infused by a complex blend of the competing sentiments and insecurities about Minangkabau heritage, identity, and place within the Indonesian state that stem from the failure of the PRRI rebellion.

PRRI and the Crisis of Minangkabau Identity

The aftermath of the PRRI failure was tangible and pervasive in the 1960s (see chapter 3). Although there are individuals unwilling to talk about this period, there are historical accounts and personal narratives that suggest it is an important part of Minangkabau history. The events activated ethnic sensibilities, a palpable awareness that one was affiliated with the category of Minangkabau and not a member of another ethnic category, regardless of whether an individual supported the rebels' cause or not. That failure, some like Edy Utama argue, led to a crisis of Minangkabau identity, where some people were so concerned about being identified by others as Minangkabau that they changed their names or gave their children Javanese names.

More important, Edy argued that this crisis and insecurities about being Minangkabau translated into musical preferences. He claimed this was why some Minangkabau people were heavily invested in pop Minang, which had no basis in indigenous practices, such as the music played by the bands Orkes Gumarang and Kumbang Tjari (see chapter 1). This was the definitive music for many cosmopolitan Minangkabau, in both the homeland and the rantau. Edy saw people's investment in the new talempong idiom as part of the same trajectory: not wanting to engage with Minangkabau musical forms that were heavy in Minangkabau markers (interview, 2004).

Several of my interlocutors explicitly connected the development of the diatonic talempong style to the failure of the PRRI, including

Edy and then director of STSI, Zulkifli. For proponents of this theory, the arts, supported by the government, became a way to rebuild Minangkabau pride and find a safe way to integrate Minangkabau people seamlessly back into the state following the PRRI era. In comparison to an armed rebellion, the arts offered an innocuous expression of ethnicity. Irsjad Adam and Herawati, both of whom were of age in the late 1960s, in contrast, were reluctant to make any explicit connections between artistic developments and politics when I asked them about it. Whether or not one puts much stock in this theory, at the very least the style's architects were trying to create a new musical form that referenced indigenous Minangkabau practices yet helped define a more modern way of being Minangkabau in the late 1960s. And 1960s Indonesia was a very particular place. Minangkabau people were dealing not only with the failure of the PRRI but also with the series of major political events that rocked the country in that decade, including the downfall of Sukarno's government, the communist purge, and Suharto's seizure of power. The province and the people who lived within in it were caught up with trying to find a place in the new political order of Indonesia.

The Initial Experiment with Diatonic Talempong

In the narrative recollections of the idiom's history, there is a single event that sparked its creation. In 1968 the three-year-old institution—a sparkling new jewel in West Sumatra's crown and already the inarguable artistic authority in the province—was invited to perform at the Independence Day celebration at the governor of West Sumatra's residence. It is significant that this was just two years after Zain's appointment as governor, with his interest in supporting activities that helped reclaim Minangkabau pride (Kahin 1999).

In 2004, Murad, who had just retired from teaching at SMKN, recounted the events leading to the first-known experiment with a diatonic talempong ensemble (interview, 2004). Boestanoel Arifin Adam, director of ASKI in 1969, stipulated that the team from the institution were not allowed to present an indigenous practice for the performance at the governor's residence, but rather they were to devise something innovative based on talempong. Murad, the violinist who was retooling himself to teach indigenous musics, was put in charge. The product of Murad's experiment laid the groundwork for the style that would become known as orkes talempong and eventually the talempong kreasi ensemble (see chapter 1). Murad's account of the prototype and early evolution of the style was supplemented with the recollections of Irsjad Adam, another key participant in formulating the new style (interview, 2004). There were two others key to the endeavor: Achiar Adam, Irsjad's brother who taught at the high school; and Yusaf Rahman, who taught briefly at ASKI and then at IKIP and was the composer and codirector of Sanggar Sofyani with his choreographer wife, Sofyani. At the time of my fieldwork in 2003–4, Murad and Irsjad were the only two still alive.

Murad's prototype involved an unprecedented fusion of talempong pacik and talempong duduak into the one ensemble. He restricted the melodic range to just five pitches, thereby approximating the range of many indigenous ensembles. Tuning these five notes diatonically, by which I believe he meant using the first five notes and intervallic structure of a major scale, he claimed to approximate some of the tunings he had heard in village contexts. This is an interesting claim, given the tunings I encountered in talempong sets during my own fieldwork in nagari (see tables 2.2, 2.3), none of which are close to diatonic. By using this quasidiatonic standard to tune the instruments, Murad was choosing a neutral tuning, one that was not specific to any one nagari. Aside from tuning, the instrumental function and techniques of indigenous practices were maintained in Murad's prototype: a set of kettle gongs were set on a stand as in talempong duduak and provided melody, while a second set of gongs were divided between multiple players who held two gongs per person in their hands in the fashion of talempong pacik. However, rather than playing melodically and rhythmically interlocking parts, this pacik set provided chordal accompaniment. To play a two-note chord, the performer was required to oscillate between the pair of gongs he held in his hand. According to Irsjad Adam, nine or ten people were required on talempong pacik to cover all the chords, though he did not specify which chords those were. Therefore, the exact tuning of this set of gongs is unclear and there are no recordings to help clarify the record. At the very least, it seems they would have covered the I, IV, and V chords. The effect of this instrumentation, Irsjad suggested, was akin to *angklung* (I, shaken bamboo rattles), where a single person had one or two pitches and sounded them only when that pitch was required. As no audio documentation of this prototype exists, the memories of Murad and Irsjad reveal an important but forgotten episode in the history of the idiom. Aside from the use of indigenous instruments, nobody hearing the idiom today in its current derivatives would ever guess that it had initially been designed as a direct derivation—albeit combination—of indigenous practices, myself included.

Achiar Adam is credited with two important modifications to Murad's original concept. First, he instigated the arrangement of all the talempong on a stand, not just the duduak set. As Irsjad explained, this shift was pragmatic: it facilitated the playing of chords by allowing two gongs to be played simultaneously by one person, and therefore one player could be assigned more than two gongs, thereby streamlining the number of musicians necessary to produce the basic range of chords. However, any visual and audible connection to talempong pacik was obscured by this new arrangement. It is likely that at this stage the scale also was extended from five notes to a complete octave, which expanded the chordal possibilities. Second, and more important, Achiar was responsible for incorporating instruments and tunes from other Minangkabau genres into the style, including the use of winds, such as bansi and saluang. These additions expanded the form's power to convey Minangkabau ethnicity, but that is getting ahead of the story. For now, it is important to note that the idiom moved from Murad's form, which referenced indigenous-style talempong in the instrumental technique, to Achiar's form, where such references were virtually eliminated. This shift was not problematic to the individuals involved because developing indigenous arts meant making them more palatable and contemporary for what was largely a cosmopolitan audience.

By the time Margaret Kartomi visited ASKI, in 1972, this prototype had morphed into what was called orkes talempong. Herawati, an ASKI student in the early 1970s who performed orkes talempong and went on to teach talempong kreasi there, related how a group of prominent intellectuals, artists, and budayawan aspired to have a Minangkabau art form that would garner as much attention as Javanese and Balinese gamelan on the national stage (interview, 2004), a narrative that jibes with Djaruddin Amar's account of the institution as an attempt to bring greater recognition to West Sumatra (interview, 2004). These visionaries wanted an ensemble that was comparable in size and stature to a large bronze gamelan, but nothing like that existed in Minangkabau practice. Indigenous Minangkabau talempong ensembles were small, featuring five to seven players at most. The reformers needed to create something new, modifying and augmenting indigenous practices in order to create a large, impressive ensemble so that Minangkabau arts might enjoy some of gamelan's prestige. According to Herawati, the large ensemble was also designed to attract attention that would materialize in fiscal support for the development of ASKI and Minangkabau arts. According to her account, it had some success in this regard, at least initially. While it undoubtedly helped raise the profile of West Sumatra, orkes talempong and its successors have never garnered the same attention as gamelan, either within or outside Indonesia.

As much as the architects of the form wanted to attract attention from outsiders, they were simultaneously targeting cosmopolitan Minangkabau, who had disengaged from indigenous practices because they found them outdated. The style's inventors aspired to reengage these Minangkabau in their heritage through modifying, updating, or, in short, reforming the indigenous arts. It is useful at this point to turn to Turino's explanation of cultural reformism to understand how the individuals behind orkes talempong—not just Murad and Achiar as arrangers, but also Boestanoel, who oversaw the arrangements behind the scenes and conducted the orchestra—constructed it to project a sense of Minangkabau modernity. In reformist projects, local elements are plugged into foreign frameworks. Particular elements of indigenous practices—for example, talempong—are selected for their symbolic value. These practices are then divorced from their original contexts, aesthetic frames, and value systems as they are "'reformed' in light of modernist ideas, aesthetics, practices, and contexts." Detached from their deeper ethos, the indigenous features become shallow references at best (Turino 2000, 107). Before I get into an analysis of the local and foreign features of the orkes talempong style, a cautionary note about this framework. In addition to showing how these reformist projects co-opt indigenous practices, they should be approached and analyzed for the aesthetic value and meaning for the people who invest in them. I will return later to a discussion of the processes and mechanisms through which orkes talempong comes to accrue meaning for some people who have identified as Minangkabau.

In the analysis that follows I consider which elements of the new form functioned as references to indigenous practices and which were designed to articulate the Minangkabau character of the music, along with what modernist ideas and frames were brought to bear on the model. This includes instrumentation and physical aspects of the ensemble, along with other features of the style, including tuning, texture, and structure. This approach will help not only to clarify how the form was shaped by the background and training of the innovators and arrangers in Western music (cf. Ramstedt 1992, 69), but also to understand how it helped forge a new way of being Minangkabau.

Talempong was clearly at the center of the style, but why was it chosen as the main instrument to use in a form explicitly designed to represent Minangkabau people en masse? First, talempong's wide distribution throughout West Sumatra made it a logical choice. Second, as Herawati stressed, it was more accessible to listeners than genres such as saluang jo dendang, where poetry was central to the form. Using her adult children as an example, she pointed out that even "Minangkabau people don't always understand" the literary references in the genre (interview, 2004). The use of a regional language such as Minangkabau presented an obstacle to the founders' desires for broad appeal outside Minangkabau communities; instrumental styles were considered more translatable across cultural barriers.

Third, while the initial conception of the form was based exclusively on talempong, orkes talempong came to incorporate references to other indigenous practices, instruments, and genres, including the tunes and flute of saluang jo dendang. Its inclusive nature helped articulate an encompassing, collective definition of who Minangkabau people were that transcended local differences. Most significantly, however, talempong was chosen because the instruments—including the gong row and the metallophone—physically resembled gamelan instruments. The talempong jao, the Javanese talempong, here made from bronze, was even named for its resemblance to a saron, an instrument used in Central Javanese gamelan. This ensemble was the closest a Minangkabau practice could get to the paragon of traditional musics from Indonesia—gamelan—while remaining Minangkabau at the same time. Orkes talempong's inventors hoped to accrue the same prestige gamelan enjoyed for their new musical style.

Orkes Talempong: A Style Analysis

From the time of Murad's first experiment through its subsequent development, the ensemble was significantly larger than its indigenous talempong counterparts. Kartomi's 1979 article, based in part on the 1972 trip that took her to ASKI, includes the first scholarly mention of this style, identified as orkes talempong, and provides a list of the instruments in a footnote (35n12).[1] The Sumatra Music Archive at Monash University, which houses Kartomi's field recordings, holds the only extant recordings of orkes talempong and the most extensive collection of photographic evidence of the ensemble from this time. I have extrapolated a rough approximation of the instrumentation of the orkes talempong in 1972 (see table 4.1) by consulting a series of five slides and Kartomi's footnote, along with the recollection of Herawati (interview, 2004).[2]

As table 4.1 illustrates, instrumental function was divided into melody, harmonic accompaniment, bass, and rhythm. It also shows that there was doubling on the most important parts and a spread of register with instruments in three octaves with *canang* (M, flat kettle gong

TABLE 4.1
Instrumentation of *orkes talempong*

Function	Instrument	Description	Musicians /part	Pitch range (relative)
Melody	Talempong	Rack of 9 kettle gongs	3	b–c″
	Talempong jao	Metallophone with 9 keys	2	b″–c‴
	Winds *Bansi*	Small end-blown flute	1	Highest octave
	Saluang	Oblique flute used to accompany *dendang*	1	Middle octave
Harmonic accompaniment	Talempong	Rack of 8 kettle gongs divided into two rows of four each	3	c′–c″
	Canang dasar	Rack of 4 larger, flatter gongs	2	c–f
	Canang tinggi	Rack of 4 larger, flatter gongs	2	g–c′
Bass	Gong		1	
Rhythm	Tambourine	Tambourine with skin head	1	
	Conga		1	

with a larger diameter than talempong) in the lowest octave, talempong in the middle, and talempong jao in the highest. This spread of register helped showcase individual instruments in the dense texture of the ensemble. The pitch range given in table 4.1 is relative rather than absolute. The tuning of the ensemble aimed to be diatonic, even if the recordings suggest the instruments were not precisely tuned to this standard.

Why did the term *orkes* (I, musical group) come to be attached to this ensemble? It is possible it was adopted because of textural resemblance to *orkes Melayu* (I, Melayu bands), or pop bands such as Orkes Gumarang, which featured melody, harmonic accompaniment, bass, and rhythm. The orkes talempong also resembles other experiments in Indonesia to expand the size and scope of indigenous ensembles, including the Bugis *sinfoni kacapi* (I, symphony of two-stringed lutes) in Sulawesi (Sutton 2002, 55). Kartomi (1979, 24) provides several reasons why *orchestra* might even be the appropriate translation of *orkes,* including the use of notation, "the application of the concerto principle," and a conductor.

Figure 4.1 (also see webfig. 4.1), while containing only part of the ensemble, provides a sense of its physicality and the stage presence it commanded. Examining this and other photographic evidence where the talempong, canang, and talempong jao were mounted on elaborately carved wooden frames with the players standing behind, the orkes talempong indeed looked, as Kartomi remarks, "like a rather high Javanese *gamelan*" (1979, 24). The frames from this time were elaborately carved using patterns found on rumah gadang. The performers, in a radical departure from indigenous practice—where talempong groups consist of either women or men, but never a mix—included both men and women, all of whom wore colorful, glossy costumes that referenced ceremonial practice for the women and typical performers' outfits for the men. Complete with a conductor standing in front with a baton (see webfig. 4.2), the ensemble *looked* something like a Minangkabau orchestra. At the very least, the form's sheer physicality had to help increase the visibility of Minangkabau people.

Kartomi's archival recordings of four pieces[3] from 21 January 1972 are useful in extrapolating some structural features of the diatonic talempong idiom in the 1970s because there are some key differences from its contemporary derivative, talempong kreasi. The kinds of instruments incorporated in orkes talempong were, for the most part, indigenous Minangkabau ones, including talempong; canang; the wind instruments: bansi, saluang, and sarunai; and the gongs. The

FIGURE 4.1. *Orkes talempong* with *talempong jao* in the second row. ASKI, Padang Panjang, 1972. Photo by H. Kartomi. Used with permission.

pictures taken during Kartomi's 1972 visit suggest that the drums, including a conga and a tambourine with a skin head, were not indigenous at this time. The ways in which the instruments were used, however, departed from indigenous practice, including the sheer size of the ensemble, the combination of instruments from distinct genres (e.g., using a bansi or saluang with talempong) (Kartomi 1979, 24), and the principles of orchestration (e.g., the doubling and tripling of some parts). By mixing instruments from different genres in the one ensemble, Herawati has suggested, its creators wanted to "enrich the timbres" of Minangkabau music (interview, 2004), a word choice that hints at an agenda to improve previous practices. Instrumental technique was for the most part maintained, as indigenous instruments were incorporated into the orchestra, but some extended instrumental techniques providing timbral diversity were developed, such as playing on the *pinggir* (I, edge)—that is, the face rather than the boss—of the talempong and canang. The physical presentation of the instruments, with their high frames encouraging a standing posture, was also different from indigenous practice, where groups either moved in procession or sat on the ground. While this presentation of the musicians made the distinctions between performer and audience clearer, it was also a sharp break from indigenous practices, where sedentary events are still conducted at ground level and standing in the presence of those sitting is rude. I see this as a shift to more cosmopolitan values, as the audience members no longer sat on the ground but on chairs.

An important modification of the instruments from their use in indigenous practices was the diatonic tuning. While Murad's prototype used just five pitches for the melody, by the time of these recordings, the range had been expanded to a full octave or more. The main melody instruments—the talempong, which I shall call *talempong melodi* (I, melody talempong, *tm* for short) following Herawati's lead, and the talempong jao—had nine notes each, which probably stretched from scale degree 7 to scale degree 1, two octaves above (see fig. 4.1, front row left and center for talempong melodi and the talempong jao directly between them in the following row). From the photographic evidence, the accompanying talempong part, which I shall call talempong accompaniment (*ta*), in order to distinguish it from the melody part, included an octave set divided into two rows of four gongs, or a tetrachord, each (see fig. 4.1, player to the far left). However, with only two mallets, each player would only have been able to play two notes simultaneously. The canang part appears to be an octave divided into two sets of four gongs each (see fig. 4.1, woman in the last row). Herawati identified these as *canang dasar* (I, low canang), covering the first tetrachord, and *canang tinggi* (I, high canang), covering the second.

Tuning the kettle gongs diatonically so as to allow functional harmony was one of the reforms designed to convey modernism. Diatonicism had the added benefit of being a theoretically neutral system in West Sumatra: by showing affiliations to no specific nagari, it came to stand for a pan-Minangkabau identity. Moreover, as Irsjad explained, outsiders—meaning other Indonesians—would more readily accept diatonicism than the tuning standards of indigenous practices because they were already familiar with it (interview, 2004). Irsjad and Djaruddin both commented on how diatonic tuning had been the great equalizer in the music of the Indonesian nationalist movement.

Some of the melodies used as the basis for orkes talempong arrangements were freshly created, but other pieces drew on well-known dendang that were or could be replicated diatonically, such as Achiar Adam's "Tak tontong" (a children's song referencing onomatopoeic sounds of drums and talempong) (audio 4.1 for the dendang, accompanied by the talempong jao; audio 4.2 for the orkes talempong arrangement of it; the melody starts at 00:57) (Kartomi 1979, 24). This incorporation of existing local material is somewhat akin to the use of *dolonan,* Javanese children's songs, as a basis for Javanese kreasi baru (Becker 1980; Benamou 2010). The recordings suggest that at this time, despite the range of the melodic instruments just over an octave, most of the melodies are largely contained within the span of a fifth, much like dendang and some indigenous talempong practices. But while the melodies sometimes referenced indigenous genres, the arrangements of these melodies were novel: they were orchestrated in parallel thirds, sixths, or octaves, and set to harmonic accompaniment that drew almost exclusively on chords I, V, and (less frequently) IV. Sometimes the melodies were combined into medleys, such as "Tak tontong," which combined the dendang of that name with one called "Indang Payakumbuh." Cosmopolitans were attracted to the new style, Herawati suggested, because the melodies were arranged in novel ways that departed from indigenous modes (interview, 2004). The use of functional harmony was one way that arrangers reinterpreted and presented indigenous practices in a frame that Minangkabau with cosmopolitan tastes could understand and appreciate; they were otherwise disdainful toward indigenous practices because they considered them outdated and backward. Cosmopolitans were engaged, Irsjad contended, only when talempong was revamped in the form of orkes talempong (interview, 2004). These practices of diatonic tuning and functional harmony, identified as Western, were internalized by Minangkabau cosmopolitans, including Murad and Boestanoel, as their own, the second stage in Turino's theory of cosmopolitanism. Culturally reformist projects, where the best of the local features are plugged into foreign frameworks, such as orkes talempong, could be considered the third stage, where a cosmopolitan formation uses local markers to distinguish it from others (Turino 2000; 2003).

In addition to the diatonic tuning of the instruments, the arrangement of dendang for a talempong orchestra required some fairly drastic modifications of the indigenous practices. The use of harmony resulted in considerably different textures than either dendang or talempong in their indigenous contexts. In saluang jo dendang, the flute and vocal line are delivered heterophonically, and chapter 2 illustrated how indigenous talempong styles involve interlocking patterns and melody layered over rhythmic ostinati. The shift to homophony in orkes talempong involved a shift from an emphasis on horizontal relationships in indigenous practices to one on verticality, which is emphasized by block chords sustained by tremolos on the talempong and canang that were a distinctive characteristic of the early orkes talempong style.

To illustrate more specifically how orkes talempong pieces were put together I draw on the piece "Kambang cari." The analysis that follows illustrates how the arrangers of orkes talempong pieces were paying considerable attention to the presentation of material with textural and timbral contrasts to engage the listener. Variety and contrast, as Turino asserts, provide the means to gain and retain audience attention that is central to the success of presentational forms of music, one of the four fields of music that he outlines for their distinctive approaches to the "frame of interpretation, values, responsibilities, practices, sound features, and distinct conceptions of what music is" (2008, 21; 2000). These orkes talempong arrangements provide a stark contrast with indigenous talempong practices, where the constancy of sound is advantageous to the context where the music is necessary to the keramaian of a ceremony yet remains in the background. In contrast, in orkes talempong, the music—and any dance it accompanied—was the focal point of the event. Skilled musicians—trained at the institution—played for a distinct audience, sometimes physically separated by a stage or seating arrangements. Such distinctions are not always clear in indigenous contexts.

I have included a full transcription of "Kambang cari" (music example 4.1), along with a structural outline of it in music example 4.2, below (see audio 4.3 for the recording). As the outline suggests, the

MUSICAL EXAMPLE 4.1. Transcription of the *orkes talempong* piece "Kambang cari." (*page 1*)

MUSICAL EXAMPLE 4.1 *(cont.)*. Transcription of the *orkes talempong* piece "Kambang cari." *(pages 2–3)*

MUSICAL EXAMPLE 4.1 (*cont.*). Transcription of the *orkes talempong* piece "Kambang cari." (*pages 4–5*)

MUSICAL EXAMPLE 4.1 (*cont.*). Transcription of the *orkes talempong* piece "Kambang cari." (*pages 6–7*)

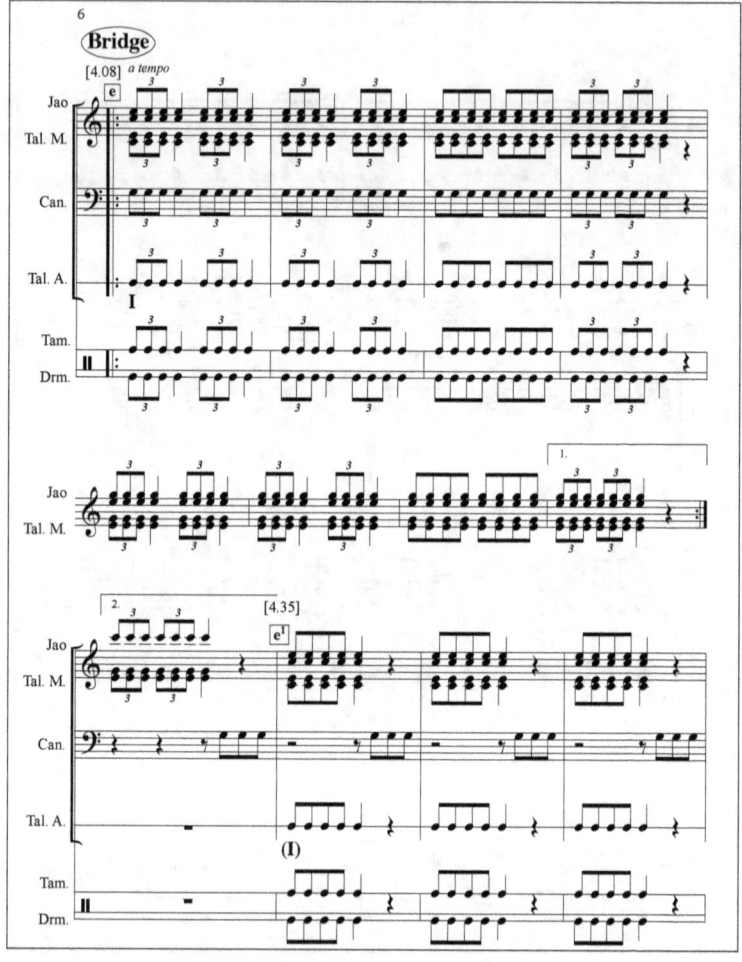

MUSICAL EXAMPLE 4.1 (*cont.*). Transcription of the *orkes talempong* piece "Kambang cari." (*pages 8–9*)

MUSICAL EXAMPLE 4.1 (*cont.*). Transcription of the *orkes talempong* piece "Kambang cari." (*pages 10–11*)

MUSICAL EXAMPLE 4.1 (*cont.*). Transcription of the *orkes talempong* piece "Kambang cari." (*pages 12–13*)

MUSICAL EXAMPLE 4.1 (*cont.*). Transcription of the *orkes talempong* piece "Kambang cari." (*pages 14–15*)

MUSICAL EXAMPLE 4.1 (*cont.*). Transcription of the *orkes talempong* piece "Kambang cari." (*pages 16–17*)

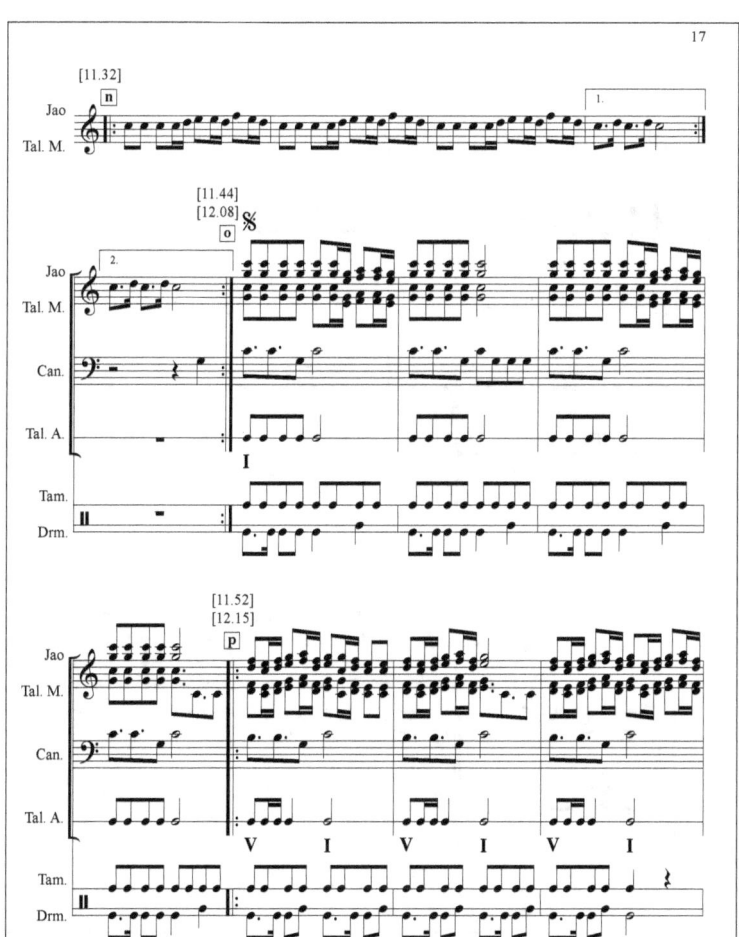

MUSICAL EXAMPLE 4.1 (*cont.*). Transcription of the *orkes talempong* piece "Kambang cari." (*pages 18–19*)

MUSICAL EXAMPLE 4.1 *(cont.)*. Transcription of the *orkes talempong* piece "Kambang cari." *(page 20)*

Time	Large Section	Melodic Phrase	Instrumentation		
			All*	Melody Instrument/s	Accompaniment Style
0.00	Intro	ax2	X		ta & c: block chords with tremolos
0.34	A	bx4	X	tm & jao in call & answer	ta: block chords; c: bass line, pattern 1
0.50	A	cx2	X		ta: block chords; c: bass line, pattern 1
1.20		c¹x2		bansi	t: pinggir, pattern 2
1.51		cx2	X		ta: block chords; c: bass line, pattern 1
2.22		cx2		jao, bansi, saluang & drum	ta: block chords; c: bass line, pattern 3
2.51		c²		saluang & jao	
3.04		d		saluang, bansi, and jao	ta: tremolo block chords
3.21		c²		saluang & jao	
3.35		d		saluang, bansi, and jao	ta: tremolo block chords
3.51		c³		bansi & saluang	
4.08	Bridge	ex2	X		ta & c block chords, alternating with just ta block chords
4.35		e¹	X		ta: block chords; c: bass line
4.49		e²		jao: rhythmic drone	
4.56		e³		bansi & saluang	
5.06		e⁴		canang: rhythmic drone	
5.21	B	fx2	X	tm & jao	ta: block chords; c: bass line, pattern 4
5.36		gx2		jao, bansi, saluang & drum	ta & c: pinggir, pattern 5
5.49		fx2	X		ta: block chords; c: bass line, pattern 4
6.03		gx2		jao, bansi, saluang & drum	ta & c: pinggir, pattern 5
6.17		f¹x2		bansi, saluang & drum	ta: block chords; c: bass line, pattern 6
6.32		g¹x2		jao in call & answer with bansi & saluang, plus drums	
6.45		gx2	X		ta & c: block chords
6.58	Bridge	h	X		ta & c: block chords and tremolos
7.40				drum solo	
7.53				tambourine joins drum	
7.58	C	i		loosely metered saluang	solo talempong ostinato
9.10	D	jx2	X		ta & c: block chords, pattern 7
9.38		kx2		jao, bansi, saluang & drum	ta & c: pinggir, pattern 8
10.03		jx2	X		ta & c: block chords, pattern 7
10.27		kx2		jao, bansi, saluang & drum	ta & c: pinggir, pattern 8
10.52		j	X		ta & c: block chords, pattern 7
11.06		lx2	X		Tremolo block chords
11.17		mx2		bansi & saluang	
11.32		nx2		jao solo	
11.44		o	X		ta & c: block chords, pattern 9
11.52		px2	X		ta & c: block chords, pattern 10
12.08		o	X		ta & c: block chords, pattern 9
12.15		px2	X		ta & c: block chords, pattern 10
12.32		o		jao	ta & c: pinggir, pattern 10
12.39		px2		bansi, saluang, & talempong	
12.55	Coda	p¹	X		ta & c: block chords
13.20	End				

*all = talempong melodi, talempong jao, talempong accompaniment, canang, drum, tambourine. Everything but bansi and saluang. Melody in these sections, unless otherwise specified, is on talempong melodi and the talempong jao.
tm = talempong melodi, ta = talempong accompaniment, c = canang
Pinggir = gongs played on the face, not the boss.

MUSICAL EXAMPLE 4.2. Structural outline of "Kambang cari."

form of this piece is linear, with a number of distinct sections. This is a clear departure from the cyclical structures of indigenous talempong practices. In my analysis, each large section marked by a capital letter is predicated on a different melodic idea, while other sections are more transitional, such as the bridges or the coda. Different melodic phrases within a section are expressed by lowercase letters, with a prime number indicating slight variation in melodic or rhythmic material of that phrase. Most of these phrases are four or eight measures long. Any phrases longer than that are typically transitional.

The arrangers of these pieces exploited instrumental, textural, and occasionally metrical contrasts. For example, arrangers worked with the alternation between denser textures, involving the whole orchestra (minus the winds) (e.g., phrases *a, c, f,* and *j*), and thinner textures, involving a solo instrument (e.g., bansi in c^1, talempong jao in e^2, *n,* and *o*) or groupings of instruments, where they played with different combinations of timbres. For example, the breathy saluang is combined with the vibrant, piercing timbre of the talempong jao in phrase c^2 and with the mellow sounds of the bansi at other moments (e.g., phrases c^3, e^3, and *m;* see fig. 4.2; webfig. 4.3). The arrangers also played with orchestration in other ways, such as devising call-and-response phrases between different instrumental sections where timbral and register differences were juxtaposed; for example, the talempong trading phrases with the talempong jao, which is an octave higher and has a much brighter timbre, in phrase *b,* or the talempong jao trading phrases with the wind instruments in g^1. The arrangers also played with parallel melodic lines. When the talempong or talempong jao had the melody, it was often delivered in parallel thirds (e.g., phrases *a, b, c,* and c^2). When the bansi and the saluang played together, they never played at the same pitch level, which helped emphasize their distinct timbres: most often they played in parallel octaves, but sometimes in parallel compound minor sixths and once in out-of-tune parallel perfect fourths.

Another element of the orchestration of these pieces was the arrangement of the accompanying parts. Most often the accompanying talempong and canang parts played block chords, each player contributing two notes of the chord. Sometimes, however, the canang outlined a simple bass line instead. To provide contrast, the arrangers played with the rhythm of the accompanying parts, changing it from phrase to phrase. These patterns have been marked in music example 4.2. When the talempong and canang were used to accompany the winds or the talempong jao (or both), as in phrases c^1, *g, k,* and *o,* they switched to playing on the pinggir. This resulted in a flatter, tinnier timbre but also reduced the dynamic level so the instruments soloing were more audible.

FIGURE 4.2. The *bansi* (*left*) and *saluang* (*right*) take a solo in *orkes talempong*, ASKI, Padang Panjang, 1972. Photo by H. Kartomi. Used with permission.

The manipulation of contrasting accompanying patterns rhythmically, timbrally, and texturally is even more explicit in the piece "Tak tontong" in the setting of the dendang "Indang Payakumbuah" (audio 4.2, starting at 03:28).[4] As seen in music example 4.3, there are four different accompaniment patterns with variation in rhythm, timbre, and texture for six iterations of the melody. The talempong and canang parts played block chords following the chordal changes indicated, while the canang sometimes also outlined a distinct bass line. On the first two repeats when the talempong held the melody, the talempong played on the down beat every measure while the canang had its own pattern. On the third repeat, when the bansi and saluang held the melody, the accompanying parts switched to play every beat but played on the pinggir. On the fourth repeat, there was a more elaborate two-measure pattern under the talempong jao. On the fifth repeat, the melody returned to the talempong and the same pattern as in repeats 1 and 2 was used. On the final repeat, the accompanying parts featured a new measure-long pattern under the talempong.

Another way variety was created in these pieces was through metrical contrasts or referencing indigenous practices. For example, the

```
Melody:        5 ||: 5  5̄4̄ 54 | 4̄ 4̄4̄ 34 54 | 5  5̄4̄ 43 | 3  3̄1̄ 21 | 2̄3̄ 32 2̄1̄ |  1  1̄2̄ 3
Chords:              I              V              I           I          V              I
Accomp. 4th repeat: xx xx xx | x   o   o  | xx xx xx | x  o  o | xx x  x | x  o  o


| 4̄ 4̄4̄ 32 34 | 43 31 21 | 2̄3̄ 3̄2̄ 31 | 1  1̄2̄ 32 | 2  2̄1̄ 31 | 2  2  2  | 2  o  5 :||
      V            I           V          I           V          V          V
| xx   x   x  | x  o   o | xx x   x  | x  o   o | x  o   o | x  x  x  | x  o  o |
```

Accompaniment pattern 1st and 2nd repeats:

    Talempong: ||: x o o :||

    Canang: ||: o xx x :||

Accompaniment pattern 3rd repeat:

    Talempong & : ||: x x x :||
    Canang

Accompaniment pattern 4th repeat:
(see above)

Accompaniment pattern 5th repeat:

    Talempong: ||: x o o | x o o :||

    Canang: ||: x o x | x o x :||

Accompaniment pattern 6th repeat:

    Talempong: ||: xx x o | xx x o :||

    Canang: ||: x o x | x o x :||

MUSICAL EXAMPLE 4.3. Accompaniment patterns for *dendang* "Indang Payakumbuah" in "Tak tontong."

first section of "Tak tontong" (audio 4.2) is in the duple meter more characteristic of Minangkabau music, but the later section that involves the arrangement of the dendang "Indang Payakumbuah" (as seen in music example 4.3) is in triple meter (at 03:17). "Kambang cari," like other orkes talempong pieces, references indigenous practices. For example, the saluang in phrase c^2 references a figuration used in the Singgalang category of songs—songs said to originate near or around Mt. Singgalang—within the saluang jo dendang repertoire. Section

C is styled on a nonmetrical saluang part akin to something heard in the *ratok* (M, sad) category of songs, though what is new here is the combination with a metrical talempong ostinato. In the piece "Tari barabah," one section also references talempong pacik.

This analysis of orkes talempong pieces has illustrated the balance between repetition and contrast at a melodic, textural, and timbral level. While there was not a lot of melodic complexity to a piece, diversity was maintained through the orchestration, including varying timbral combinations of instruments, changing rhythmic patterns underneath melodies, and dynamic changes when the winds were featured and talempong were played on the pinggir.

While orkes talempong was designed to entertain an audience, the style also served an ideological end. Its founders and supporters in the early years hoped it would gain some visibility and prestige for Minangkabau people on the national stage, though it never did in the way they wished. A handful of people also explicitly connected its rise to the failure of the PRRI and loss of cultural confidence. While the voice of the minority, the connection of orkes talempong with the PRRI is, I think, an important part of the discourse to include. In the project to sonically represent Minangkabau ethnicity, the style referenced indigenous Minangkabau practices through instruments, melodies, and instrument frames. But the style did not just passively reflect Minangkabau ethnicity, it also had the effect of ushering in a new way to be Minangkabau, even if not everybody agreed with it in retrospect.

By refusing specific nagari associations of indigenous talempong styles—including tunes, instrumentation, and tunings—in favor of incorporating references with broader signification—diatonic tuning and well-known dendang, orkes talempong actively contributed to the construction and maintenance of a broad Minangkabau identity that transcended the nagari and regional differences. The cultural reformism that drew on diatonic tuning, functional harmony, linear arrangements, and textural and timbral contrasts helped forge an image of Minangkabau modernity. For some people, there was more

Minangkabau essence in the orkes talempong version of Minangkabau modernity than the one offered by pop Minang of the time, such as Orkes Gumarang, which featured Minangkabau lyrics set to Latin rhythms. The people in the business of creating, managing, and listening to orkes talempong thought of themselves as Minangkabau as they engaged with it. In other words, for those individuals, a sense of ethnicity was activated, brought into focal awareness, and momentarily eclipsed the many other identities they simultaneously held.

Turino's work on Peircian semiotics helps explain how an art form can actively create a new identity. For example (1999, 236), he shows how the mass media and advertising deliberately create signs to signal shared experiences, helping create a sense of what the theorist Benedict Anderson termed "imagined communities." In Benedict Anderson's ([1983] 1991) model, people do not know each other personally but can imagine their connection through a shared discourse or other shared signs. The performance of this style in contexts where Minangkabau identity was being represented made "the imagined possibility materially patent and public, thus helping to bring the possibility to fruition" (Turino 1999, 245). This new musical style helped create an "imagined community" of cosmopolitan Minangkabau who imagined their connection to others like them, even if they did not know them personally. In other words, orkes talempong helped carve out a space for a new way of being Minangkabau—a cosmopolitan and modern one—in the new political and social order of the late 1960s and early 1970s in Indonesia. For the cosmopolitans in the process of redefining what it meant to be Minangkabau in this period, the diatonic talempong idiom came to be imbued with an emotional salience.

By the 1980s, when proponents of the PRRI theory claimed the fear of repercussions from being "too Minangkabau" had receded, orkes talempong had gained a strong foothold among the cosmopolitan Minangkabau population, making way for the aesthetic ascendancy of its successor, talempong kreasi, as the musical representation of Minangkabau ethnicity, underscoring the ways in which an art—talempong in this case—can become a mechanism that activates and actively articulates a sense of ethnicity.

In one example of how the tensions between the preservation of a tradition and its development were resolved, I have illustrated how the aesthetic transformations to take talempong from a communal expression to one that articulated a pan-Minangkabau identity were considerable. The concept of producing a form that also expressed modernity, as it was thought about in the 1960s, also shaped the resultant form, as did the musical background and training of the style's inventors in Western practices. In the next chapter, I present different solutions to this negotiation and how the pressures of the free-market economy and the reemergence of regional politics in Reformation Indonesia shaped the practice of talempong.

Chapter 5

TALEMPONG IN THE MARKETPLACE

In the late 1960s and 1970s talempong was restyled from a form that expressed local identity to a form that expressed ethnicity. This chapter continues the interest in the diatonic talempong idiom as an expression of Minangkabau ethnicity, but shifts the focus onto transformations connected with the political economy of the New Order and Reformation eras including the cultural politics of the state interested in display; the strengthening of a free-market economy in which artistic and cultural goods were exchanged for economic capital at tourist shows, government functions, and private events; and the reemphasis on tourism as a source of economic revenue under regional autonomy. This chapter, then, is focused on money matters: how concerns of the market shape the arts or, put another way, how arts are modified and framed in order to be viable in the marketplace and respond to the needs of the paying clientele.

Continuing the exploration of talempong styles, I trace the ways talempong has been aesthetically reshaped by these market forces and how it is packaged with other arts, including the transformation of orkes talempong into talempong kreasi at the institution in the 1980s, its subsequent adoption by sanggar, and the emergence of the most popularized version of talempong to date, talempong goyang. The tonal palette of the idiom, however, has been expanded from the diatonic major of orkes talempong to include more chromatic notes that allow for minor keys and modulation. I explore the ways these new talempong practices have encouraged people to listen to and engage with the music in ethnic terms. The chapter also traces the emergence and proliferation of sanggar, the performance and cultural troupes that have packages at the ready for any occasion, and the involvement of graduates of the institution on the lookout for ways to make a living. Therefore, here I continue the conversations about the consequences of institutionalization and the related professionalization of Minangkabau arts as graduates, faculty, and students of the institution are involved in these activities and venues.

After the fall of Sukarno's government, the purging of some half million to one million suspected communists, and Suharto's assumption of power, in 1967, the country settled into a period of relative political stability. The new government, known as the New Order, to distinguish it from the previous presidency of Sukarno, began to target national development, including the growth of the economy, industry, and improvements to education and living standards. As the country experienced a period of economic growth, economic modes in West Sumatra continued to diversify from subsistence to capitalism, with a greater percentage of the population needing—and wanting—access to economic capital. During the New Order, which lasted until Suharto's ousting, in 1998, there was an increasing professionalization of the workforce and the subsequent growth of the middle class. Moreover, some artistic and cultural practices, driven by the cultural politics of the New Order and the development of the tourist industry, accrued explicit fiscal value and were incorporated into a developing market as individuals and communities looked to hire performers for their events.

Cultural Politics and the Rise of Tourism

If the cultural policies of Sukarno's government (1945–65) were characterized by trying to craft expressions representative of the new nation, those of Suharto's New Order (1967–98) were concerned with celebrating, at least nominally, the country's cultural diversity. Scholars offer differing opinions about this switch in policy. On the one hand, Michel Picard (1997, 196–97) points out that the assumption of national unity enabled the celebration of regional diversity, albeit within a prescribed framework. Rita Kipp (1993), on the other hand, argues that regional expressions were cultivated because they diffused political expressions of independence. Ultimately, however, they both argue that the displays of difference were crafted and monitored so the stability of the nation was not threatened. I am interested in the act of cultural display as another mechanism through which a sense of ethnicity was engaged and articulated, although its expression was deliberately manipulated, contained, and framed.

Arts were selected and crafted for display in a process that I call the packaging of ethnicity. When indigenous artistic practices, such as music and dance, were chosen, they were refined, modified, modernized, sanitized, simplified, recontextualized, or resignified (Kuipers 1998; Pemberton 1994; Rutherford 1996; Taylor 1994; Yampolsky 1995). As Anna Tsing comments, local practices had to transform into "harmless, officially sanctioned 'entertainment'" (1993, 245–46). Some artistic forms that were culturally reformist in nature, such as orkes talempong and its derivative, talempong kreasi, were designed explicitly for this purpose. Cultural difference was performed at theme parks, museums, and festivals, with comparable items—costumes, knives, cooking pots—presented side by side from each cultural group or region. The performative equivalents featured packages of music, dance, and ritual fused into pretty spectacles. But ethnic difference, even in its innocuous form, was sometimes subsumed by representation at the provincial level. For example, Taman Mini Indonesia Indah (I, Beautiful Indonesia in Miniature Park) has a pavilion for each of the twenty-seven provinces that existed when it opened, in 1975. Selecting which items would represent an ethnically diverse province has been a politically loaded business. Even in West Sumatra, where 88 percent of the population identified as Minangkabau in the 2000 census, Minangkabau people represent the province at the expense of the Mentawaians living on the islands off the southern coast.

Packages virtually identical to those presented for displays of the state were presented for tourist events, with some tourists present at the former. In 1969, with the release of the first REPELITA (I, Rencana Pembangunan Lima Tahun, Five-Year Development Plan), the central government started investing in the development of Indonesia's tourism potential, seeing the international market as an important source of external revenue and the domestic one as a way of strengthening national sentiments and providing employment opportunities (Adams 2006; Booth 1990; Picard 1997). However, the growth of the industry in the 1970s was hampered in part by the high value of the rupiah in connection with the oil boom and tourist visa requirements (Booth 1990, 46, 48). The numbers of foreign tourists increased significantly from the 1970s, with slightly fewer than 900,000 total in the first REPELITA (1969–74) to over 4.5 million in the fourth (1984–89) (Oka 1990, 23–24). By 1989 the tourism sector was the second-highest source of foreign income revenue outside oil and gas and was predicted to become the largest sector by the end of 1990s (Booth 1990, 52–53).

The history of cultural tourism in West Sumatra has received little attention, compared with more famous stops on the tourist route: Bali (e.g., Picard 1996; Dunbar-Hall 2006; Noszlopy 2007), Java (Hughes-Freeland 1993b), and the Torajan highlands in Sulawesi (Adams 1998, 2006). This paucity of information may stem from a comparatively small number of tourists visiting West Sumatra in comparison to these other areas (Soedarsono 1999, 373). Although I do not have access to figures from West Sumatra for the 1970s or 1980s, an examination of the numbers shows an increase through the 1990s from almost 50,000 foreign tourists and just over 400,000 domestic ones in 1990 to a peak in 1996 of over 100,000 foreigners and 850,000 domestic tourists (BPSPSB 1998, 392). In comparison, the Toraja highland had more than double the number of foreign tourists at its peak in the mid-1990s (Adams 2006, 15), while Bali received the lion's share, with 1.5 million foreigners visiting in 1994 (Picard 1997), myself included.

Although I do not have data for the numbers of tourists in West Sumatra in the 1970s, there are several accounts that mention the emergence of the tourism industry. Soedarsono (1999, 386), for example, claims tourists started traveling to the province in the 1970s, especially as passengers on cruise ships. They disembarked at the port of Teluk Bayur, stayed in Padang, and watched shows at the Taman Budaya.[1] Kartomi (1979, 24) also mentions the rise of the industry during this decade, identifying the audience as largely domestic or from nearby countries. The tourists stopped at the institution to see performances. Herawati recalled how orkes talempong was designed, in part, to capture the attention of the tourist market (interview, 2004). In 1984 a space especially for tourist performances was built in the highland town of Bukittinggi (Soedarsono 1999, 386). While there are no definitive numbers of tourists from this period, the establishment of this space suggests that the growth of tourism—if not the numbers of visitors—in West Sumatra was in line with that of the industry in other parts of the archipelago.

By the time of my first visit to West Sumatra, in 1998, the number of tourists—both domestic and foreign—had seriously declined. The Asian financial crisis of 1997 precipitated widespread rioting that resulted in dictatorial Suharto's ousting as president in May 1998, after thirty-one years of claiming the office. In the following years, a period characterized as the Reformation Era, Indonesia experienced a period of political and economic instability. The tourism industry suffered from these national events but was dealt a further blow by terrorist attacks in Indonesia in the wake of September 11, including the 2002 Bali bombings, in which more than two hundred people, mostly foreigners, lost their lives, and the bombing of other Western interests, including the Marriott in Jakarta in 2003 and the Australian embassy in 2004 (cf. Adams 2006). In West Sumatra, figures show a decrease in foreign tourists from 108,676 in 1996 to 37,762 in 2008, with significantly lower numbers in 1999–2002, right after the economic crisis and ensuing political instability. In 2008 over 80 percent of those foreign tourists were Malaysian (BPSBSP 2009, 433). In 2003 the central government was heavily promoting domestic tourism around the archipelago to overcome the economic shortfall in the national budget from the declining numbers of foreign visitors.

The provincial, regional, and local governments of West Sumatra also saw the tourism industry as a solution to economic problems following the implementation of *otonomi daerah* (I, regional autonomy) in 1999, a decentralization policy that was spurred by demands made "to an autocratic regime that had consistently accumulated wealth and power in the centre" at the expense of the regions (Benda-Beckmann and Benda-Beckmann 2001, 2). Resource-rich provinces, such as Aceh and Papua, demanded not only more equitable distribution of the profits but also greater political autonomy. Laws 22/1999 and 25/1999 were designed to decentralize "administrative authority, fiscal autonomy and control over resource management to local regencies and municipalities" (Hainsworth, Turner, and Webster, 2007, 43–44; see Aspinall and Fealy 2003 for a general overview; Smith 2008 for an incisive analysis of the political motivations behind the law).

The fiscal implications of this new arrangement for cultural and artistic practices were considerable. When visiting government offices and agencies concerned with culture and the arts in West Sumatra in 2003–4, I constantly encountered the claim that there was little or no money since the implementation of regional autonomy for cultural activities. West Sumatra, in comparison to other regions, was relatively resource poor: as Asnam Rasyid, employee of Taman Budaya Padang, commented to me, "We only have cement, coal, and people." According to him, the difference was also manifest in arts budgets: Riau had Rp 1.8 billion, whereas West Sumatra had just Rp 75 million (interview, 2004). As fiscal responsibility for the Taman Budaya was transferred from the central government to the provinces with regional autonomy, Taman Budaya Padang had to manage with an even smaller budget than it had in the past.

As parts of a relatively resource poor province, the provincial, regional, and local governments were forced to think creatively about raising the revenue necessary to subsist: they saw economic salvation in tourism. By packaging West Sumatra, with its unique natural and cultural resources, as the gateway to western Indonesia and Sumatra, the provincial Department of Tourism, Arts, and Culture hoped to turn tourism into the major economic resource of the province. The numbers suggest that while they were not successful in attracting foreign tourists to return to the region, the domestic market was dramatically increasing. After a parallel decline in domestic tourism from

1997–2002, the numbers of domestic tourists dramatically increased—from 858,652 in 1996 to 4,843,822 in 2007 (BPSPSB 2009, 433–34).

The reemphasis on tourism meant there was an increased interest from all stakeholders in the market viability of the arts: the glitzier the spectacle, the better its commercial success. Asnam Rasyid recounted some of the changes: "Before, we used to prioritize art for the sake of the arts. Maybe there was much research, documentation, examination, also lots of arts workshops because arts were under [the] education [department]. . . . Now that we are under tourism, *art is for sale*. It's different. There's more commercialization of the arts" (interview, 2004, my emphasis). This focal shift meant privileging the kinds of artistic and cultural practices that could be packaged for entertainment purposes, including the glossy packages offered by sanggar, of which talempong kreasi, a streamlined version of orkes talempong, was a part. According to Sutton, there is a "belief that traditional performing arts, however refigured and reinterpreted in contemporary contexts, constitute one of the most important components in the package Indonesia can offer to attract foreign tourists" (2002, 22). By the time I left Indonesia in 2004, talempong goyang was also gaining traction, used by the institute in outreach events and in demand for private events because it was more fashionable and could cover songs from many different genres. Returning in 2010 gave me the opportunity to follow up on these issues. In both cultural policies and the private sector, the emphasis was clearly on the marketability of the arts. I found, however, that the discourses about arts for sale had also gained a foothold even in nagari where musicians and administrative figures were increasingly thinking about how they could participate in the arts marketplace, some even aspiring to "go international."

To summarize, by the mid-1980s there were a number of new markets for the arts, including two with overlapping concerns: elaborate cultural displays of the state and tourist events. Both these markets demanded arts that could entertain, were in touch with the times, and yet were representative of Minangkabau ethnicity. Along with the demand for sanggar to perform at tourist events, theme parks, and government functions, there were increasing requests from people and communities, both in the homeland and the rantau, with the economic resources to hire sanggar for life-cycle ceremonies, such as weddings and circumcisions, and other communal events. All markets were subject to fluctuations in the Indonesian economy, both the public and private sectors seeing a decline in available resources, and thus in activity, during the krismon, starting in 1997. The markets started to gradually recover during the Reformation era: while the state invested fewer resources in cultural displays and the tourist market had changed, the demand for gigs in the private sector had significantly increased as the economy strengthened. More of the middle class now had the resources to participate in the gig economy.

The Emergence of Minangkabau Sanggar

Sanggar, what I have loosely defined as performing arts troupes until now, were a phenomenon that in West Sumatra began to emerge in the 1960s and blossomed through the 1980s to fill the various demands of the growing markets for new kinds of Minangkabau arts. One of the earliest sanggar dedicated to Minangkabau arts was established on 15 February 1962 by a group of students from West Sumatra who attended a cultural festival in Bali: this group became known as Sanggar Tari Sofyani, and was directed by choreographer Sofyani and her composer husband, Yusaf Rahman. Herawati recalls that when she was a student at ASKI in the early 1970s, teams from the college performed weekly around the province: "sometimes just for entertainment, sometimes for a wedding, sometimes at the ceremony to install a titled man" (interview, 2004). The demand was high because at the time there were very few groups for hire that offered the new, modernist versions of Minangkabau arts, such as orkes talempong.

In the Minangkabau context, the word *sanggar* takes on different associations than it does in other Indonesian contexts. In the Indonesian language, the definition of *sanggar* is quite broad: usually a studio for some kind of artistic or athletic activity. Sanggar can also be places to train new artists. Jonathan McIntosh (2012), for example, discusses one such dance studio in Bali. While *sanggar seni* (I, arts studio) of this nature do exist in West Sumatra, the most common application of the term in my experience there since 1998 is to mean performance troupes that offered packages tailored to a client's needs, whether that client was an individual, the state, or the local tourist office. These packages, fusing ritual, music, dance, and theater, celebrate and reify Minangkabau cultural practices and performing arts. The use of the term *sanggar* itself is a general indicator of aesthetic approach: such a group privileges the music and dance styles that emerged at the institutions in response to demands for the preservation and development of Minangkabau traditions. In short, sanggar offer glossy spectacles that include aestheticized versions of Minangkabau rituals, such as "Tari pasambahan" or "Tari galombang," ritualistic dance offerings with the delivery of betel to distinguished guests; colorful costumes; dramatic items designed to dazzle the audience, such as the version of tari piring where dancers stomp on broken shards of glass with their bare feet (video 5.1) or self-defense displays where two individuals engage in a fight scene that escalates and involves the drawing of a knife; and talempong kreasi ensembles playing arrangements of dendang and pop Minang (see video 1.1, where Lansano Entertaint play a cover of the dendang "Mudiak arau," which has been incorporated into the pop Minang repertoire).

Sometimes sanggar do include items referencing indigenous practices, such as Saayun Salangkah's program for tourists in Bukittinggi. On 8 May 2004, their program included *bansi tunggal* (I, solo bansi), saluang jo dendang, talempong pacik, and a piece that referenced talempong duduak but did not directly resemble a particular practice. In the latter two cases, the gongs were borrowed from the diatonically tuned set, talempong pacik's processional applications referenced by walking in circuitous routes around the stage. Sanggar packages sometimes also involve the staging of cultural and religious practices that are discursively labeled cultural attractions, including wedding processions and fashion shows of ceremonial costumes. Saayun Salangkah's program included an item called "Manggua tabuah" (M, to hit the drum). Using a large drum such as those mounted outside mosques, the sanggar demonstrated the various signals that would announce the call to prayer, a death, or Idul Fitri (I, the feast celebrating the end of Ramadan; also known in Indonesia as Lebaran). Even when sanggar packages incorporate cultural items or indigenous practices, talempong kreasi and the choreographed dances it accompanies remain the core offering. Moreover, in the promotional literature, program notes, and the interpretive narratives of emcees, these packages are discursively presented as traditional. I will return to the implications of that framing later.

Because these displays are designed to represent Minangkabau ethnicity, those individuals orchestrating them, including directors of sanggar along with the composers and choreographers involved, exemplify Rogers Brubaker's (2002, 166) concept of "ethnopolitical entrepreneurs," specialists who live "off" and "for" ethnicity. Involved in selecting and packaging practices for display, they have a hand in the way that the category of Minangkabau is shaped, presented, and perceived. They are involved in the business of ethnicity. Minangkabau people who watch these displays are encouraged to think of themselves and to listen in ethnic terms; those who are not Minangkabau themselves are encouraged to take the shows on faith as representations of what it looks and sounds like to be Minangkabau.

It is no accident that the music and dance styles connected with the institutions are at the center of sanggar aesthetics, as the people primarily populating the ranks of sanggar are students, faculty, and alumni. Students participate in sanggar as an extracurricular exercise to earn pocket money and gain experience that might help them land gigs once they graduate. Many sanggar directors I knew were alumni seeking to make a living, and others were faculty wishing to augment relatively modest incomes. For example, the husband-and-wife team Rafiloza, who taught in the traditional music department, and Rasmida, who taught in dance, directed Sanggar Seni Titian Aka. Sulastri Andras, one of the earliest ASKI graduates, who taught dance at SMKN, directed Sanggar Satampang Baniah. In fact, in addition to teaching in the public-school system, working in a sanggar was one of the most common, though not generally lucrative, lines of work open to graduates. The institution's curriculum provided students the skills and raw material necessary to enter the sanggar market. Students in the traditional music department pursuing this path needed to study talempong kreasi, the derivative of orkes talempong.

Talempong Kreasi Baru

If the diatonic talempong idiom had initially started at the institution, by the 1980s it was flourishing outside as the expanding cadre of graduates took what they learned out into private enterprise, working with or establishing their own sanggar (see Muchtar 2005). By the 1980s the idiom was known as *talempong kreasi baru,* a term in keeping with artistic developments at the time elsewhere in Indonesia. *Talempong kreasi baru* has since been abbreviated to *talempong kreasi,* the term by which the style still taught at ISI and SMKN is known. Comparing the style of orkes talempong in 1972 as we know from Kartomi's recordings with the talempong kreasi style I learned at the institute in 1998–99 and 2003–4, there are some significant stylistic changes. It is unclear, however, just when these changes took place and whether they neatly coincided with the change in terminology, though it is likely they were in place by the 1980s. What were the aesthetic continuities and departures?

An important continuity with orkes talempong, of course, was that the instruments remained for the most part diatonically tuned: in the 2004 talempong kreasi class that I sat in on, all the accompanying parts were tuned to a major scale but the talempong melodi part had some chromatic notes added. The first significant difference between talempong kreasi and orkes talempong is size of the ensemble: rather than the doubling or tripling of melody and harmony parts found in orkes talempong, the new form featured just one person per part. Some instruments, including the talempong jao and hanging gongs, were abandoned altogether. One performer now covered all the wind instruments, trading off between them as the composition demanded. The approximately eighteen-person ensemble had been reduced to a streamlined ensemble of seven that no longer needed a conductor. The term *orchestra* no longer seemed so appropriate. Table 5.1 illustrates the new lineup.

TABLE 5.1
Instrumentation of *talempong kreasi* at the arts institutions

Function	Part	Pitch range
Main melody	Talempong melodi	b–f"
Harmonic-rhythmic support	Talempong dasar	c'–f'
	Talempong tinggi	g'–c"
	Canang dasar	c–f
	Canang tinggi	c–c'
Rhythm	Gandang	
Melody	Winds: *Bansi, Sarunai, Saluang*	

In addition to the changes in instrumentation, there are some stylistic changes from the orkes talempong compositional style I discussed in the last chapter. Like orkes talempong, the new style features homophonic textures with harmonized arrangements of tunes and sectional form. But in talempong kreasi greater emphasis is placed on tutti sections, rather than solos or playing with timbral combinations of different instruments. This structural change, as Herawati suggested, made the idiom a more appropriate ensemble for pedagogical contexts: more students could continuously participate in the music making (interview, 2004). One of the most important stylistic transformations from the orkes talempong compositions I analyzed above is the shift in the nature of the accompanying talempong parts. Rather than playing block chords in rhythmic unison, each part is given a distinct rhythmic pattern. The talempong dasar, talempong tinggi, and canang dasar, each covering the range of a tetrachord, plays two notes of the chord. The canang tinggi, which covers a whole octave, functions as the bass line. Rather than varying, the accompanying patterns often stayed the same throughout the piece, the pitches changing according to the harmonies. One can hear how these principles of orchestration are applied in the piece titled "Minangkabau" (audio 5.1). The notation the students received for the piece at STSI in 2004 involved a combination of cipher notation, chordal patterns (although using the roman numerals I, II, and III in place of I, V, and IV, respectively), and rhythms for the accompanying parts written out not in cipher notation but in standard Western notation. I have translated this combination into staff notation for easy reading (music example 5.1).

Sanggar have developed, altered, and expanded the institutional version of the talempong kreasi ensemble according to their needs, budget, and the times. The adjustment to the times and a changing market is most evident in the incorporation of synthesizers, electric bass, and even djembe (for example, Lansano Entertain in video 1.1). In 2003–4, three out of the five sanggar I tracked had a synthesizer

MUSICAL EXAMPLE 5.1. Transcription of the *talempong kreasi* piece "Minangkabau."

and two of those three also had an electric bass and djembe. It seems these groups had traded the canang, which provided a bass line in the institutional version, for a bass. During that period, the djembe was so in vogue in Indonesia they were being made locally. Only one sanggar I worked with, Saayun Salangkah, one of the original four that performed in the 1980s in Bukittinggi, had a lineup very similar to the version found at the institutions. For efficiency of personnel some sanggar, such as Gadih Ranti, based in Jakarta, had one musician covering two parts, alternating between winds and talempong

accompaniment. At one wedding I attended where the group played, there were just four instrumentalists. Other sanggar ensembles, such as that of Satampang Baniah, were designed to impress through size: the ensemble had the most musicians of any sanggar I saw and thus made the greatest visual impact. Sixty talempong were arranged in neat rows across the front of the ensemble, with the remainder of the ensemble seated on a riser behind them. As one individual suggested, the size helped the sanggar "fill up on money" (see video 5.2, in which they play a cover of the same tune, "Minangkabau," that STSI students played in audio 5.1).[2]

The repertoire for sanggar ensembles involves both pieces to accompany discrete dance items, such as "Tari pasambahan" or "Tari piriang," and purely instrumental arrangements of dendang or pop Minang. In video 5.3, Sanggar Saayun Salangkah plays a medley of tunes, which even includes "She'll Be Coming 'Round the Mountain." Aside from quirks like this that I am at a loss to explain, the overlap in the repertoire between one sanggar and the next is considerable. In some cases, they even use the same choreographies and arrangements for a particular item. When discussing the homogeneity of sanggar offerings with Asnam Rasyid, he offered a compelling explanation: "They only look for that which sells well. They are not brave in trying other things. Because if they did research for new dances, they wouldn't raise funds [through performances] as much as they would incur costs [from conducting research and developing new dances]" (interview, 2004).

Many sanggar arrangements and commercially available recordings of talempong kreasi capitalize on tunes familiar to most Minangkabau, such as "Mudiak arau" (see video 1.1), "Lubuk sao," "Talago biru," "Ayam den lapeh," "Baju kuruang" (audio 5.2), and "Kelok Sembilan" to draw in listeners. While the arrangements sometimes obscure the character and ornamentation of a dendang, the tune is still recognizable through melodic contour. The incorporation of these tunes helps market the style—both live performance packages and recorded media—toward migrants nostalgic for the homeland and cosmopolitan Minangkabau who hold romanticized images of their Minangkabau heritage. At sanggar performances, I often sat next to people who happily sang or hummed along with the tune.

The style had appeal for these people because of its capacity to reference—yet update—indigenous practices. Most sanggar, for example, include an arrangement of talempong pacik in their repertoire. For Satampang Baniah, an arrangement of talempong pacik was used to accompany part of the choreography for a dance, "Dantiang balinduang," that fuses two iconic Minangkabau dances, tari piriang and *tari payung* (I, umbrella dance) (see video 5.1). Hajizar, a faculty member at the institute, composed the music in the period when he taught at SMKI with Sulastri Andras, from 1982 to 1984. When I played him a video recording of the item performed at a wedding in 2004, he was quick to point out there had been some aesthetic modifications to his original composition. This statement was part of his rhetorical move to politically and aesthetically distance himself from talempong kreasi.

Hajizar explained to me how his methodological approach to composition—then and now—was to use various components (melodies, rhythms, instruments, tunings) of indigenous practices (or what he and most of his colleagues called *traditional music*) and arrange them in novel ways. The idea was not to be traditional but "to resemble authentic tradition." He rationalized the aesthetic departures from the original by claiming composers have to "consider the needs of the composition, not the needs of tradition" (interview, 2004). In the part of the work I am discussing, Hajizar referenced the talempong pacik piece "Gua tari piriang," used to accompany the plate dance in Bungo Tanjueng, his home nagari, part of the repertoire his younger brother, Elizar, taught in the talempong class discussed in chapter 3.

The aesthetic differences between the original and his composition are brought into relief through a comparison of recordings of the piece rendered in an indigenous context and the contemporary version of his composition as performed by Satampang Baniah in 2004. In Bungo Tanjueng, they used three pairs of talempong, or six talempong in total; while in Satampang Baniah, they used sixty talempong, a fairly significant difference. In the former, they used a pupuik batang padi; in the latter, a sarunai. The timbre is relatively similar between the two instruments, so the difference is not so drastic. The other significant difference in instrumentation was with the expansion of the percussion section: a double-headed drum and a frame drum in the former, and two double-headed drums, two djembes and a tambourine in the sanggar version. Moreover, the modifications extended beyond instrumentation to other elements of style. Hajizar related how he exchanged the drum pattern used in Bungo Tanjueng with a pattern from another dance, in addition making the drum section louder through its expansion in size (the use of the djembe was not his modification but a later one). While the nagari version of the piece is cyclical, with the number of repetitions determined by context, in Hajizar's arrangement the repetitions were determined by the formal choreography.

In the original arrangement, Hajizar kept the local tuning system, what he considered a critical marker of indigenous frames. But by 2004 the sanggar was using the diatonically tuned talempong kreasi set because the instruments were there and, according to Hajizar, it was too much hassle to tune the instruments to a different standard or have them on hand. This modification of his composition troubled him because the "musical feeling of the diatonically tuned gongs playing 'Gua tari piriang' are very different from those that are not diatonically tuned playing it" (interview, 2004).

In other words, the aesthetic elements of the indigenous practice were maintained to some extent in Hajizar's arrangement but were manipulated in service of the novelty and originality of the composition and, thus, even of the sanggar and its coffers. While he did not intend the piece to be a talempong kreasi composition, it became one over the years. However, with sanggar audiences largely constituted by international tourists, fellow Indonesians, and Minangkabau with a cosmopolitan cultural outlook, few, if any, people hearing this piece have any exposure to or knowledge of the indigenous practices inspiring it and similar adaptations. They therefore uncritically absorb the rhetoric that projects talempong kreasi and the choreographed dances that it accompanies as Minangkabau tradition.

Talempong kreasi as performed by sanggar, such as Satampang Baniah, becomes a complex sign vehicle in which multiple references— instruments, tunes, and other genres—of Minangkabau identity coalesce. Perhaps the genre maintains such strong appeal precisely because it incorporates several different references. For cosmopolitans, talempong kreasi is traditional Minangkabau music, presented in an aesthetic frame that is more contemporary and accessible than the frames of indigenous practices. During my fieldwork in 2003–4, those with the means to do so engaged sanggar to perform at weddings and other life-cycle and communal events; the combination of familiar tunes played on Minangkabau instruments, as opposed to the lone synthesizer in orgen, held great appeal. The form engendered a deeper engagement than orgen with what it sounded like to be Minangkabau.

Sanggar Economics

Sanggar belong largely to the private sector and are therefore subject to the vagaries of the market. In the period I tracked them, from 2003 through 2010, some sanggar had regular gigs for tourists, but that work was far from lucrative. The declining numbers of visitors and shift to the domestic market had consequences for a group's finances. In 2003–4 the tourism office in Bukittinggi organized a show every night of the week. They rotated between five local sanggar, including Puti Limo Jurai and Saayun Salangkah, both of which were populated by people affiliated with the institutions. In 2010 the office was still offering nightly shows. Officially, they needed a minimum of ten guests to run the show, but I witnessed shows staged for less. The sanggar were lucky to break even on the costs, let alone make a profit: they had to pay a fee to rent the space, pay for transporting the performers to the venue (many of them from the nearby town of Padang Panjang, where the institute is located), and provide a modest honorarium to each performer. In 2004 tickets were Rp 20,000; the expenses incurred by the sanggar, one member estimated, were Rp 120,000 without the honoraria. Many sanggar tried to augment their meager income by selling recordings and instruments at their shows. Alfalah, who had been a member of Saayun Salangkah for twelve years and was one of the musical directors in 2004, told me he participated for personal satisfaction, not commercial benefit. With approximately twenty-five members in the sanggar (though not all performed in the one show), honoraria were minimal (interview, 2004; cf. Hughes-Freeland 1993a, 2001).

By 2003–4, sanggar could no longer rely on the tourism industry and the cultural displays of the state, which provided the majority of their work in the past. Some may have maintained official affiliations with local tourism and cultural offices, but few had regular or lucrative gigs. For the most part sanggar survived by freelancing, patching together opportunities as they went, and relying on word of mouth for promotion. Constantly occurring, weddings offered one of the most reliable sources of work, especially as personal finances improved after the krismon. Groups were also hired to perform for product launches, malls, business functions, and on private TV stations, most of these opportunities available only in Jakarta. In West Sumatra, some sanggar, including Indojati, Sofyani, and Puti Limo Jurai, supplemented income generated from performance with commercial recordings. Some, such as Titian Aka, also offered music and dance lessons or comprehensive packages for weddings, including costume, hair styling and makeup, catering, and video documentation.

If the kinds of opportunities for sanggar have increased over the years, so have the number of groups willing to provide the services. The supply far outweighs the demand, engendering fierce competition among the groups—especially in urban centers such as Padang or Jakarta—over the limited opportunities to perform and, ideally, make money. The most coveted gigs—because they are the most prestigious *and* the most lucrative—are cultural missions abroad. In 2004, Lansano Entertaint was invited to travel to Ethiopia. They did so under the auspices of the Padang Office of Tourism and Culture, but there was political intrigue surrounding their selection.

In order to give themselves an advantage in the marketplace, some sanggar deliberately tried to brand themselves as unique. As Sulastri attested, Satampang Baniah recognized the need to separate themselves from the flock by presenting their own choreographies or fusions of the classics, such as "Tari dantiang balinduang," that combined tari payung with tari piring. They also offered a series of *sendratari* (I, dance dramas) related to local folktales. Like Sanggar Satampang Baniah, Lansano ventured into unique arrangements with their staged presentation of randai involving an eight-minute adaptation of what was historically and in some places, like Gunung Rajo, still is an all-night and often multinight performance (Pauka 1998). Their adaptation featured the dramatic pants-slapping movements of the form while completely omitting the theatrical aspects that are absolutely critical to the art yet alienating to people who do not understand literary Minangkabau. The accompanying music involved a talempong kreasi composition that incorporated the dendang typically affiliated with a randai performance (though many in the audience would not be able to make that connection). Sanggar modifications of this kind, like pedagogical approaches at the institute, thoroughly detach indigenous practices from the contexts and value systems within which they are embedded.

In order to survive, some sanggar, such as Metro Minang in 2004, simply offer a wide range of practices, from the indigenous (such as rabab Pasisia, rabab darek, saluang, kacapi, and even talempong sambilu) to the cosmopolitan (orgen and rock band). While Metro Minang initially formed to "maintain the vitality of traditional arts," as indicated in discussions with several members, financial need drove them to offer such a wide array of services and be willing to accept virtually any gig.

Other individuals addressed the shifting market by offering an updated version of diatonic talempong, one that has stronger pop influences and shifted the emphasis from a primarily instrumental form that accompanied dance to one that accompanied vocals. Some scholars and musicians see the new style as a direct outgrowth of talempong kreasi and contest the need for terminological distinction because of considerable overlap in terms of instrumentation and aesthetic approach. Other people, such as Alfalah, a key proponent of the new style, suggest that it was not simply a direct outgrowth of talempong kreasi but that its inspiration partially lay elsewhere. Below I examine the origin narratives, functions, and aesthetic priorities of the new version of talempong in order to establish why categorical distinction is warranted.

As an ethnographer it is my duty to pay heed to the discourses and investments of the people with whom I worked. But even for the people who see the need for distinction, there is no agreement on the appropriate term for the new style. The musicians I worked with in the highland region around Padang Panjang and Bukittinggi call it talempong goyang, while the musicians in Padang call it *talempong taleno* (M, sleepy talempong) and those in Jakarta are reluctant to use either of these labels (Muchtar 2005, 69, 71). One of my contacts in Jakarta, for instance, claimed the style arose around the same time there as it did in West Sumatra, thereby also contesting its place of origin. It is important to keep in mind, then, that there is no singular narrative about this style but rather multiple opposing ones offering different accounts of its origins and rationales. I privilege the version of the musician I worked with most closely, Alfalah, who is a faculty member at ISI but continues to play talempong goyang around the West Sumatran highlands.

The Origins of Talempong Goyang

In this account, the name and form of talempong goyang can be traced to the nagari of Koto Kaciak, in the Payakumbuh region (Alfalah 2007, 96) and a particular musician, Admiyah, who has since passed on. Alfalah was a member of Admiyah's group in the 1990s. "The framework was simple," Alfalah recalled, "but it was already asyik [I, cool]." In 1999, Alfalah established his own group in Padang Panjang and put his own stamp on the style (interview, 2004; 2010). The term *goyang* means shaky or wobbly, but in performance contexts it has long been employed to refer to "the swaying movement of the hips, waist, and buttocks" of dancers (Weintraub 2010, 22). While I have personally never seen people dance in this manner at talempong goyang gigs in West Sumatra (except for one particularly energetic male tambourine player), talempong goyang ensembles cover dangdut songs, and *goyang* is a term strongly associated with this genre. Its use in the title of the talempong ensemble and style is explicitly to reference these associations while also indicating the repertoire and pop aesthetic of the style. When I asked Alfalah about the term in 2004, he acknowledged that it was deliberately used as a marketing tool to make the style more attractive to potential clients (interview, 2004).

There are some discrepancies regarding the impetus of the style in the written and oral accounts. Both scholarly and practitioner accounts suggest that talempong goyang's development was a consequence of concerns circulating in Indonesia among intellectuals and cultural officials about the damaging effects of Euro-American-influenced practices, such as rock bands and orgen, on indigenous ones. Paradoxically, talempong goyang, which itself is predicated on Euro-American idioms and instruments, is seen as part of the solution to saving indigenous talempong practices, not part of the threat. Its ability to do so, however, as I will demonstrate below, is highly contested by opposing sides of the argument: proponents claim it stems from indigenous practices; critics claim it does not.

Involving one to several vocalists, often female, backed by a synthesizer complete with rhythm machine and programmed for karaoke, orgen groups crank out classic pop Minang tunes and the latest hits in a range of popular genres, all pumped through massive speaker systems. While rock bands covering pop Minang repertoire were all the rage at weddings in the 1980s (cf. Blackwood 2000, 114, 143), they were displaced by orgen. During the krismon, few hosts could afford the services of a band. Orgen offered a more economically viable and practical replacement because of limited gear and personnel (Alfalah 2007; Muchtar 2005; cf. Weintraub 2010, 204). During the last decade or so, orgen has become the most popular style of live music at weddings, especially in urban areas.

But orgen has also become one of the most contentious styles of Minangkabau music. In moderate Muslim circles orgen's performance challenges Muslim propriety because the vocalist's style of dance and skimpy dress are considered provocative and morally corrupt, leading to a slew of negative behavior, including dancing between opposite sexes, the consumption of alcohol, and the outbreak of fights, some fatal, between male youths competing for the affections of the vocalists (Alfalah 2007; Muchtar 2005). While many communities condone the performance of orgen today, especially if dress standards are suitably modest and vocalists avoid dance moves considered erotic by local standards, others have taken a more extreme stance and banned it outright.

In the dominant origin narrative, talempong goyang was designed to redress the dominance of Western musics: it was envisioned as the ideal replacement for orgen. Like orgen, it privileges a pop aesthetic and features vocals. But the difference is that it is more explicitly Minangkabau in character, or at least it is according to its proponents. As Alfalah claimed, it aims to draw people back to their cultural roots through references to indigenous Minangkabau practices but puts those references into a form that "appeals to the needs and tastes of the masses" (2007, 97). The narrative is markedly similar to that surrounding the emergence of orkes talempong in the late 1960s; the parameters for the appealing frame, however, have changed since then. Ironically, although the new style was envisioned as a means to fight against the influx of Western music, the style itself was dependent on structural and aesthetic frames derived from Euro-American practices. Regardless of one's aesthetic evaluation of the style, talempong goyang is seen to obviate the moral concerns raised by orgen because its vocalists and instrumentalists are dressed appropriately. Although people might *bergoyang* (I, shake their hips) in relation to talempong goyang, it is "just to the degree necessary, it is not excessive, and those dancing are singers and players with the goal of bringing a festive atmosphere" (Hanefi et al. 2004, 76). This is very different from the dancing that occurs with orgen, which can involve *berjoget* (I, a kind of social dance between singers and audience members) (cf. Spiller 2010). Talempong goyang, therefore, is considered to more directly embrace Minangkabau values and ethics.

When I asked Alfalah directly about his approach to the style, he did not begin with the defense against the incursion of Euro-American practices but rather his interest in reforming so-called tradition:

I was oriented toward *kesenian tradisi* (I, traditional arts) involving talempong . . . but they were . . . *monoton* (I, monotonous) in form . . . if we look at it the next day, it is the same thing, there are no changes or developments, the instruments are the same. It will definitely bore people. . . . How can these traditional arts be developed so we can play them almost everyday?

In other words, Alfalah was invested in tradition but thought that it needed updating. It needed some zing, some variety to attract interest and be successful in the marketplace. He searched for a one-size-fits-all solution to the problem, something that would "recruit all parties, the old, kids, young people, and middle-aged people," something that he considered traditional yet modern at the same time. In conceptualizing the formula, he considered two possibilities: incorporating what he called contemporary instruments (synthesizer and guitar) into indigenous talempong practices, or incorporating talempong into a conventional band (interview, 2010).

The problem with the first model, according to Alfalah, was that the tuning of indigenous instruments was not appropriate to cover the pop repertoire. Recall table 2.3, which illustrated the distance of talempong sets in the nagari from diatonic standards. The pop repertoire, in contrast, demands a diatonic tuning at the very minimum and ideally a fully chromatic system. Alfalah therefore decided to go with the second model: incorporating talempong into a band. In this narrative, then, he is suggesting that talempong goyang should be seen more as a continuity of band and orgen than one of talempong kreasi, which he had cited as inspiration back in 2004 (interview, 2004). In many ways the aesthetic priorities of the style support this reading. However, it is perhaps best to think of talempong goyang not as an outgrowth of any one style but rather a confluence of multiple influences: band with talempong, a more Minangkabau version of orgen, an updating of so-called monotonous indigenous practices, and an outgrowth of talempong kreasi. It has appeal in part because it covers so many bases. As I worked closely with Alfalah's group, Alfa Musik, in 2003–4 and again in 2010, Alfa Musik provides the basis for the following discussion about the aesthetic priorities of the style.

FIGURE 5.1. Halim with Alfa Musik, Padang Panjang, 17 June 2010. *Left to right:* Seprinaldo, drum set; Timen, guitar; Alfalah, *talempong melodi;* Faril, bass; Halim, vocals; Asep Saeful Haris, Sundanese drums.

The Aesthetics of Talempong Goyang

At one 2010 wedding I attended, Halim (see fig. 5.1; webfig. 5.1), the emcee of Alfa Musik, explained the style of talempong goyang to the audience. He used the Minangkabau language with the occasional English word thrown in.

> This here is named talempong goyang. It is the talempong that goyang [I, shake] or the people that goyang [I, move their hips].... The meaning, the songs, the music: it's *enjoytainment. Musik entertain enjoy sekali* [entertainment music that is very enjoyable]. It's flexible ... we can do Western songs, Arabic songs, Japanese songs, *lagu urang awak* [M, songs of our people].... Here is an Indian song, "Saibah."

His perspective as a practitioner and key member of the ensemble provides considerable insight into the purpose and orientation of the ensemble: entertainment. One of the primary ways talempong goyang responds to the market for entertainment is through instrumentation

FIGURE 5.2. Alfa Musik looking like a rock band with *talempong,* Padang Panjang, 17 June 2010. *Left to right:* Alfalah, *talempong melodi;* Timen, guitar; Faril, bass; S. Anton, *talempong pengiring*.

choices. This is clear in the changes in the lineup of Alfa Musik, Alfalah's group, from 2004 to 2010. In 2004 the group's lineup overlapped more with talempong kreasi: it did not include drum set or electric guitar. But by 2010, Alfa Musik looked and sounded more clearly like a rock band with talempong (see figs. 5.1, 5.2).

Talempong in the Marketplace   201

TABLE 5.2
Tuning of the *talempong* in Alfa Musik

Top row L–R	d'#	b	a	g	a#	f'#	g'#	a'#	c'#	e"
Bottom row L–R	c'#	c'	d'	e'	f'	g'	a'	b'	c"	d"

The melody section included one to three vocalists (both male and female; see webfig. 5.3 for Alfalah's sister, Wilda Aviva), talempong melodi with two rows of kettle gongs, an electric guitar, a synthesizer, and a series of winds, including saluang, sarunai, bansi, the transverse flute used in dangdut, and the transverse flute used for Bollywood tunes. The tuning of the talempong was chromatic with even consistent intervals of half steps, as illustrated in the layout of the gongs represented in table 5.2, adapted from Alfalah (2007, 102). Note that the talempong are not laid out from a scalar perspective but a kinesthetic one to facilitate playing.

The *talempong pengiring* (I, talempong that accompanies) provided harmonic accompaniment on two rows of kettle gongs (see fig. 5.2; webfig. 5.2), an electric bass provided a bass line, and the rhythm section included different percussion, including a drum set, Sundanese drums that were used for variety of tone color (played by Asep Saeful Haris, who was Sundanese and taught Sundanese gamelan at the institute), and tambourine. At one 2010 wedding I attended, the group was short one player in the beginning, so the talempong pengiring player pictured in figure 5.2, Anton, who is now a faculty member at ISI, started on synthesizer, thereby suggesting that instrument was more critical to the overall mix. The synthesizer is highly valued for its capacity to imitate other instruments and easily produce the effect of an orchestra or ensemble playing (Hanefi et al. 2004, 73n6). A key feature of the style is that it is pumped, like orgen, through massive speaker systems, often at volumes that make it difficult to talk and socialize at an event.

The talempong goyang ensemble, as Halim declared at the 2010 wedding, covers songs from a wide range of genres, both indigenous and popular. The ensemble has no repertoire exclusive to it but borrows entirely from external genres. The bulk of the indigenous material adapted is songs from saluang jo dendang (see webfig. 5.4, video 5.4), material that may have originated in the cultural heartland but has become popular throughout the province and the rantau through a vibrant performance scene and rich representation in the recording industry. Alfa Musik has also adopted a handful of tunes from other regional vocal traditions, including indang. The repertoire, however, focused primarily on classic songs of Minangkabau popular genres, including pop Minang (audio 5.3, "Mudiak arau," and audio 5.4, "Kelok Sembilan"), *dangdut Minang* (I, the Minangkabau-language variant of the national genre), *saluang dangdut* (M, the pop version of saluang jo dendang that incorporates the instrumentation and rhythms of dangdut), and gamaik.

The group also threw in covers of national genres, such as *pop Indonesia* (I, a genre of popular music in the Indonesian language), dangdut, and *qasidah* (I, Arabic-influenced Islamic pop), into the mix. As Alfalah states, they explicitly tried to cover "songs that are *ngetop (glemor)* [I, the top hits] of this age in order to make this art more alive according to the tastes of contemporary society" (2007, 99), for example a dangdut Minang hit "Arek-arek lungga" in 2004 (audio 5.5), and in 2010 "Lupa-lupa ingat," a pop Indonesia hit from 2009 (audio 5.6). Moreover, as a Jakartan musician told me, and Alfalah endorsed, the flexible nature of the ensemble allows it to cater to ethnically diverse audiences, incorporating instruments and hits from other Indonesian regions, such as Sulawesi, Sunda, and North Sumatra. The ensemble even has the capacity to incorporate Bollywood tunes, though they were already a part of the pop Minang repertoire themselves (video 5.5). Finally, while the focus of talempong goyang is primarily vocal, the ensemble also has the capacity to incorporate indigenous instrumental genres, including talempong pacik for processional moments or bansi used to establish nostalgia for the homeland (Muchtar 2005, 71).

To convey the feel of the different genres incorporated into the repertoire, Alfa Musik made deliberate choices regarding instrumentation and the vocalist. Halim, for instance, switches flutes to indicate the respective repertoire and Alfalah suggested that he hires specific vocalists because of the particular repertoire they can cover. For example, Fitri, a thirty-eight-year-old mother of three with a series of albums to her name, covered pop Minang (audio 5.4) and dangdut at a wedding I attended on 17 June 2010. At another wedding ten days later, Rina Oktavia, then a current student at ISI and an active vocalist on the saluang jo dendang performance circuit, covered the dendang repertoire (see webfig. 5.4).

Variety is key to the marketing of Alfa Musik. The repertoire is deliberately broad to cater to the diverse interests and demands of audiences and to reach the widest possible market. Alfalah wants to encourage people of all generations and walks of life to appreciate the style, even if they cannot afford to hire the ensemble for their own event. Banking on the affective appeal of the music, Alfalah tailors the material to fit the demographics of the majority audience at any given moment: they play the latest pop hits to draw in the youth; dendang or *lagu kenangan* (I, nostalgic songs), the well-known classics of pop Minang, to draw in the older generations (Fraser 2011). The group also maintains a sizeable repertoire—approximately one hundred songs—in order to perform, as is sometimes required, for up to twelve hours or more. They also have to be prepared to tailor a performance to the specific requests of a host (some, for instance, prefer Islamic-themed repertoire while others request predominately pop Minang or saluang jo dendang); take song requests from the guests or staff; and accompany anyone present who wants to take a turn at singing. As Alfalah points out, talempong goyang is a style driven by and oriented toward the market (2007). The more responsive to the shifting demands of the market, the greater the economic riches to be reaped by the group and its members, or at least those in key positions. If the presence of a new truck with advertising for Alfa Musik—including pictures I had taken in 2010, some of which are included here—in front of Alfalah's house in June 2013 was anything to go by, the market had been good to him.

So why hire a talempong goyang group? It covers the same repertoire offered by orgen groups, but has the capacity to cover an even broader range of genres, including songs from indigenous practices. Clients appreciate this style over and above orgen for its "strong Minangkabau nuance," greater modesty in clothing of the performers, and its affective capacity and ability for references to indigenous practices (Muchtar 2005, 71), sentiments I found echoed in statements of people I talked to in both rural and urban areas. When I asked Suryanti, my host mother, about the presence of talempong goyang at her daughter's wedding, she responded, "Although it is modern, there are still traditions. It is more Minang. Orgen is just *barat* [I, Western]" (pers. comm., 14 July 2010). While the detractors of the style—intellectuals and artists invested in other aesthetic frames—question the Minangkabau character of the music, the clients of Alfa Musik find the instruments, tunes, and language strong enough references to mark the music as Minangkabau. For these people, choosing talempong goyang is a deliberate investment in their ethnic identity. While some people hire the ensemble simply because they like the sound, many others engage with it because the sound helps them feel more Minangkabau than choosing orgen. This is not to say that orgen groups playing pop Minang do not help other people feel Minangkabau, but talempong goyang is seen as a *more* explicit engagement with that identity.

The presence of an emcee during performances, usually one of the band members, underscores the music's objective to entertain an audience. The emcee mediates, explains, and embellishes the musical performance, filling in breaks between songs with chitchat, humor, and "topical matters relating to the song, the singer, the audience, or the bridal couple" (Hanefi et al. 2004, 76–77), commentary that is typically delivered in Minangkabau language. The role of the emcee is to increase the sociability of the event, make the guests feel welcome, solicit their participation by inviting them to sing, bolster the host's pride, and enhance the overall entertainment value. At one gig I attended, Halim, the emcee, mentioned my presence as evidence that the invitations to the wedding extended overseas. As Alfalah later commented, this provided the host with "enthusiasm and respect" (pers. comm., 28 June 2010). Alfa Musik also uses emcee commentary to do a little marketing, publicizing its services or those of other businesses involved in staging an event, along with the albums of group members.

The Economics of Talempong Goyang

The group fulfills requests to play not only for weddings but also for batagak pangulu, circumcisions, fundraisers, and other life-cycle and communal celebratory occasions, in addition to government functions. Hiring a talempong goyang group cost more than any other kind of music I encountered at weddings. Partially this is because of the sheer number of instruments, musicians, and equipment required, but the greater part of the expense can be explained by the kind of musicians involved, most of whom are formally trained and try to make their living primarily from music. Talking about money in West Sumatra is a sensitive issue. I am therefore grateful to the individuals who are willing to disclose concrete information about the cost of various musical practices. The figures I provide reflect their interpretations of prices, not hard evidence. It would have been inappropriate to cross-examine wedding hosts about how much they paid the musicians.

Rather than charge a fixed rate or use a formula based on the number of performers, time, and distance required for a gig, Alfalah's fee to perform is variable. He offers a discount for friends, neighbors, and colleagues and has a sliding scale for other clients based on his personal appraisal of their financial capacity. In other words, he understands and has a facility with the "mechanics of turning music into money" (Stokes 2002, 143). The different costs are sometimes manifest in the presentation of the ensemble, including the attire of its members (compare the shirts the men are wearing in webfig. 5.1 with webfig. 5.4, for example). Packets—how long the group performs, how many performers, what kind of repertoire, and so on—also are customer driven, fashioned according to the needs and budget of the client. This approach is not unusual: I talked with other service providers who have a sliding scale and determine fees based on their estimation of the client's ability to pay.

In 2010 the minimum Alfalah charged for a gig in Padang Panjang was Rp 3 million (approximately US$300), while the higher end was more than twice that: Rp 7 million. To put this figure in perspective, in 2010, Rp 4 million was the monthly wage of a high-level faculty member at the institute while the poverty line in West Sumatra was Rp 180,669 per month (BPSPSB 2009, 185). In other words, it was a substantial amount of money. Alfalah explained that the margin of profit was lower for out-of-town gigs (the transportation necessary for musicians and equipment incurred higher costs, which ate into the payment received for performing) so he considered fulfilling requests on a case-by-case basis. Occasionally, Alfalah explained, they take on a gig where they barely cover operational costs, for the purposes of promotion. This was clearly an investment strategy for the business: to book its next gigs Alfa Musik relied largely on exposure and word of mouth, along with low-key marketing at gigs through banners (evident in the background of webfigs. 5.2 and 5.4) and business cards. While Alfalah participated for the money, along with genuine enjoyment of the music, I do not have any gauge of the profit margin. It is also unclear how much group members get paid for gigs: I was not able to survey the different members for a comparative account of their individual earnings. Based on my familiarity with the hierarchy of the personnel, however, it is likely that the faculty members earned more than the students, the vocalists with albums more than the instrumentalists. Back in 2004, however, I asked friends of mine, students singing with the group, why they participated; the pocket money they earned (Rp 30,000–50,000) was not the main incentive for a long day where they sang only occasionally. They participated because they were asked by faculty members and for the experience that it offered.

Certainly, the cost of talempong goyang is inflected by the kinds of musicians involved. Alfalah is a graduate of, and full-time faculty member in, the Department of Traditional Music at ISI. In 2004 he was the most junior person in the department. Civil servants' pay is in accordance with rank and longevity in the position. To supplement his income, he operated Alfa Musik. Many of the members of the group, both in 2004 and 2010, also were affiliated with the department. In

2010 these members included fellow faculty members M. Halim and Asep Saeful Haris; recent alumni S. Anton, Seprinaldo, and Wilda Aviva (they were all students in 2004; Anton is now a faculty member); and student Rina Oktavia. Noticeably those individuals not affiliated with the institute—Timen, Faril, and Bana Baram—played the rock instruments: guitar, bass, and drums, respectively. None of the members were contracted exclusively to the group. Most of them had other gigs or operated in other musical scenes. The legitimacy garnered from affiliation with the institute, along with market viability of some member's albums, lent considerable weight to the value of the product, helping sell the ensemble to the clients and audiences. The people who can afford to hire Alfa Musik are from relatively affluent backgrounds. They are mostly, but by no means exclusively, from urban areas. Over the years, I have attended talempong goyang gigs at the homes of bureaucrats (including the mayor and the principal of a primary school in Padang Panjang), businessmen, doctors, and academics. Alfalah relates he once even played for the governor of West Sumatra, then Gamawan Fauzi.

Some of the artistic elite, faculty at the institute, and cultural critics such as Edy Utama, consider the style crassly commercial: a popular music that functions as entertainment where the audience is not concerned with the artistry involved. Others had some reservations about the aesthetics of the style yet hire a goyang group for their own weddings. Faculty who participate in its performance are sometimes criticized for doing so. A discussion with Halim—the wind player, vocalist, and emcee of Alfa Musik—in 2010 exposed some of the tensions and conflicts involved for talempong goyang musicians. One day during the lunch break at a wedding, he launched, entirely unsolicited, into a defense of why he participated in the style. In addition to his duties as a faculty member, Halim was an active composer and performer in the contemporary music scene and sought after as a saluang player in the recording industry. There was nothing particularly remarkable about his participation in multiple scenes; lots of artists did it. However, my discussion with Halim suggests that while these musicians themselves were musically comfortable making the switch between genres and styles across the aesthetic spectrum, there were tensions below the surface. Halim's critics, he hinted, thought his participation in talempong goyang would compromise what they considered his more serious artistic endeavors and sensibilities, especially his involvement in the contemporary music scene. In 2010, Alfalah mentioned he had also received criticism from colleagues at the institute who considered playing music at weddings a low-status gig, though ironically some of those very critics had done so themselves in the past or even engaged Alfa Musik to play at the weddings of their children. Certainly, there was an underlying discourse about the artistic value of practices that were driven by market concerns.

For the musicians who participate in the talempong goyang scene, their involvement is driven by a variety of reasons, and often multiple ones, including investment in and enjoyment of its aesthetic frame, in addition to an interest in the economic benefits that participation provides. As Halim commented, he wanted to "enjoy all the arts!" Halim's rationalization, however, was also centered on the economic dimensions. He explained that he had a large nuclear family to support and also was expected, as the oldest sibling, to support his parents and other family members back in his home nagari. In other words, Halim was implying that he did not have the luxury of participating *only* in the art music world and that his critics were in denial about the economic realities driving artistic activities. Although I encountered musicians in other contexts who were engaged in styles they found aesthetically distasteful to make ends meet, including saluang dangdut (cf. Buchanan 2006, 178), some people also actively liked this music.

It is ironic, then, that while some individuals affiliated with the institute are leveling critiques at talempong goyang musicians operating in the private sector, the style was sometimes adopted by the institute in its outreach performances. Talempong goyang was the privileged musical style in the program of both outreach performances I attended in 2003–4, although the style was not part of the curriculum at the time. The ensemble at the Sungai Batang program in Agam in May 2004 was clearly identified as such, but at the first program in Limau Paruik in Pariaman in December 2003, the ensemble was identified as talempong kreasi rather than talempong goyang, underscoring the contested nature of the latter term. In spite of the terminology, I consider the style, instrumentation, and function more in line with talempong goyang than talempong kreasi. In both instances, the lineup included two sets of talempong (melody and accompaniment); a series of flutes, including saluang, bansi, the transverse flute for dangdut, sarunai; a range of percussion including local drums, *gendang oyak* (I, what my consultants called the drum used in dangdut), and tambourine; and, most significantly, a keyboard and bass guitar. Both ensembles accompanied dances (a function more in line with talempong kreasi) and a series of tunes from a range of popular genres, including pop Minang and dangdut Minang (a function more in line with talempong goyang). The benefit of talempong goyang over and above talempong kreasi was that the one ensemble could successfully do both. The more compelling reason to identify both ensembles as talempong goyang was the aesthetic frame: the incorporation of instruments (keyboard, bass, tambourine, gendang oyak) and material (pop songs) that were not part of talempong kreasi classes at the institute at the time.

The institutional version of talempong kreasi had a considerably different lineup than the one presented at the outreach programs. But the instrumentation at these programs *was* virtually identical with the lineup of Alfa Musik at that time. Like Alfa Musik, the wind and percussion instruments were modified in each song to convey the appropriate flavor of the piece. At the Sungai Batang performance, the particular constellation of individuals also had considerable overlap with the personnel of Alfa Musik at that time. Although these outreach events were designed as experiences for students to showcase their skills, the team of musicians included several faculty members, including Alfalah himself on lead talempong, Asep on Sundanese drums, and Halim as emcee, flute player, and vocalist. Some of the other participants were neither faculty nor students, but recent alums or other members of Alfa Musik. Most of the student participants also were already (or would become) members in Alfa Musik (see audio 5.5, where Wilda sings "Arek-arek lungga"; by 2010 she was a regular member of the ensemble). The personnel and the repertoire at the Sungai Batang performance in 2004 resembled that of the group hiring itself out for gigs in the private sector at that time.

In short, the talempong goyang segments of the program were more in line with extracurricular activities of faculty and students than a representation of curricular emphasis. At the workshop the day after the Sungai Batang performance, Ediwar, who oversaw these programs as head of the DUE-like program (see chapter 3), explained the program choices to the village hosts. It was possible my queries about the presence of popular styles not part of the curriculum had encouraged him to do so. He explained to the villagers present that at the institute there were

> the [preexisting] traditions [and] there are those that are developed. At this time there are people who call these kreasi, but they are still strong in Minangkabau nuance. Although the orgen [synthesizer] is mixed with talempong goyang . . . it is simply combined with talempong, so in the end this nuance is still the nuance of *ke-Minangkabauan* [I, Minangkabau-ness]. The songs have the aroma, the dances have the aroma, of still being strong in the nuance of *adaik basandi syarak, syarak basandi kitabullah* [M, adat is based on Islam; Islam is based on the holy book].[3] (speech, 23 May 2004)

It is important to note here the classic defense of talempong goyang offered by its advocates and apologists: that the style had at least the nuance of Minangkabau practices. But, as critics rail, are these superficial references *enough*? Another defense of the genre and deliberate linkage with indigenous practices, as offered by then director of STSI, Zulkifli, in his speech at the opening of the event, quoted at the opening of the last chapter, was that arts needed to adapt to the times. These outreach programs, as his speech suggested, were concerned with educating host communities about the endangered state of indigenous arts, endangered because communities preferred to "consume arts that come from elsewhere" (read: Euro-American pop), never mind that the primary form presented at this event was predicated on the very thing to which he objected. His rhetoric, an attitude supported by proponents of talempong goyang, suggested the best way to reengage the general populace in indigenous arts was to present them with popular forms, such as talempong goyang, that had what they considered a basis in indigenous practices (Zulkifli, speech, 22 May 2004). But this basis is highly contested by detractors of the style. Moreover, nobody representing the institute at this event was concerned with the apparent contradiction that the style privileged was not at that time part of the curriculum. This institutional endorsement of popular styles was not without critique. Edy Utama, for instance, declared,

> If educational institutions such as STSI develop talempong goyang as a section of their program, I think this already violates, right?, departs from the idea, the original concept of an institution that offers alternatives better for the life of the culture itself. It should no longer support or give support to pop forms of art like that! (interview, 2004)

But his voice and those who agreed with him, including some faculty within the institutions, were in the minority.

The adoption of talempong goyang at this program, moreover, played into the interests of the local government. The regent of Agam, a high-ranking elected official below only the governor of the province, gave a speech at the opening of the event indicating that his primary interest was in reinforcing the link between arts and tourism, an emphasis in local cultural policies at the time (speech, 22 May 2004). This discourse underscores the ways in which state, provincial, and local cultural policies were leaning toward the position that arts were not viable unless they attracted tourists, thereby helping fill empty coffers. Talempong goyang is the kind of style that people think balances the demands of the market and the representation of Minangkabau identity. In a world of tough choices, it is a better option than others.

Both talempong kreasi and talempong goyang continue to polarize the community of intellectual and professional artists, creating a divide between those individuals who believe these talempong styles encapsulate the essence of Minangkabau music and those who believe that they are superficial at best. The question of which music should represent people who understand themselves to be Minangkabau remains a politically loaded question, involving debates about the nuance of what is called tradition and which elements of style—instruments, tuning, texture, and so on—should have bearing on the evaluation. For the proponents of the diatonic-chromatic idiom, including Murad, Herawati, and Alfalah, whose livelihoods were and continue to be partially contingent on the continued existence of these new styles, and cosmopolitan audiences who appreciate them, the *warna* (I, color) of Minangkabau music is established through the instrumentation and the incorporation of dendang. Critics of these styles, however, such as Hajizar and Edy Utama, find any such references very superficial and believe instrumentation alone is not enough to determine the Minangkabau character of the music. For Edy, Minangkabau essence is more in the melodies and rhythms of indigenous practices than the instruments themselves (pers. comm., 21 June 2004). For dissenters, the reliance on functional harmony also immediately compromises any claims to a basis in indigenous frames. People who believe talempong kreasi is Minangkabau in character, Hajizar emphasized, simply do not know any better (interview, 2004). I find nothing in the style aside from instruments that connects it with the aesthetics of indigenous practices or, more important, the ethos from which they come.

While it is important to acknowledge the aesthetic preferences of people invested in talempong goyang, it is equally important to understand just what they are buying into: it might have come to constitute tradition for them, but it is a version that leaves no room for people and practices from the nagari. For people in the nagari, as explained in chapter 2, tradition is about practices handed down from their ancestors, the way things have always been done. For the apologists of talempong goyang, tradition is merely something that is more Minangkabau, at least on the surface, than other pop music practices, like orgen or band. This discussion brings me back full circle to my host father's assertion, raised in chapter 1, that people are quick to claim identity as Minangkabau but they do not understand the values attached to that identity. The depth of engagement from cosmopolitans is simply not the same as it is for someone invested in nagari life. Cosmopolitans fail to recognize that the tradition they are buying into is not the same thing as indigenous practices and the value systems within which they are embedded in the nagari. In these modifications, the history of talempong, its grounding in rural practice and embeddedness within a community, and its stylistic features of nondiatonic tunings, cyclical structure, and horizontal textures, have disappeared. The twelve melodies telling the legend of how talempong came to Unggan is replaced by the pop Minang song "Ayam den lapeh." "The past," to borrow a phrase from Philip Yampolsky, "is reduced to pop" (pers. comm., January 2014).

For some people who identify as Minangkabau, listening to talempong kreasi and talempong goyang mobilize their engagement with ethnic identity; they unquestioningly accept this representation of what it sounds like to be Minangkabau. But as I have suggested, there are other people who actively resist that representation. I am less concerned with declaring a right and a wrong side than acknowledging that these talempong styles engender ethnic engagements—a heightened awareness of being Minangkabau—for a part of the population who understand themselves to be Minangkabau. However, it is important to recognize that their engagements with what it means to be Minangkabau are qualitatively different from those of people engaging with that category in indigenous contexts. The different ways of engaging with these talempong styles—whether for, against, or indifferent—also articulate some of the different ways of understanding oneself as Minangkabau at the beginning of the twenty-first century. As Ediwar stated, there are different kinds of Minangkabau people: the people in the nagari are *asli* Minangkabau, meaning they are more authentic, implying they are different from Minangkabau in towns and cities (interview, 2014).

While the critics of these diatonic-chromatic styles see the markers of indigenous practices as superficial, the very same markers are effective in signifying the traditional to an entirely distinct subset of people. As Efrinon, celebrated pop singer and faculty member at the institute, told me once, there was such a thing as "too much tradition." When she uses indigenous tunes as the basis for a song, she makes sure to set them within a popular frame, otherwise, "if it is too traditional . . . the sales market will be languid" (interview, 2010). This brings me back to the key point of the chapter: how talempong, an expression of Minangkabau identity, gets shaped in response to pressures of the free-market economy. It is clear how the market drove the change to greater inclusion of popular material. It is also clear that some individuals did not appreciate—both aesthetically and ideologically—the results. They consider artists who respond to the demands of the market as selling out. But with the institutions pumping out increasing numbers of academically trained musicians in need of a job, those artists are often dependent on the market to make a living and, more significantly perhaps, some even actively liked the music they play.

Chapter 6

MULTIPLE WAYS OF SOUNDING MINANGKABAU

This book has offered a case study in art as an expression of ethnic identity. It has traced how talempong, a Minangkabau musical form, has changed over the last sixty years and how it was transformed in response to a number of different forces, including political events, the institutionalization and the related professionalization of the arts, and the pressures of a free-market economy. I have illustrated how talempong shifted from a musical practice that represents a local community to also something that, with the advent of orkes talempong, not only expressed but also actively helped create an awareness of and investment in Minangkabau ethnicity, a pan-Minangkabau identity that transcended nagari affiliations.

The institutionalization, professionalization, and monetization of Minangkabau arts has, moreover, brought about a diversification of talempong styles, including the emergence of new styles, such as orkes talempong, talempong kreasi, and talempong goyang that coexist, to some extent, with the older styles still found in indigenous contexts. Nonetheless, it is important to note that these indigenous practices are endangered: the arts institutions, sanggar, and cosmopolitan audiences largely reject the musical idioms, sounds, and repertoire of indigenous genres, including talempong practices of the nagari, substituting radically different idioms, sounds, and repertoire in their place. In indigenous contexts the future of these indigenous practices is precarious. When the older generation dies, sometimes a practice dies with them, as in Sialang (see chapter 2). Sometimes just the repertoire is threatened: for example, in Unggan the young generation is interested only in the newer material drawing on dendang and pop Minang, while in Paninjauan the young generation has mastered only two out of twenty songs in the repertoire. I fear that knowledge will be lost with the older generation. So while there are currently vibrant talempong practices in some nagari, on the whole indigenous talempong practices are in decline and face a precarious future. Therefore, while all of the talempong styles I have discussed, with the exception of orkes talempong, whose legacy continues in the current diatonic and chromatic styles, were extant at the time of research in 2003–4, 2010, and again in 2014, will that be true in another ten or twenty years?

Just as there is a diversity of talempong styles coexisting, at least for now, there is a diversity of ways to think about music in relation to money: for example, the ways in which indigenous practices are still embedded within a gift economy even though fiscal remuneration is involved, compared with the ways in which market forces completely drive the aesthetics of talempong goyang and the laboring of musicians dependent on its economic rewards. Just as there are multiple styles and ways of thinking about money in relation to them, there also are different kinds of musicians. Not everyone receiving money in exchange for performance thinks about herself as a professional. Income and skill are not the only elements determining whether one is considered a professional musician in Minangkabau contexts. The *framing* of the act, I have argued, is paramount. Rather than uncritically importing concepts from elsewhere, it is important to ground terms used for analysis, such as *professional*, in the particulars of the ethnographic context and pay attention to what people say and do.

In the Minangkabau case, the institutionalization of the arts has resulted in the production of a new class of musicians who think of, purport themselves to be, and are perceived as seniman. Their formal training confers a particular kind of artistic authority, which is very different from the criteria used outside institutional contexts where musicians considered professionals specialize in one genre, such as saluang jo dendang or rabab Pasisia. For the graduates, their formal training confers the label *professional,* but the skill set does not involve specialization in one genre but generalization in many. For a handful of artists outside the institutional system, expertise and skill allow them to seek a primary part of their living from performance. They think of themselves as professionals because of the combination of skill and income, but for graduates of the institutions the criteria are different. This is where the framing of the act becomes critical. Whether or not graduates make enough money to sustain a living from artistic activity alone, it is the way they frame their experiences—or their hopes—that matters: they think about performance or related careers in arts and culture industries—what gets labeled *kesenian* and *kebudayaan*—as a career path and orient their lives around it. This is qualitatively different from the talempong performers in Paninjauan who are similarly desirous of the income generated from performing at events but think about playing as an avocational activity and their contribution to those events as part of community spirit. This is not to say that there are no musicians in indigenous talempong contexts who aspire to make performance their primary economic and occupational activity—Siti Aisah in Unggan is one such example—but that it is still relatively rare.

Gongs and Pop Songs, moreover, offers a case study in the cognitive view of ethnicity. Rather than considering ethnicity as something inherent within people, it asks when and why people claim ethnic identifications. The book has traced some of mechanisms in West Sumatra that mobilize a sense of ethnicity in individual and collective lives, including the PRRI and its fallout; the cultural policies of the state and the nominal celebration of diversity; and the tourist industry. Each of these mechanisms has fueled the expression of Minangkabau ethnicity, encouraging people to think of themselves as Minangkabau in those particular moments and places. *Gongs and Pop Songs* has emphasized that expressive practices are absolutely critical venues to this process through which ethnicity is actively engaged and articulated, yet their power to do this has been neglected in cognitive approaches to date.

Institutionalization, Professionalization, and Monetization of the Arts in Indonesia

The processes of institutionalization, professionalization, and monetization are not unique to West Sumatra. There are interesting parallels in these processes in the way institutions in Bali, Bandung, Banyumas, Sulawesi, Surabaya, Surakarta, and Yogyakarta have engendered standardized styles, homogenized fragmented musical scenes, accrued artistic authority, and privileged artists with academic training. In most of these cases, institutionalization was partially a response to concern over the decline and quality of indigenous arts. However, by privileging formalized pedagogical approaches and epistemologies involving explicit knowledge and rational methods, such as notation and analysis, these very practices have changed. In short, the preservationist objectives of the institutions have failed. In the Minangkabau case, the institutionalization of indigenous arts has not addressed or mitigated this decline as the founders hoped. In many ways, the Institute of Indonesian Arts in Padang Panjang has done more to undermine than preserve them: first, by decontextualizing these arts and stripping them of embedded value systems; second, by pedagogical approaches to teaching these practices that dilute their aesthetic content; third, by producing a class of musicians who dismiss the value of rural practices and the accomplishment of indigenous practitioners; and last, by encouraging the development of indigenous arts and the creation of new musical styles nominally predicated on them.

The sentiment that the institution had somehow failed in its original mission was echoed in a conversation I had in 2010 with a young silek practitioner at an event on the shores of Lake Maninjau. Curious to gather commentary on the perception of the institution within the wider arts scene, I asked him what he thought its role was and should be. He responded that the institution was great for the new creations, for combining things that are "taken from traditions." But, he asserted, these new creations no longer contain the *inti* (I, core values) of the original practices that inspired them. At the time, we were watching an excerpt of randai; he pointed out that every single movement in randai has symbolic significance, but those symbolic meanings are the kinds of things lost with the institutionalization of the arts. Occasionally, one even hears this critique from *within* the institutional system, but those individuals tend to be labeled *kuno* (I, antiquated) for their attitudes. For the silek practitioner, the bigger danger of institutionalization was that lots of *asli* (I, autochthonous) arts were being ignored with the focus on new creations.

One of the most enduring new creations put out by the institution was orkes talempong, which was developed in part to create a Minangkabau genre that was as prestigious as Javanese and Balinese gamelan. While I do not believe the style was successful in this respect, it did create an enduring legacy of talempong styles based on diatonic and chromatic tuning standards, though the ensemble lineup and nomenclature have changed over the years. West Sumatra, however, is certainly not unique for the presence of diatonic-chromatic musical styles mixed with indigenous practices; *campur sari* (I, gamelan mixed with keyboard and other instruments) in Java is similar in some ways to talempong goyang. However, as Benamou (2010, 13) writes, musicians at ISI Solo actively reject the practice while ISI Padang Panjang, according to Ediwar (pers. comm., 21 February 2014), has started including talempong goyang in the curriculum. Moreover, the pervasive talempong style developed at the institution has, arguably, included more pop culture references than styles emphasized at comparable institutions.

Talempong is far from the only Minangkabau genre, however, that has been popified. Sometimes pop songs are used in the place of dendang during the scene breaks in randai performances, which encourages hip-swaying dance movements in the place of silek, and sometimes the gendang oyak are used to enhance the effect. There is also a pop version of saluang jo dendang: saluang dangdut. As the name suggests, it combines saluang jo dendang with the repertoire, instrumentation, and aesthetics of dangdut. In saluang dangdut the usual flute and vocal ensemble is augmented with dangdut drums, tambourine, frame drum, and other percussion. In contrast to talempong goyang, saluang dangdut, Ediwar asserted, would not be appropriate for inclusion in the curriculum because of its low moral standards.

Another enduring legacy of the institutionalization of the arts in Indonesia is that there are occupational opportunities to carve out an economic existence from musical and cultural practices that simply did not exist a hundred years ago. However, some opportunities to make a living from the arts differ between Bali, Java, and West Sumatra. Although there have been fluctuations in the tourism industry across the archipelago, a stronger emphasis on cultural tourism and a more vibrant tourist industry in general in both Java and Bali seemingly offer more sustainable avenues of employment for graduates from institutions in those places than in West Sumatra. In her research on the comparable institution in Bali, Brita Renée Heimarck (2003) found evidence of a close connection between art and tourism in curricular development, something to which ISI Padang Panjang is increasingly paying attention. I have illustrated how the focus of cultural policies in West Sumatra is also shifting in the direction of "art that sells," especially following the implementation of regional autonomy and the need to fill coffers. The institute, as the outreach performance discussed in chapter 5 illustrates, is complicit in this endeavor. Bali, at least, also seems to have a thriving privatized arts scene where many children are sent to learn Balinese dance and music at sanggar where most of the instructors are graduates of the institutions (McIntosh 2012). There is no such equivalent scene in West Sumatra, in part because local arts are not seen as critical to cultural heritage or an avenue for social mobility.

A key part of the professionalization process I have discussed in the book is the privileging of musicians with academic credentials in cosmopolitan contexts over and above indigenous musicians, including teaching at the institution and performing at tourist events, bureaucratic settings, and weddings of the elite. More alarmingly yet, people affiliated with the institute and the high school sometimes even come to represent the indigenous perspective in these contexts. For example, the program notes for the SCP Theater in Bukittinggi, a short-lived, high-class tourist production that I saw in 1998, included a group of male faculty members representing Unggan's female-only talempong practice. At Taman Mini, I also saw photographs of people affiliated with the institute mixed in with groups representing one of West Sumatra's regencies. These stories illustrate just how pervasive the artistic authority of the institute is.

Graduates of these arts institutions—both the institute and the high school—are key in disseminating and helping entrench institutional styles. I have shown how alumni were instrumental in transferring talempong kreasi from the institutional setting into the sanggar world as they established or joined troupes upon graduating. They also bring these styles into schools. In 2004 a friend from my studies at ASKI in 1998 had just begun at a grade school where she taught arts to small groups of students as an addition to the regular curriculum. Making use of the school's set of talempong kreasi instruments, she focused on teaching talempong kreasi pieces she herself had learned during her studies at ASKI. She began with giving the students notation, encouraging them to memorize it and perform it on *pianika* (I, small keyboard powered by breath, known best in the United States as a melodica) before they transferred it to talempong themselves (pers. comm., 26 May 2004).

That talempong kreasi has become deeply embedded in the Minangkabau musical landscape illustrates the "transformational effect" of reformist projects backed by powerful institutions (Turino 2000, 107). For some people, talempong kreasi and talempong goyang are what it sounds like to be Minangkabau. For some of these people, it has even become an enduring tradition. Take, for example, a CD released by Department of Traditional Music faculty member Junaidi called *Nada talempong klasik* (vol. 1) (I, Sounds of Classical Talempong), where talempong kreasi covers of classic dendang and pop Minang tunes are listed as "*Musik khas daerah Sumatera barat*" (I, Characteristic Music of the West Sumatra Region). In short, the educational institutions for the arts in West Sumatra, ASKI/STSI/ISI and SMKI/SMKN, have unequivocally and irrevocably shaped the contours of the Minangkabau musical landscape. Whether this has been positive, negative, or neutral very much depends on whom you talk to.

In the book I have illustrated how different combinations of gongs and pop Minang mobilize people's understanding of themselves as Minangkabau, encouraging them to think of themselves, listen, and engage in ethnic terms. Individually, talempong, dendang, and pop Minang songs each reference what it means to be Minangkabau. While kettle gongs are found throughout the archipelago, talempong is a uniquely Minangkabau phenomena, found only among communities that identify themselves as Minangkabau, though there is much diversity from one nagari to the next. Likewise, dendang—songs in the Minangkabau language and its dialects—are found throughout the Minangkabau area. While the Minangkabau content of pop Minang is contested by some intellectual and artistic elite, millions of other people who understand themselves as Minangkabau invest in the genre as a powerful sonic representation of what it means to be Minangkabau (Fraser 2011). When these pop songs and dendang are combined with gongs, in styles such as orkes talempong, talempong kreasi, or talempong goyang that are designed to reference music of the past within a contemporary frame, the capacity for listeners to create emotional attachments to the form increases. The various combinations of these elements in the talempong styles included in the book have and continue to help forge new paths and ways of being Minangkabau. People's investment in one talempong style over another does not make them more or less Minangkabau but speaks to differing levels of engagement with the category—whether it is more or less focal—and, more important, to multiple ways of being and understanding oneself as Minangkabau at the beginning of the twenty-first century.

Finally, the diverse styles of talempong coexist not just because people have aesthetic preferences for one over another but because they are embedded within communities that are guided by radically different value systems and worldviews. The indigenous and cosmopolitan styles of talempong—respectively talempong pacik and talempong duduak, and talempong kreasi and talempong goyang—operate in distinct spheres. The consumers and performers in one sphere are not, for the most part, the same as in the other. But there are exceptions: some people in the nagari would hire a talempong goyang ensemble if they could afford it. However, on the flip side, most cosmopolitans have no interest in watching or listening to any indigenous styles of music, such as talempong duduak, if indeed they have any exposure to them at all. They are disparaging of musical practices associated with nagari life because they feel they are outdated. But they are not willing to discount the past entirely—they want to update it by importing the symbolism and aesthetics of pop.

These personal investments in different musical styles, including talempong, are strategic: they help people articulate who they are and what matters to them. The variety of options suggests multiple ways of sounding Minangkabau today and in today's world, it is important to be attuned not just to the moments of sameness that a particular category evokes but also to the differences within it, along with the various mechanisms—including music—that mobilize feeling, being, and thinking in ethnic terms.

Notes

Chapter 1: Ethnicity, Gongs, and Pop Songs

1. I use the term *Western* as a direct translation of the term *barat* (I) that my interlocutors used. In references to music, Minangkabau people were referring primarily to structural features involving diatonic (or chromatic) tuning and functional harmony. Sometimes the term was also shorthand for kinds of instrumentation, such as a synthesizer, guitar, or bass. Therefore, when the word *Western* appears in the text I am invoking local uses of the term. I am personally hesitant to use the term because as a geographical term just where "the West" is located is contingent on where one is standing and the suprageographical criterion used for membership is vague at best. The term is also problematic because these practices are as natural for some Minangkabau people as they are for many people living the United States, France, or Australia.

2. There is no Minangkabau equivalent of *kesenian* or a collective term for performing arts. The term *pamainan anak nagari* (M, games of the children of the nagari—the Minangkabau concept for a village), comes the closest, but I have mostly heard it invoked to refer to an evening of performances, not a convenient shorthand for a range of practices.

3. However, the data are not as accurate as they could be: when respondents marked dual language preferences, BPS privileged the language that matches the marked ethnic category (Ananta et al. 2013, 24).

4. In recent census data a minuscule percentage of people who self-identified as Minangkabau (0.28%) did not identify as Muslim but as Catholic, Protestant, or Buddhist (Ananta et al. 2013, 21).

5. Although there is a Minangkabau term for *adat—adaik*—most people tended to use the Indonesian word in everyday parlance and in conversation with me. Hence, I tend to use the Indonesian form here.

Chapter 2: Talempong and Community

1. This was an institutional connection. Asma, who passed away in the summer of 2011, was the mother of Ediwar, a faculty member at ISI.

2. I stayed in Unggan several times during fieldwork in 2003–4 and visited again in 2010. I started visiting Paninjauan in June 2004, after a team visited STSI for a three-day workshop the previous month. I have returned frequently since then, including trips in the summer of 2010 and most recently in 2014. In both Unggan and Paninjauan, I took lessons to learn the more challenging talempong melody parts. Padang Alai, in contrast, proved a more difficult site in which to study talempong when I visited in 2004 because I needed to have a group of friends in order to learn the interlocking talempong parts of talempong pacik.

3. When he was initially a student, ASKI granted only three-year diplomas. He went back for an additional year to earn his bachelor's degree.

4. Ironically, this legend features male figures bringing talempong to Unggan, though the practice, for as long as anyone can remember, has been a women's tradition.

5. Elsewhere the same instrument is called the *pupuik batang padi* or *pupuik gadang,* but in Paninjauan they use a different term because of the particular way the coconut frond is wound.

6. Until February 2014 this piece had always been referred to as "Talempong bana." I just understood it to have two different versions: the one played by Yusni and the other by Mariani. Although their versions required a different order of the gongs, including a different placement of the talempong paningkah player, I did not think much about it as everyone always called both versions "Talempong bana." Then in February 2014, Yusni referred to her version as "Tupai bagaluik." In order to honor this latest information, I have decided to retain her most recent preference for the title, as it is her version that I analyze and discuss here.

7. Plates were actually used in the past for this function, but they were often broken, so once glass bottles were accessible, a switch was made. Both help enhance the sound so it can be heard far away (interview with Asma, Jenni Aulia, Mardiani, and Yusni, 2004).

8. The transcription is based on a different recording than video 2.1 in which there was no frame drum player. Individuals also vary the basic patterns—e.g., tambourine—so a transcription of a different recording of this piece would likely look different.

9. The tuning of Paninjauan comes from a 2010 field recording, Unggan from a 2003 field recording, and tunings of the extinct Sialang practice from Mahdi Bahar's (2009, 339) research.

10. My analysis of tunings aligns with that of Mahdi Bahar (2009, 338–41), who includes tuning charts of talempong ensembles from fourteen different nagari in his book, including both talempong duduak and

talempong pacik ensembles. None of these tuning systems adheres to diatonic standards in intervallic structure.

11. It was not clear, however, what her motivations were for doing so. It was also not the only instance where she used terminology clearly outside an indigenous frame; other examples include *ritem* (I, rhythm) and *pola* (I, pattern).

12. David Salisbury (2009, 4) explains the relationship in a structuralist homology using a metaphor provided by a collaborator. *Tali nan bapilin tigo* (M, three strings entwined) refers to important social categories within adat: the nephews and nieces, uncle and mother, and male and female leader. My host father used a similar phrase but used a different metaphor to explain the three interlocking parts found in talempong pacik: he likened it to the nagari leadership structure with three strands of guidance combined together: the *ulama* (I, Islamic leader), the *pangulu* (M, lineage leader), and the *cerdik pandai* (I, intellectual leader).

13. There were some chronological inconsistencies here in that the groom had already been at the house all day but must have returned to his parent's house before being "collected."

14. Yusni told me that in the past, when the couple processed individually, rather than together, there was different music for each procession: four small hanging gongs were used for the bride, and gandang tambua with the pupuik gandang for the groom (pers. comm., 9 June 2004). Now, all processions in Paninjauan incorporate the latter option.

15. I refer to dances that have specific choreographies the way I refer to the names of musical pieces (placing them in quotes), thereby distinguishing them from genres of dance, for which I do not use quotes and which I italicize the first time I mention them.

16. *Uaik*, meaning older woman in the singular, is the spelling of the term on the wooden rack that holds the talempong, but Jenni Aulia (2011) spells the term *uwaik* in his undergraduate thesis, reflecting the nonstandardized spellings for local Minangkabau terms.

Chapter 3: Institutionalizing Minangkabau Arts

1. The arts are also incorporated into curricula at state-run teacher-training universities, called IKIP (I, Institut Keguruan Ilmu Pendidikan, Teacher Training Institute), including the one in Padang. Its status has now been upgraded to UNP (I, Universitas Negeri Padang, Padang State University).

2. A state-sponsored high school conservatory was established in South Sulawesi in 1974 (Sutton 2002), but there was never a college-level

counterpart. There is an arts institution in Pekanbaru, Riau, but it is, to my knowledge, privately funded. There is also an effort underway, at the time of writing, to establish an institution for the arts in Banda Aceh, Aceh.

3. This was the oldest handbook I was able to access.

4. The state currently officially recognizes six religions: Islam, Protestantism, Catholicism, Buddhism, Hinduism, and Confucianism. Each of these is or was made to be monotheistic: in the case of Hinduism, the multiplicity of gods collapsed into one main figurehead; in Buddhism, Buddha becomes God. The class in religion is not about learning tolerance for other religions, however, but deepening the understanding of one's own religion so as to become a more pious citizen. The focus on Islam at the institute assumes that all students are Muslim.

5. By the time of my visit in 2010 the curriculum had been revised yet again. There were now six required semesters of talempong under Karawitan Practice in Melodic Percussion: two of talempong kreasi, two of talempong pacik, and two of talempong duduak (one each of styles from Sialang and Unggan).

6. While students still visited communities for service in 2003–4, the flow of knowledge had reversed: rather than learning from the community, they were teaching it.

7. A Taman Budaya was established in every province following a 1980 decree and they were putatively funded, at least back then, by the central government (interview, Asnam Rasyid, 2004).

Chapter 4: Reforming Talempong

1. There appear, however, to be some discrepancies between this list and archival evidence, along with some inconsistencies in the naming of instruments: for example, the *talempong lao* [not talempong jao] is described as a series of kettle gongs. The recordings and photographs, however, show metallophones and suggest the keys were made of bronze, not like the instrument called *talempong jao* in Unggan, the keys of which are made from old oil drums.

2. Herawati's account had some minor differences in terms of instrumentation, which may indicate changes since Kartomi's documentation of the form or a lapse in memory. For the most part, I follow the photographic evidence.

3. Two of these pieces are instrumentals: "Kambang cari" (audio 4.3) and "Tak tontong" (a children's song referencing onomatopoeic sounds of drums and talempong; audio 4.2), which is a piece derived from the

dendang of the same name and for which Kartomi provides a partial transcription in her 1979 article. The other two pieces were, and still are, used to accompany dances: "Tari piriang" and "Tari barabah" (M, Dance of the shrike), a piece I learned on talempong kreasi in 1998 during the class in Music to Accompany Dance.

4. Interestingly, this same dendang is also incorporated into "Tari barabah."

Chapter 5: Talempong in the Marketplace

1. According to Asnam Rasyid, long-term employee and director of Taman Budaya in 2010, in the 1970s the space was known as Pusat Kesenian Padang (I, Padang Center for the Arts) until the 1980 decree to establish Taman Budaya in every province throughout the archipelago (interview, 2004).

2. It is not surprising that Satampang Baniah covers the same tune, as the director of the sanggar, Sulastri Andras, was one of ASKI's earliest graduates and many members of the ensemble were faculty, students, or alumni of the high school.

3. An aphorism frequently invoked as a pillar of Minangkabau values.

Glossary

Indonesian and Minangkabau noun plurals are typically identical to the singular forms.

adaik	M, the Minangkabau equivalent of *adat*.
adat	I, most frequently glossed as custom or tradition; in the Minangkabau case, *adat* is understood as a social code by which to live; see *adaik*.
aguang	M, gong; typically a substantially larger gong than a *talempong*; also the name of a part in the *talempong pacik* practice of Padang Alai.
Alam Minangkabau	M, the Minangkabau World.
ASKI	I, Akademi Seni Karawitan Indonesia, Academy of Indonesian Traditional Arts.
ASTI	I, Akademi Seni Tari Indonesia, Academy of Indonesian Dance.
baju kuruang	M, a style of women's clothing featuring long blouses over skirts or a wrap.
bako	M, paternal relatives.
bansi	M, a small end-blown bamboo flute; originally associated only with the Solok region.
baralek	M, the main ceremonial reception at a wedding.
barzanji	I, a pan-Indonesian Islamic vocal genre with texts recounting the Prophet Muhammad's life.
batagak pangulu	M, the ceremony to install a lineage or clan leader.
batino	M, lit., female; one of the gongs or parts in *talempong pacik* from Bungo Tanjueng.
botol	I, lit., bottle.

BPS	I, Badan Pusat Statistik, Central Board of Statistics.
budayawan	I, a cultural authority.
canang	M, a flat kettle gong with a larger diameter than a *talempong*.
canang dasar	I, the part in an *orkes talempong* or *talempong kreasi* ensemble that covers the first tetrachord of the major scale; see *canang tinggi*.
canang tinggi	I, the part in an *orkes talempong* ensemble that covers the second tetrachord of the major scale; the part in a *talempong kreasi* ensemble that covers a whole octave; see *canang dasar*.
chromatic	a term used to refer to a scale that consists entirely of half-step intervals, or a way of tuning instruments based on that scale. This is unlike a diatonic scale, which involves a series of whole- and half-step intervals.
dangdut	I, a pop style with influences of Hindi-film music and Arabic and Western pop.
dangdut Minang	I, the Minangkabau variant of *dangdut* that is sung in the Minangkabau language.
darek	M, the cultural heartland of the Alam Minangkabau.
dendang	M, any indigenous Minangkabau song and a specific repertoire from the *darek* that is sometimes referred to as *dendang darek*.
dendang Pauah	M, a vocal genre accompanied by a flute called the *saluang Pauah* from the region called *Pauah* that surrounds Padang, the capital of West Sumatra.
diatonic	lit., two tones; a scale and way of tuning that involves a series of whole- and half-step intervals; see chromatic.
dikia rabano	M, an Islamic vocal genre accompanied by frame drums.
dol	M, a large barrel-shaped drum that is used in *gandang tambua* ensembles.
Dt.	M, Datuak; a traditional honorific.

functional harmony	chord progressions based on harmonic function, where the tonic (I), subdominant (IV), and dominant (V) chords are central.
gamaik	M, the Minangkabau version of *orkes Melayu*.
gambus Melayu	I, the Melayu-style strummed lute.
gandang	M, a drum; generally a double-headed drum; also *gondang*.
gandang sarunai	M, a genre from the Muaro Labuah area that combines a pair of drums with a *sarunai*.
gandang tambua	M, a drum ensemble using a flat kettle drum (*tasa*) and large double-headed drums (*dol* or *tambua*); found in the Pariaman and Maninjau regions.
gendang oyak	I, what Minangkabau people called the characteristic *dangdut* drums.
giriang	M, the name for a tambourine.
gondang	See *gandang*.
I	Indonesian language.
IKIP	I, Institut Keguruan Ilmu Pendidikan, Teacher Training Institute.
indang	M, a vocal genre with Islamic associations that uses drumming and movement; distinct versions exist in Pariaman and Solok.
INS	Indonesisch Nederlandesche School.
ISI	I, Institut Seni Indonesia, Institute of Indonesian Arts.
jantan	I, lit., male; one of the gongs or parts in *talempong pacik* from Bungo Tanjueng.
jorong	M, subdivision of a *nagari*; usually based around a *suku* (clan).
kaba	M, epics.
kacapi	M, the kind of zither that is used in the Minangkabau genre of *sijobang*.

karawitan	a word coined in the beginning of the twentieth century to refer to Javanese refined arts, especially court-style gamelan; now applied to other indigenous musics (or performing arts) in Indonesia.
kebudayaan	I, culture, especially elements that can be displayed.
keramaian	I, festive atmosphere, ideally with lots of noise and color.
kesenian	I, the arts, usually referring to performing, literary, and plastic arts.
KOKAR	I, Konservatori Karawitan, Conservatory of Traditional Music.
kreasi	I, a shortening of *kreasi baru*.
kreasi baru	I, new creations; often shortened to *kreasi*.
krismon	I, *krisis moneter*, the Indonesian monetary crisis of 1997.
Lebaran	I, the day of celebration following the end of the fasting month, though often used to refer to the following whole week.
M	Minangkabau language.
mamak	M, mother's brother.
Melayu Deli	M, an east coast Melayu musical style that involves violin, accordion, vocals, and frame drum.
nagari	M, a village federation.
orgen	I, a shortening of *orgen tunggal*.
orgen tunggal	I, lit., stand-alone keyboard; an ensemble that features vocalists backed by a synthesizer programmed to imitate a wide variety of instruments and pumped through massive speaker systems.
orkes Melayu	I, ensembles that comprise vocalists, violin, a lute called *gambus*, and drums performing harmonized songs.

orkes talempong	I, lit., *talempong* orchestra, a reformist style of *talempong* developed at ASKI in the late 1960s involving an expanded ensemble size and melodies backed by harmony.
Pak	I, a polite term of address for an older man or a man in a position of authority; Mr. or Sir. Shortened from Bapak.
pambao	M, the one who brings; used for *talempong pambao* to mean the one who brings the melody and *gandang pambao*, the drummer who brings the basic pattern.
pangulu	M, lineage leader.
paningkah	M, lit., elevator; one of the parts in *talempong pacik* from Bungo Tanjueng.
pantun	I, a poetic form with rhyming couplets.
panyaua	M, lit., interlocker; the elaborating part in *talempong pacik* from Bungo Tanjueng.
pasambahan	M, ritual speech.
pasisia	M, coastal; generally refers to the southwestern coast.
pinggir	I, lit., edge; a term used to refer to the extended technique of playing on the face of the *talempong*.
polong	M, lit., channel; one of the two-gong parts in *talempong pacik* from Padang Alai.
pop Indonesia	I, a popular music genre performed in the Indonesian language.
pop Minang	I, pop music genre performed in the Minangkabau language.
PRRI	I, Pemerintah Revolusioner Republik Indonesia, the Revolutionary Government of the Republic of Indonesia; associated with the 1958–61 rebellion.
pupuik batang padi	M, a loud aerophone made from a coconut palm frond and rice stalk.
pupuik gadang	M, lit., big pipe.

pupuik solo	M, the name for *pupuik batang padi* in Paninjauan.
rabab darek	M, a two-stringed bowed fiddle with a flat, round body specific to the *darek*, used to accompany *dendang*.
rabab Pariaman	M, a three-stringed coconut shell fiddle specific to the Pariaman region, used to accompany vocals.
rabab Pasisia	M, a four-stringed fiddle modeled on the violin and specific to the southwestern coastal region called Pesisir Selatan; accompanies *kaba*.
rabano	M, frame drum.
randai	M, a theater form incorporating *silek*, *talempong*, and *saluang jo dendang* and performed in a circular format.
rantau	M, 1) lit., lowland; the part of the Minangkabau world that is defined as all the areas outside the *darek*; 2) migratory areas outside West Sumatra, including Jakarta.
rapa'i	M, a small frame drum, often with cymbals.
rendang	I, spicy beef curry.
REPELITA	I, Rencana Pembangunan Lima Tahun, Five-Year Development Plan.
Rp	I, rupiah; the official currency of Indonesia.
rumah gadang	M, longhouse; customary house; home to a sublineage and characterized by *gonjong*, sweeping horn-shaped roofs.
salawat dulang	I, two vocalists using mostly Islamic texts, accompanying themselves with brass serving trays.
saluang	M, a bamboo oblique flute; without a classifier *saluang* usually refers to the *saluang darek*, the most common type of *saluang*.
saluang darek	M, a flute made from a bamboo tube with four finger holes and a slightly beveled edge at the head; it is played with circular breathing.
saluang dangdut	M, the pop version of *saluang jo dendang* that incorporates the instrumentation and rhythms of *dangdut*.

saluang jo dendang	M, lit., flute with song; a vocal genre originating in the *darek* with several vocalists and one flute player; texts rely on *pantun*.
saluang panjang	M, lit., long flute; a ring flute from Muaro Labuah.
saluang Pauah	M, an end-blown block flute from the region around Padang.
sampelong	M, an end-blown bamboo flute from the Limapuluh Kota region that has mystical associations.
sanggar	I, usually a studio for some kind of artistic or athletic activity; in West Sumatra, a performing arts troupe; often a shortening of *sanggar seni*.
sanggar seni	I, a performing arts troupe.
saron	A type of metallophone used in Javanese gamelan where the keys are suspended over a wooden trough.
sarunai	M, a single-reed bamboo pipe.
sarunai bibia	M, lit., *sarunai* of the lips; harmonica.
saua	M, interlocking; one of the two-gong parts in *talempong pacik* from Padang Alai.
seniman	I, an artist, often with the connotation of professional.
seniman tradisi	I, lit., traditional artist; often used to refer to artists in indigenous contexts and those without academic training.
sijobang	M, a vocal genre from Payakumbuh that uses *kaba*, accompanied historically by a matchbox, now by a *kacapi*.
sikatuntuang	M, the name for the instrument in Padang Alai that alludes to the mortar and pestle used for pounding rice.
silek	M, the art of self-defense.
sirompak	M, a flute used in the Payakumbuh region for mystical purposes.
SMKI	I, Sekolah Menengah Karawitan Indonesia, High School of Indonesian Traditional Arts.

SMKN	I, Sekolah Menengah Kejuruan Negeri, State Vocational High School.
STSI	I, Sekolah Tinggi Seni Indonesia, Higher Institute of Indonesian Arts.
talempong	M, a small bronze or brass kettle gong; also the name for an ensemble or a musical style.
talempong batu	M, lit., stone talempong; a large lithophone.
talempong batuang	M, a xylophone made of bamboo.
talempong dasar	I, the *talempong* part in a *talempong kreasi* ensemble that covers the first tetrachord of the major scale; see *talempong tinggi*.
talempong duduak	M, lit., seated *talempong;* a musical style with *talempong* arranged on a rack.
talempong goyang	I, a mix of *talempong* with rock instruments.
talempong jao	M, lit., Javanese *talempong;* a metallophone like a Javanese *saron*.
talempong kayu	M, lit., wooden *talempong;* a xylophone, usually with loose keys.
talempong kreasi (baru)	I, lit., new-creation *talempong;* a reformist style with roots in *orkes talempong*.
talempong melodi	I, the lead *talempong* part that plays the melody in an *orkes talempong, talempong kreasi,* or *talempong goyang* ensemble.
talempong pacik	M, lit., hand-held *talempong*.
talempong pambao	M, lit., the bringer of *talempong;* the melody part in a *talempong duduak* ensemble.
talempong paningkah	M, lit., the *talempong* that elevates; the repetitive part in a *talempong duduak* ensemble.
talempong pengiring	I, the accompanying *talempong* part in a *talempong goyang* ensemble.
talempong sambilu	M, a bamboo tube zither.
talempong tinggi	I, the *talempong* part in a *talempong kreasi* ensemble that covers the second tetrachord of the major scale; see *talempong dasar*.

Taman Budaya	I, Culture Park.
Taman Mini	I, Taman Mini Indah Indonesia, Beautiful Indonesia in Miniature Park.
tambo	M, mythical origin story of the Minangkabau.
tambua	M, a large, barrel drum.
tari piriang	M, plate dance; see *tari piring*.
tari piring	I, plate dance.
tari payung	I, umbrella dance.
tingkah	M, elevator; the name of a single-gong part in the *talempong pacik* practice of Padang Alai.
urang awak	M, my people, our people.
USU	I, Universitas Sumatera Utara, University of North Sumatra.
Western music	A translation of the term *musik barat* (I), which my interlocutors used to refer primarily to structural features involving diatonic (or chromatic) tuning and functional harmony. Sometimes the term was also shorthand for kinds of instrumentation.

References

Adam, Boestanoel Arifin. 1990. "Talempong: Musik tradisi Minangkabau." *Jurnal masyarakat seni pertunjukan Indonesia* 1 (1): 53–75.
Adams, Kathleen M. 1998. "More than an Ethnic Marker: Toraja Art as Identity Negotiator." *American Ethnologist* 25 (3): 327–51.
———. 2006. *Art as Politics: Re-crafting Identities, Tourism, and Power in Tana Toraja, Indonesia*. Honolulu: University of Hawai'i Press.
Alfalah. 2007. "Talempong goyang: Musik alternatif pengaruh budaya popular." *Ekspresi seni: Jurnal ilmu pengetahuan dan karya seni* 9 (1): 92–107.
Ames, David W. 1973. "Igbo and Hausa Musicians: A Comparative Examination." *Ethnomusicology* 17 (2): 250–78.
Ananta, Aris, Evi Nurvidya Arifin, M. Sairi Hasbullah, Nur Budi Handayani, and Agus Pramono. 2013. "Changing Ethnic Composition: Indonesia, 2000–2010." Paper presented at the 27th International Union for the Scientific Study of Population International Population Conference in Busan, Republic of Korea, 26–31 August.
Andaya, Leonard Y. 2008. "Ethnicization of the Minangkabau." In *Leaves of the Same Tree: Trade and Ethnicity in the Straits of Melaka*, 82–107. Honolulu: University of Hawai'i Press.
Anderson, Benedict R. O'G. (1983) 1991. *Imagined Communities: Reflections on the Origin and Spread of Nationalism*. London: Verso.
Anwar, Khaidir. 1999. "The Minangkabau and Their Culture." In *Walk in Splendor: Ceremonial Dress and the Minangkabau,* edited by Anne Summerfield and John Summerfield, 55–63. Los Angeles: UCLA Fowler Museum of Cultural History.
ASKI (Akademi Seni Karawitan Indonesia). 1985–86. *Buku pedoman ASKI Padang Panjang*. Padang Panjang: Sekolah Tinggi Seni Indonesia Padang Panjang, Departemen Pendidikan dan Kebudayaan.
———. 1997–98. *Buku pedoman ASKI Padang Panjang*. Padang Panjang: Sekolah Tinggi Seni Indonesia Padang Panjang, Departemen Pendidikan dan Kebudayaan.
Aspinall, Edward, and Greg Fealy, eds. 2003. *Local Power and Politics in Indonesia: Decentralisation and Democratisation*. Singapore: Institute of Southeast Asian Studies.

Aulia, Jenni. 2011. "Talempong Uwaik-Uwaik Nagari Paninjauan Kecamatan Tanjung Raya, Kabupaten Agam (Tinjauan Perkembangan)." Undergraduate thesis, Institut Seni Indonesia, Padang Panjang.

Bahar, Mahdi. 2009. *Musik perunggu nusantara: Perkembangan budayanya di Minangkabau*. Bandung: Bumi Grafika Utama.

Baily, John. 1988. *Music of Afghanistan: Professional Musicians in the City of Herat*. Cambridge: Cambridge University Press.

Barendregt, Bart. 2002. "The Sound of 'Longing for Home': Redefining a Sense of Community through Minang Popular Music." *Bijdragen tot de taal-, land- en volkenkunde* 158 (3): 411–50.

Barth, Fredrik. 1969. Introduction to *Ethnic Groups and Boundaries: The Social Organization of Cultural Difference*, edited by Barth, 9–38. Boston: Little, Brown.

Bauman, Thomas. 1991. "Musicians in the Marketplace: The Venetian Guild of Instrumentalists in the Later 18th Century." *Early Music* 19 (3): 345–55.

Becker, Judith O. 1980. *Traditional Music in Modern Java: Gamelan in a Changing Society*. Honolulu: University of Hawai'i Press.

Benamou, Marc. 2010. *Rasa: Affect and Intuition in Javanese Musical Aesthetics*. Oxford: Oxford University Press.

Benda-Beckman, Franz von, and Keebet von Benda-Beckman. 2001. "Recreating the Nagari: Decentralisation in West Sumatra." Max Planck Institute for Social Anthropology Working Papers, no. 31.

Blackwood, Evelyn. 2000. *Webs of Power: Women, Kin, and Community in a Sumatran Village*. Lanham, MD: Rowman and Littlefield.

Booth, Anne, 1990. "The Tourism Boom in Indonesia." *Bulletin of Indonesian Economic Studies* 26 (3): 45–73.

Bowen, John Richard. 1996. "The Myth of Global Ethnic Conflict." *Journal of Democracy* 7 (4): 3–14.

BPSPSB (Badan Pusat Statistik Propinsi Sumatera Barat). 1998. *Sumatera Barat dalam angka*. Padang: BPSPSB.

———. 2009. *Sumatera Barat dalam angka*. Padang: BPSPSB.

Brinner, Benjamin E. 1995. *Knowing Music, Making Music: Javanese Gamelan and the Theory of Musical Competence and Interaction*. Chicago: University of Chicago Press.

Brubaker, Rogers. 2002. "Ethnicity without Groups." *Archives européénnes de sociologie* 43 (2): 163–89.

———. 2009. "Ethnicity, Race, Nationalism." *Annual Review of Sociology* 35: 21–42.

Brubaker, Rogers, and Frederick Cooper. 2000. "Beyond 'Identity.'" *Theory and Society* 29 (1): 1–47.

Brubaker, Rogers, Mara Loveman, and Peter Stamatov. 2004. "Ethnicity as Cognition." *Theory and Society* 33 (1): 31–64.
Buchanan, Donna A. 1995. "Metaphors of Power, Metaphors of Truth: The Politics of Music Professionalism in Bulgarian Folk Orchestras." *Ethnomusicology* 39 (3): 381–416.
———. 2006. *Performing Democracy: Bulgarian Music and Musicians in Transition.* Chicago: University of Chicago Press.
Byl, Julia. 2014. *Antiphonal Histories: Resonant Pasts in the Toba Batak Musical Present.* Middletown, CT: Wesleyan Press.
Collins, Megan. 2002. "Bongai in Tanjung Ipoh, Negri Sembilan." *Journal of the Branch of the Royal Asiatic Society* 75 (1): 91–114.
———. 2003. "The Minangkabau Rabab Pasisia: Music, Performance and Practice in West Sumatra, Indonesia." PhD dissertation, Victoria University of Wellington.
Drakard, Jane. 1999. *A Kingdom of Words: Language and Power in Sumatra.* Oxford: Oxford University Press.
Dunbar-Hall, Peter. 2006. "Culture, Tourism, and Cultural Tourism: Boundaries and Frontiers in Performances of Balinese Music and Dance." In *Ethnomusicology: A Contemporary Reader,* edited by Jennifer Post, 55–65. London: Routledge.
Fanany, Ismet. 2003. "The First Year of Local Autonomy: The Case of West Sumatra." In *Autonomy and Disintegration in Indonesia,* edited by Damien Kingsbury and Harry Aveling, 177–88. London: Routledge Curzon.
Fraser, Jennifer. 2011. "Pop Song as Custom: Weddings, Entrepreneurs, and Ethnicity in West Sumatra." *Ethnomusicology* 55 (2): 200–228.
———. 2013. "The Art of Grieving: West Sumatra's Worst Earthquake in Music Videos." *Ethnomusicology Forum* 22 (2): 129–59.
Hadler, Jeffrey. 2008. *Muslims and Matriarchs: Cultural Resilience in Indonesia through Jihad and Colonialism.* Ithaca: Cornell University Press.
Hainsworth, Geoffrey, Sarah Turner, and David Webster. 2007. Introduction to "Indonesia's Democratic Struggle: *Reformasi, Otonomi* and *Participasi.*" *Asia Pacific Viewpoint* 48 (1): 41–46.
Hanefi. 1999. "Traditional Minangkabau Music." In *Walk in Splendor: Ceremonial Dress and the Minangkabau,* edited by Anne Summerfield and John Summerfield, 297–311. Los Angeles: UCLA Fowler Museum of Cultural History.
———. 2011. "Perubahan pertunjukan talempong yang inklusif ke pertunjukan talempong yang eksklusif." Master's thesis, Universitas Negeri Padang.

Hanefi, Ediwar, Hajizar, Ardipal, Ernida Kadir, and Deni Hermawan, eds. 2004. *Talempong Minangkabau: Bahan ajar musik dan tari.* Bandung: Pusat Penelitian dan Pengembangan Pendidikan Seni Tradisional, Universitas Pendidikan Indonesia.

Heimarck, Brita Renée. 2003. *Balinese Discourses on Music and Modernization: Village Voices and Urban Views.* New York: Routledge.

Hendri, Yon. 2005. "Dendang tradisi dan lagu pop Minang: Sebuah lintasan sejarah." *Ekspresi seni: Jurnal ilmu pengetahuan dan karya seni* 7 (7): 128–43.

Herawati. 2003. *Transformasi teknik permainan talempong.* Padang Panjang: Sekolah Tinggi Seni Indonesia.

Hough, Brett. 1999. "Education for the Performing Arts: Contesting and Mediating Identity in Contemporary Bali." In *Staying Local in the Global Village: Bali in the Twentieth Century,* edited by R. Rubinstein and L. Connor, 231–63. Honolulu: University of Hawai'i Press.

Hughes-Freeland, Felicia. 1993a. "*Golek Menak* and *Tayuban:* Patronage and Professionalism in Two Spheres of Central Javanese Culture." In *Performance in Java and Bali: Studies of Narrative, Theatre, Music and Dance,* edited by Ben Arps, 88–120. London: School of Oriental and African Studies, University of London.

———. 1993b. "Packaging Dreams: Javanese Perceptions of Tourism and Performance." In *Tourism in South-East Asia,* edited by Michael Hitchcock, Victor T. King and Michael J. G. Parnwell, 138–54. London: Routledge.

———. 2001. "Performers and Professionalization in Java: Between Leisure and Livelihood." *South East Asia Research* 9 (2): 213–33.

Jensen, Joli. 1998. *The Nashville Sound: Authenticity, Commercialization, and Country Music.* Nashville: Vanderbilt University.

Kafsir, Sidney Littlefield. 1999. "Samburu Souvenirs: Representations of a Land in Amber." In *Unpacking Culture: Art and Commodity in Colonial and Postcolonial Worlds,* edited by Ruth B. Phillips and Christopher Burghard Steiner, 67–83. Berkeley: University of California Press.

Kahin, Audrey. 1999. *Rebellion to Integration: West Sumatra and the Indonesian Polity.* Amsterdam: Amsterdam University Press.

Kahn, Joel S. 1980. *Minangkabau Social Formations: Indonesian Peasants and the World Economy.* Cambridge: Cambridge University Press.

———. 1993. *Constituting the Minangkabau: Peasants, Culture, and Modernity in Colonial Indonesia.* Providence: Berg.

Kartomi, Margaret J. 1979. "Minangkabau Musical Culture: The Contemporary Scene and Recent Attempts at Its Modernization." In

What Is Modern Indonesia Culture? edited by G. Davis, 19–36. Athens: Ohio University Press.

———. 1980. "Musical Strata in Sumatra, Java and Bali." In *Musics of Many Cultures: An Introduction,* edited by E. May, 111–33. Berkeley: University of California Press.

———. 1990. "Taxonomical Models of the Instrumentarium and Regional Ensembles in Minangkabau." In *On Concepts and Classifications of Musical Instruments,* 225–34. Chicago: University of Chicago Press.

———. 1998. "Sumatra." In *Southeast Asia,* edited by S. Williams and Terry E. Miller, 598–629, vol. 4 of *The Garland Encyclopedia of World Music.* New York: Garland.

———. 2012. *Musical Journeys in Sumatra.* Urbana: University of Illinois Press.

Kipp, Rita Smith. 1993. *Dissociated Identities: Ethnicity, Religion, and Class in an Indonesian Society.* Ann Arbor: University of Michigan Press.

Klopfer, Lisa. 1999. "Ceremonial Foods for the Celebration of Marriage." In *Walk in Splendor: Ceremonial Dress and the Minangkabau,* edited by Anne Summerfield and John Summerfield, 257–70. Los Angeles: UCLA Fowler Museum of Cultural History.

Kuipers, Joel C. 1998. *Language, Identity, and Marginality in Indonesia: The Changing Nature of Ritual Speech on the Island of Sumba.* Cambridge: Cambridge University Press.

Levine, Hal B. 1999. "Reconstructing Ethnicity." *Journal of the Royal Anthropological Society* 5 (2): 165–80.

Manan, Imran. 1984. "A Traditional Elite in Continuity and Change: The Chiefs of the Matrilineal Lineages of the Minangkabau of West Sumatra, Indonesia." PhD dissertation, University of Illinois at Urbana-Champaign.

Martamin, Mardjani, Alwir Darwis, Syafruddin, Buchari Nurdin, Refrizal M, Nur Jaul, Larandi A. Tamin, Zamasri, and Muslim. 1997. *Sejarah pendidikan daerah Sumatera Barat.* Jakarta: Departemen Pendidikan dan Kebudayaan RI.

McIntosh, Jonathan. 2012. "Preparation, Presentation and Power: Children's Performances in a Balinese Dance Studio." In *Dancing Cultures: Globalization, Tourism and Identity in the Anthropology of Dance,* edited by H. N. Kringelbach and J. Skinner, 194–210. New York: Berghahn.

Muchtar, Asril. 2005. "Mensiasati sebuah perubahan budaya: Kasus talempong goyang kemasan musik tradisi bernuansa 'pop.'" *Jurnal penkajian dan penciptaan seni tabuik* 1 (1): 63–75

Murgiyanto, Sal. 1991. "Moving between Unity and Diversity: Four Indonesian Choreographers." PhD dissertation, New York University.

———. 1993. "Moving between Unity and Diversity: Indonesian Dance in a Changing Perspective." *Drama Review* 37 (2): 131–60.

Naim, Mochtar. 1973. "Merantau: Minangkabau Voluntary Migration." PhD dissertation, University of Singapore.

Navis, A. A. 1984. *Alam takambang jadi guru: Adat dan kebudayaan Minangkabau.* Jakarta: Grafiti.

———. 1999. *Yang berjalan sepanjang jalan.* Jakarta: Grasindo.

Neuman, Daniel M. 1985. "Indian Music as a Cultural System." *Asian Music* 17 (1): 98–113.

Noll, William. 1991. "Economics of Music Patronage among Polish and Ukrainian Peasants to 1939." *Ethnomusicology* 35 (3): 349–79.

Nor, Mhd. Anis. 2011. "From Matrilineality to Post-colonial Gazes: Hybridity in Minangkabau Art Dance and Music." *Proceedings of the 1st Symposium of ICTM PASEA Study Group, Singapore, 10–13 June, 2010.*

Noszlopy, Laura. 2007. "Freelancers: Independent Professional Performers of Bali." *Indonesia and the Malay World* 35 (101): 141–52.

Oka, Anak Agung Gde, ed. 1990. *Buku pedoman penerangan kepariwistaan Indonesia.* Jakarta: Ministry of Information.

Pätzold, Uwe. 2001. "Das 'Talempong Batu' von Talang Anau: Ein musikalisches Erbstück einer Megalithkultur in West-Sumatera, Indonesien." In *Perspektiven und Methoden einer systemischen Musikwissenschaft: Bericht über das Kolloquium im Musikwissenschaftlichen Institut der Universität zu Köln 1998,* edited by Klaus Wolfgang Niemöller and Bram Gätjen, 277–91. Frankfurt am Main: Peter Lang.

Pauka, Kirstin. 1998. *Theater and Martial Arts in West Sumatra: Randai and Silek of the Minangkabau.* Athens: Ohio University Center for International Studies.

Pemberton, John. 1994. *On the Subject of "Java."* Ithaca: Cornell University Press.

Perlman, Marc. 2004. *Unplayed Melodies: Javanese Gamelan and the Genesis of Music Theory.* Berkeley: University of California Press.

Phillips, Nigel. (1981) 2009. *Sijobang: Sung Narrative Poetry of West Sumatra.* Cambridge: Cambridge University Press.

Picard, Michel. 1996. *Bali: Cultural Tourism and Touristic Culture.* Singapore: Archipelago Press.

———. 1997. "Cultural Tourism, Nation-Building, and Regional Culture: The Making of a Balinese Identity." In *Tourism, Ethnicity, and the State in Asian and Pacific Societies,* edited by Michel Picard and Robert E. Wood, 181–214. Honolulu: University of Hawai'i Press.

Qureshi, Regula Burckhardt. 2002. "Mode of Production and Musical Production: Is Hindustani Music Feudal?" In *Music and Marx: Ideas, Practice, Politics,* edited by Qureshi, 81–105. New York: Routledge.

Ramstedt, Martin. 1992. "Indonesian Cultural Policy in Relation to the Development of Balinese Performing Arts." In *Balinese Music in Context,* edited by E. D. Schaareman, 59–84. Winterthur, Switzerland: Amadeus.

Rice, Timothy. 2007. "Reflections of Music and Identity in *Ethnomusicology.*" *Muzikologija/Musicology* 7:13–38.

———. 2010. "Disciplining *Ethnomusicology:* A Call for a New Approach." *Ethnomusicology* 54 (2): 318–25.

Ricklefs, M. C. 1993. *A History of Modern Indonesia since c. 1300.* London: Macmillan.

Rutherford, Danilyn. 1996. "Of Birds and Gifts: Reviving Tradition on an Indonesian Frontier." *Cultural Anthropology* 11 (4): 577–616.

Salisbury, David A. 2000. "Aspects of Musical and Social Identity in the Talempong Musical Tradition of the Payakumbuh Region, West Sumatra, Indonesia." PhD dissertation, University of New England.

———. 2009. *Tali nan bapilin tigo (Three Strings Entwined): A Study of the Minangkabau Talempong Tradition in West Sumatra, Indonesia.* Saarbrücken, Germany: Lambert Academic Publishing.

Sanday, Peggy Reeves. 2002. *Women at the Center: Life in a Modern Matriarchy.* Ithaca: Cornell University Press.

Sargeant, Lynn M. 2004. "A New Class of People: The Conservatoire and Musical Professionalization in Russia (1861–1917)." *Music and Letters* 85 (1): 41–61.

Smith, Benjamin. 2008. "The Origins of Regional Autonomy in Indonesia: Experts and the Marketing of Political Interests." *Journal of East Asian Studies* 8 (2): 211–34.

Soedarsono, R. M. 1999. *Seni pertunjukan Indonesia dan pariwisata.* Bandung: Masyarakat Seni Pertunjukan Indonesia.

Spiller, Henry. 2010. *Erotic Triangles: Sundanese Dance and Masculinity in West Java.* Chicago: University of Chicago Press.

Stokes, Martin. 2002. "Marx, Money, and Musicians." In *Music and Marx: Ideas, Practice, Politics,* edited by Regula Burckhardt Qureshi, 139–63. New York: Routledge.

Suryadi. 2003. "Minangkabau Commercial Cassettes and the Cultural Impact of the Recording Industry in West Sumatra." *Asian Music* 34 (2): 51–89.

Suryadinata, Leo, Evi Nurvidya Arifin, and Aris Ananta. 2003. *Indonesia's Population: Ethnicity and Religion in a Changing Political Landscape*. Singapore: Institute of Southeast Asian Studies.

Sutton, R. Anderson. 1986. "New Theory for Traditional Music in Banyumas, West Central Java." *Pacific Review of Ethnomusicology* 3: 79–101.

———. 1991. *Traditions of Gamelan Music in Java: Musical Pluralism and Regional Identity*. Cambridge: Cambridge University Press.

———. 2002. *Calling Back the Spirit: Music, Dance, and Cultural Politics in Lowland South Sulawesi*. New York: Oxford University Press.

Sweeney, Amin. 1974. "Professional Malay Story-Telling: Some Questions of Style and Presentation." In *Studies in Malaysian Oral and Musical Traditions*, Michigan Papers on South and Southeast Asia, no. 8. Ann Arbor: University of Michigan Center for South and Southeast Asian Studies.

Taylor, Paul Michael. 1994. "The *Nusantara* Concept of Culture: Local Traditions and National Identity as Expressed in Indonesia's Museums." In *Fragile Traditions: Indonesian Art in Jeopardy*, edited by P. M. Taylor, 71–90. Honolulu: University of Hawai'i Press.

Tsing, Anna Lowenhaupt. 1993. *In the Realm of the Diamond Queen: Marginality in an Out-of-the-Way Place*. Princeton: Princeton University Press.

Turino, Thomas. 1999. "Signs of Imagination, Identity, and Experience: A Peircian Semitic Theory for Music." *Ethnomusicology* 43 (2): 221–55.

———. 2000. *Nationalists, Cosmopolitans, and Popular Music in Zimbabwe*. Chicago: University of Chicago Press.

———. 2003. "Are We Global Yet? Globalist Discourse, Cultural Formations and the Study of Zimbabwean Popular Music." *British Journal of Ethnomusicology* 12 (2): 51–79.

———. 2008. *Music as Social Life: The Politics of Participation*. Chicago: University of Chicago Press.

Usman, Abdul Kadir Dt. yang Dipatuan. 2002. *Kamus umum bahasa Minangkabau-Indonesia*. Padang: Anggrek Media.

Utama, Indra. 1999. "Traditional Dance in Minangkabau: Its Roots and Its Future." In *Walk in Splendor: Ceremonial Dress and the Minangkabau*, edited by Anne Summerfield and John Summerfield, 313–23. Los Angeles: UCLA Fowler Museum of Cultural History.

Wardlow, Holly. 2006. *Wayward Women: Sexuality and Agency in a New Guinea Society*. Berkeley: University of California Press.

Wegman, Rob C. 2005. "Musical Offerings in the Renaissance." *Early Music* 33 (3): 425–37.

Weintraub, Andrew N. 1993. "Theory in Institutional Pedagogy and

'Theory in Practice' for Sundanese Gamelan Music." *Ethnomusicology* 37 (1): 29–40.

———. 2010. *Dangdut Stories: A Social and Musical History of Indonesia's Most Popular Music*. New York: Oxford University Press.

Weiss, Sarah. 1993. " Gender and *Gendèr*: Gender Ideology and the Female *Gendèr* Player in Central Java" In *Rediscovering the Muses: Women's Musical Traditions,* edited by Kimberly Marshall, 21–48. Boston: Northeastern University Press.

Yampolsky, Philip. 1987. *Lokananta: A Discography of the National Recording Company of Indonesia, 1957–1985*. Center for Southeast Asian Studies Bibliography Series, no. 10. Madison: University of Wisconsin.

———. 1995. "Forces for Change in the Regional Performing Arts of Indonesia." *Bijdragen tot de taal-, land- en volkenkunde* 151 (4): 700–25.

———. 1996a. Liner notes For *Gongs and Vocal Music from Sumatra: Talempong, Didong, Kulintang, Salawat Dulang*. Music of Indonesia, vol. 12. Smithsonian Folkways SF CD 40428.

———. 1996b. Liner notes For *Melayu Music of Sumatra and the Riau Islands*. Music of Indonesia, vol. 11. Smithsonian Folkways SF CD 40427.

Yampolsky, Philip, and Hanefi. 1994. Liner Notes For *Night Music of West Sumatra: Saluang, Rabab Pariaman, Dendang Pauah*. Music of Indonesia, vol. 6. Smithsonian Folkways SF CD 40422.

Young, Kenneth R. 1982. "Minangkabau Authority Patterns and the Effects of Dutch Rule." In *The Malay-Islamic World of Sumatra: Studies in Politics and Culture,* edited by J. Maxwell, 63–73. Melbourne: Monash University.

Zanten, Wim van. 1995. "Notation of Music: Theory and Practice in West Java." In *Ethnomusicology in the Netherlands: Present Situation and Traces of the Past,* edited by Zanten and Marjolijn van Roon, 209–33, vol. 2 of *Oideion: The Performing Arts World-Wide*.

Zurbuchen, Mary Sabina. 1990. "Images of Culture and National Development in Indonesia: *The Cockroach Opera*." *Asian Theatre Journal* 7 (2): 27–149.

Discography

Junaidi, Ronaldi. N.d. *Nada talempong klasik,* vol 1. ND 0017. CD.

Orkes Gumarang. 1959. Lokananta ARI001. LP.

Yampolsky, Philip. 1996. *Gongs and Vocal Music from Sumatra: Talempong, Didong, Kulintang, Salawat Dulang.* Music of Indonesia, vol. 12. Smithsonian Folkways SF CD 40428.

Interviews by the Author

Adam, Irsjad, 21 July 2004, Padang Panjang.
Alfalah, 16 March 2004, Padang Panjang; 26 June 2010, Padang Panjang.
Amar, Djaruddin, 30 September 2004, Padang Panjang.
Asma and Rosani, 24 July 2010, Paninjauan.
Asma, Jenni Aulia, Mardiani, and Yusni, 6 November 2004, Paninjauan.
Asnam Rasyid, 26 August 2004, Padang.
Dt. Parpatiah nan Sabatang, 17 February 2014, Paninjauan.
Ediwar, 4 February 2014, Padang Panjang.
Efrinon, 23 June 2010, Padang Panjang.
Erianto, 12 January 2004, Pekanbaru.
Hajizar, 27 September 2004, Padang Panjang.
Herawati, 23 September 2004, Padang Panjang.
Jenni Aulia, 18 February 2014, Paninjauan.
Kamal, Zahara, 23 September 2004, Padang Panjang.
Mardiani, Mariani, and Yusni, 24 July 2010, Paninjauan.
Murad, 19 February 2004, Padang.
Nofrizal with Jenni Aulia, 18 February 2014, Paninjauan.
Rosani and Yusni, 16 February 2014, Paninjauan.
Rugusman, 14 February 2014, Gunung Rajo.
Siti Aisah and Jasril, 11 September 2004, Unggan.
Syahrul Tarun Yusuf, 25 June 2010, Balingka.
Taufik Dt. Mangkuto Rajo, 18 June 2010, Padang Panjang.
Tomi Chandra Putra, 24 July 2010, Paninjauan.
Rohana and Zuraida with Suryanti, 30 June 2010, Padang Panjang.
Utama, Edy, 25 August 2004, Padang.
Zoebir, Zuryati, 20 February 2004, Padang.

Online Resources

*Audio Examples (at http://www.ohioswallow.com/book/
Gongs+and+Pop+Songs)*

All recordings made by the author, unless otherwise noted.

1.1. "Singgalang ayak kapua," *talempong duduak,* Unggan, 31 December 2003.

1.2. "Singgalang ayak kapua," *talempong goyang,* Alfa Musik, Ombilin, 10 July 2004.

2.1. "Malam bainai," *sarunai bibia* and percussion, Paninjauan, 25 July 2010.

4.1. "Tak tontong," *dendang* and *talempong jao.* Recorded by Margaret Kartomi, 1972. Used with permission.

4.2. "Tak tontong" arranged for *orkes talempong.* Recorded by Margaret Kartomi, 1972. Used with permission.

4.3. "Kambang cari" on *orkes talempong.* Recorded by Margaret Kartomi, 1972. Used with permission.

5.1. "Minangkabau," *talempong kreasi* class at STSI, Padang Panjang, 23 March 2004.

5.2. "Baju kuruang," *talempong kreasi,* Lansano Entertaint, Jakarta, 30 October 2003.

5.3. "Mudiak arau," *talempong goyang,* Alfa Musik, Elda as vocalist, Padang Panjang, 17 June 2010.

5.4. "Kelok sembilan," *talempong goyang,* Alfa Musik, Fitri as vocalist, Padang Panjang, 17 June 2010.

5.5. "Arek-arek lungga," *talempong goyang,* STSI outreach program, Wilda as vocalist, Sungai Batang, 22 May 2004.

5.6. "Lupa-lupa ingat," *talempong goyang,* Alfa Musik, Afni, Rina, Wilda as vocalists, Padang Panjang, 27 June 2010.

*Video Examples (at http://www.ohioswallow.com/book/
Gongs+and+Pop+Songs)*

1.1. *Talempong kreasi* playing "Mudiak arau" at Tourism Expo, Lansano Entertaint, Jakarta, 30 October 2003.

1.2. *Talempong jao* with the gong part played on a cookie container, "Muaro paneh," Nurlaili and Siti Aisah Unggan, 1 December 2003.

2.1. "Tupai bagaluik," *talempong duduak,* Talempong Uaik-Uaik, Paninjauan, 10 July 2010.

2.2. *Talempong duduak,* pan shot of instruments, Talempong Uaik-Uaik, Paninjauan, 10 July 2010.

2.3. *Talempong duduak* in Unggan, 30 December 2003, including Siti Aisah on far right.

2.4. *Talempong pacik* in Padang Alai, 17 March 2004. *Left to right:* Asma on *gandang;* Rukmini, *saua;* Nurhayati, *tingkah;* Mariana, *aguang;* Barilas, *polong*. Asma's daughters, Ranti and Mimi, are playing the *sikatuntuang* but are not seen on screen.

2.5. *Talempong pacik* in wedding procession, Unggan, 31 December 2003.

2.6. *Talempong pacik* in wedding procession, Padang Alai, 18 March 2004.

3.1. "Gua cak din din," 1st level of variation, *talempong* class at STSI, 30 March 2004.

3.2. "Gua cak din din," 2nd level of variation.

3.3. "Gua cak din din," 3rd level of variation.

3.4. "Gua cak din din," up to speed.

5.1. "Dantiang balinduang," Sanggar Satampang Baniah, Padang, 21 February 2004.

5.2. "Minangkabau," Sanggar Satampang Baniah, Padang, 21 February 2004.

5.3. "Aluang bunian," Sanggar Saayun Salangkah, Bukittinggi, 8 May 2004.

5.4. *Saluang jo dendang* on *talempong goyang,* Alfa Musik, Ombilin, 10 July 2004.

5.5. "Saibah," a Bollywood tune on *talempong goyang,* Alfa Musik, Padang Panjang, 17 June 2010.

*Web Figures (at http://www.ohioswallow.com/book/
Gongs+and+Pop+Songs)*

All photographs taken by the author unless otherwise noted.

1.1. *Talempong*, 17 June 2010.

1.2. Nurlaili playing *talempong kayu*, 1 December 2003.

1.3. *Talempong jao*, 1 January 2004.

2.1. Lake Maninjau, 22 June 2013.

2.2. Women playing *talempong* at a wedding in Paninjauan, 9 July 2010.

2.3. Center of Unggan, 14 September 2004.

2.4. Outer area in Unggan, 29 December 2003.

2.5. Rice fields in Unggan, 14 September 2004.

2.6. Mountain pass into Unggan, 13 July 2010.

2.7. *Talempong pacik* as part of a *gandang tambua* ensemble with *pupuik solo* during a wedding procession, Paninjauan, 17 February 2014.

2.8. *Gandang tambua* during a wedding procession, Paninjauan, 17 February 2014.

2.9. *Gandang tambua* at another wedding in Paninjauan, 17 February 2014.

2.10. *Gandang tambua* group at wedding reception, Paninjauan, 17 February 2014.

2.11. *Talempong duduak* in Paninjauan, 10 July 2010.

2.12. Mardiani playing *aguang* with a young jackfruit, 9 July 2010.

2.13. Asma playing *gandang,* 10 July 2010.

2.14. Samsinar playing *botol,* 10 July 2010.

2.15. Rosani playing *giriang,* 10 July 2010.

2.16. *Talempong pacik* in a wedding procession in Pesisir Selatan, 1999.

2.17. Alternative ensemble in Paninjauan, 17 February 2014.

2.18. Wedding procession in Paninjauan, 16 February 2014.

2.19. Gift of uncooked rice, Paninjauan, 16 February 2014.

2.20. Bringing gifts of rice in a wedding procession in Paninjauan, 16 February 2014.

2.21. Gifts at a wedding in Paninjauan, 17 February 2014.

2.22. *Bajamba*-style food at a wedding in Paninjauan, 16 February 2014.

2.23. Women eating *bajamba* style in Paninjauan, 16 February 2014.

2.24. *Batagak pangulu*, Paninjauan, 18 January 2014.

2.25. *Talempong* group on way to a soccer game, Unggan, 14 September 2004.

3.1. The institute in Padang Panjang when it was known as STSI, 17 August 2004.

4.1. *Orkes talempong* with *talempong jao* in the second row, ASKI, Padang Panjang, 1972. Photo by H. Kartomi. Used with permission.

4.2. *Orkes talempong* with a conductor, ASKI, Padang Panjang, 1972. Photograph by H. Kartomi. Used with permission.

4.3. The *bansi* and *saluang* take a solo in *orkes talempong,* ASKI, Padang Panjang, 1972. Photo by H. Kartomi. Used with permission.

5.1. Halim with Alfa Musik, Padang Panjang, 17 June 2010.

5.2. Alfa Musik looking like a rock band with *talempong,* Padang Panjang, 17 June 2010.

5.3. Wilda, vocalist with Alfa Musik, Padang Panjang, 17 June 2010.

5.4. *Talempong goyang* at a wedding, Padang Panjang, 27 June 2010.

Web Map

1.1. West Sumatra

Index

Page numbers in italics refer to illustrations, tables, or musical examples.

adat, 14, 18–20, 44–45; and the arts, 79, 89. See also weddings in the nagari
adaik. See adat
Adam, Achiar, 100; and orkes talempong, 138–40, 147
Adam, Boestanoel Arifin, 47, 100; as director of the institution, 96, 113, 117; and orkes talempong, 137, 140; and the PRRI, 100
Adam, Hoeriah, 100, 135
Adam, Irsjad, 100–101, 117, 137; and orkes talempong, 138–39, 146–47
aesthetics, 27; and feedback interviews, 49, 63, 73; and preferences, 40, 49, 63, 77, 86, 213, 223
Agam, 12, 209, 212
Alam Minangkabau, 12, 15, 45–46
Alfalah: and Saayun Salangkah, 194; and talempong goyang, 195–210, 200–201, 213. See also Alfa Musik
Alfa Musik, 199–210, 200–203
Amar, Djaruddin, 113–14, 140, 146
Ames, David, 35
Andaya, Leonard, 9
Andras, Sulastri, xi, 114; and Sanggar Satampang Baniah, 185, 191, 194
angklung, 139
Anton, 201, 202, 208
Anwar, Khaidir, 41
"Arek-arek lungga," 203, 210
artists, kinds of, 6, 35, 217; indigenous vs. institutional training, 5, 102–4, 109, 113–16, 217–18; indigenous terminology, 102–3. See also professional musician; seniman
Arzul Jamaan, x, 14–15, 23, 40, 128, 213

ASKI Padang Panjang, 4, 93, 95, 98, 101, 120, 128, 222; and my experiences as an exchange student and ethnographer, 39, 116, 222; and Kartomi visit in 1972, 140, 142; and reform of talempong, 133–34, 140. See also institutionalization of the arts; institutions for the arts in West Sumatra
Asma, x, 37–38, 38, 42, 52, 55, 78, 226n1 (chap. 2)
Asna, 65
Asnamawarti, 119
Asnam Rasyid, xi, 45, 181–82, 190
ASTI Yogya, 93
Aviva, Wilda, 202, 208
"Ayam den lapeh," 190, 214

baju kuruang, 38
"Baju kuruang," 190
Bana Baram, 208
Baralek. See weddings in the nagari
Barendregt, Bart, 28, 30
Barth, Frederik, 20
batagak pangulu, 75, 80, 88, 206
"Batang Singingi," 49. See also music and place; Singingi River
"Batang tarunjam," 48
Benamou, Marc, 34, 91, 103–4, 118, 147, 220
Blackwood, Evelyn, xi, 18, 67, 69, 197
Brinner, Benjamin, 91, 117–18, 121, 127
bronze instruments, 2, 23, 26, 140, 142
Brubaker, Rogers, 7, 20, 130, 185
budayawan, 30, 95, 97, 140
"Buka pintu," 49

Bukittinggi, town of, 43; as headquarters of PRRI, 21–22; and tourist performances, 180, 184, 189, 193, 222

Bungo Tanjueng, *nagari* of, 121, 127; Hajizar's composition for *sanggar* Satampang Baniah, 191–92; and *talempong pacik*: "Gua cak din din," 124, *125,* 126; — "Gua tari piriang," 191–92; — "Gua sambalado lah tatunggang," *123–24;* — parts in the ensemble, 63, 122–25; — and variation, 63, 122, 124–27 (*see also under* instruments: *pupuik batang padi; rabano; rapa'i); talempong pacik* style at the institution, 63, 121–27. *See also* Elizar; Hajizar

bureaus of arts, culture, and/or tourism, 2, 66, 128, 181, 193–94

campur sari, 220

chromatic tuning, 10, 225n1 (chap. 1); and cosmopolitan styles, 60, 176–77, 220; and *talempong goyang,* 199, 202; and *talempong kreasi,* 2, 186

clans, 14, 26, 41–44, 69, 75

class. *See* social class

commercialization, 33, 84, 182. *See also* monetization: and music

commodification, 33. *See also* monetization: and music

community, 3. *See also talempong,* indigenous-style; *nagari*

Cooper, Frederick, 7, 20

cosmopolitanism, 16–17

cosmopolitan music, 16–17; forms of, 28, 30, 76, 100, 136, 195; and indigenous practices, 32, 78, 63, 135, 139–40, 147, 214, 216–17, 224. *See also talempong,* cosmopolitan-style

cultural policies of the state, 91–92; and ethnicity, 97, 130, 178; New Order, 90, 97–98, 130, 177–78; Old Order, 92–93, 97, 177; Reformation era, 176, 212, 221

cultural reformism, 140–41. *See also orkes talempong*

dance, 135, 220; and cultural display, 178; at the institution, 106, 108, 110, 112, 115; in the *nagari,* 15, 68–69, 79; and *orgen,* 196–97; and *sanggar,* 2, 184–85, 190–92, 194–95; and *talempong goyang,* 196, 198, 210–11. *See also specific titles*

"Dantiang balinduang," 191–92, 195

darek, 12, 18, 47; and *saluang jo dendang,* 29, 46. *See also dendang;* instruments: *rabab darek;* instruments: *saluang darek; saluang jo dendang*

dendang, 29; in the curriculum 106, 110–11, 130; at the institute 109, 131; and Minangkabau ethnicity, 32, 223; and place, 46–47; and *pop Minang,* 29, 31. *See also* indigenous-style *talempong; orkes talempong; sanggar; talempong duduak; talempong goyang; talempong kreasi; talempong pacik;* Unggan

Department of Traditional Music, 103–12, 115; as Jurusan Karawitan, 99. *See also* institutions for the arts in West Sumatra

Department of Western Music, 99, 109

diatonic tuning, 10, 225n1 (chap. 1); and indigenous-style *talempong,* 60, *61,* 62, 199; and cosmopolitan styles, 60, 112, 134–36, 177, 214, 217; at the institution, 100, 186; as a neutral system, 146; and *orkes talempong,* 134, 137–39, 143–44, 146–48, 173–74; in Paninjauan, 79; and *talempong kreasi,* 184, 186, *192;* in Unggan, 60, 62

Dt. Parpatiah nan Sabatang, 43

DUE-like, 116, 211

Durian Tinggi, *nagari* of, 40

economic crisis, 1, 180. *See also krismon*

economic modes of exchange: commercial transaction, 33, 84; framing of transaction, 84; gift economy and reciprocity, 33, 74–75, 84, 217

economics of music, 32–34, 84, 128, 206; and *sanggar,* 129, 193–95; and *talempong* in the *nagari*, 81–86; and *talempong goyang*, 206–9. *See also* economy, free-market; economy, gift; monetization: and music

economy: capitalist, 33–34, 177; free-market, 5, 176, 215; gift, 33, 74 (*see also under* economic modes of exchange); subsistence, 33, 177. *See also* free-market economy

Ediwar, xi, 214; and the institution, 211, 220–21; as *pangulu*, 42, 80; and Paninjauan, 75, 79, 82, 84

Elizar, xi, 63, 121–27, 191

Erianto, 120–21

Ernida, 73, 75

ethnicity: and *adat*, 44; and art, 9–10, 134–35, 174, 216, 218–19; cognitive view of, 4, 6–10, 18, 20, 134, 218–19; and cultural display, 178, 185, 218; ethnopolitical entrepreneurs, 185; and language, 7–9; mechanisms mobilizing, 7, 9, 20, 218; and migration, 20, 23; and music, 10, 18, 35–36, 174, 177, 213, 223–24; and the state, 20–21, 218; and *talempong*, 4, 10, 18, 23, 32, 35–36, 39, 105, 177, 214–16, 223–24. See also *dendang; orkes talempong; pop Minang;* PRRI; *talempong; talempong goyang; talempong kreasi*

ethnography, 33–35, 39, 84, 135, 196, 217

Faril, *200–201*, 208

fieldwork, ix, xi, 26, 39, 102, 121, 138, 193, 226n2

Fitri, 204

free-market economy, 5, 176, 215. See also *sanggar; talempong goyang; talempong kreasi;* tourism industry

Gadih Ranti, 189

gender: balance of faculty, 115; balance of students, 104, 115; and *orkes talempong*, 144; and *talempong* at the institute, 131; and *talempong* in the *nagari*, 47, 50, 57, 62; and wedding guests, 73, 75

genres
bansi tunggal, 184
barzanji, 110–11
dangdut, 65; and indigenous-style *talempong*, 65; and *talempong goyang*, 196, 202–4, 210 (*see also* genres: *dangdut Minang;* genres: *saluang dangdut*)
dangdut Minang, 203, 210; and *talempong goyang*, 203, 210
dendang Pauah, 46, 110
dikia rabano, 28, 76, 110–11
gamaik, 28–29, 203; and *talempong goyang*, 203
gambus Melayu, 110
gambus Riau, 110–11
gandang sarunai, 110–11
gandang tambua, 50, 104; in the curriculum, 110; in Lake Maninjau region, 50; in Paninjauan, 50, *51;* in Pariaman, 50; and processions, 50, 72, 227n14; and *pupuik*, 50
hiburan daerah, 29–30
indang, 47, 110–11; and *talempong goyang*, 203
Melayu Deli, 110
nasyid, 111
orkes Melayu, 29, 144
pop Indonesia, 203; and *talempong goyang*, 203
qasidah, 203; and *talempong goyang*, 203
randai, 104, 110, 220; and *sanggar*, 195
salawat dulang, 76,; in the curriculum, 110–11; as professionalized, 103–4, 108
saluang dangdut, 203, 209, 220–21; at the institution, 221; and *talempong goyang*, 203
sijobang, 46; in the curriculum, 110–11; and *saluang jo dendang*, 47; as specialized skills, 103; and *tukang sijobang*, 102; at weddings, 76 (*see also* instruments: *kacapi; kaba*)
silek, 110, 219–20
See also *dendang; orgen (tunggal); pop Minang; rabab Pasisia; saluang jo dendang; talempong*

gift theory, 84. *See also* Wegman, Rob

Gongs and Vocal Music from Sumatra (Yampolsky), 39, 53
Gunung Rajo, *nagari* of, 44, 195

Hadler, Jeffrey, 41
Hajizar, 191–92, 213
Halaban, *nagari* of, 48
Halim, 208–9; as *saluang* performer, 116, 208; and *talempong goyang*, 200, 200, 202–3, 205, 208–10
Hanefi, xi, 26, 45, 47, 62–64, 82, 90, 127–29, 135, 198, 202, 205
Haris, Asep Saeful, 201, 202, 208, 210
Heimarck, Brita Renée, 91, 221
Hendri, Yon, 29, 31
Hendrilisna, 119
Herawati, xi, 137, 183; and indigenous arts, 116, 122; and *orkes talempong*, 140–42, 145–47, 180; and *talempong kreasi*, 140, 187, 213
high school for the arts 5. *See also* institutions for the arts in West Sumatra; KOKAR; SMKI; SMKN
Hough, Brett, 91–2, 97, 102, 105, 113
Hughes-Freeland, Felicia, 129, 179, 194

identity, 14–16, 44–45. *See also* ethnicity
IKIP, 113, 227n1
"Indang Payakumbuh" 147, 171–72, 172
indigenous (term), 17, 49
Indojati, 194
INS Kayutanam, 100
institutionalization of the arts: and academic credentials, 4, 113, 115, 221; and career paths, 5, 35, 91, 103–4, 108, 127–30, 221; compared with Bali, 91, 93, 108, 113, 115, 221; compared with Java, 104–5, 108, 115, 121, 127, 129; compared with Sulawesi, 113, 227n2; compared with Surabaya, 113, 135; compared with Surakarta, 92–93, 202; compared with Yogyakarta, 93; and cosmopolitans, 89, 99–101, 114–15, 130; and development of indigenous arts, 100–101, 105, 112, 130, 133–34, 139, 211–12, 219–20; and development of indigenous arts vs. preservation, 105, 134, 175, 184 (*see also* cultural reformism; *kreasi baru*; *orkes talempong*; *talempong kreasi*); and formal training, 35, 102–4, 109, 271–78; as nationalist project, 3, 91–92, 98, 100–102; and new kind of artists, 5, 35, 91, 102–3, 217; and preservation of indigenous arts, 91, 99–101, 105–6, 109, 111, 113–14, 117, 130, 133, 219; and professionalization, 35, 102–4, 109, 132, 218, 221; and transformational effects, 3, 5, 89, 91, 104–5, 112, 133, 177, 222–23

institutions for the arts in West Sumatra, 5
and artistic authority, 116, 131, 137, 217–19, 222
and commensuration with other regions, 95, 98
and comparable institutions in Indonesia, 92–93, 94, 104, 219
and community service, 115, 228n6
critiques of, 106, 113, 117, 212, 219–20
curriculum of, 105–12, 130–31; career paths, 108–9, 112; degree tracks, 107–8; early, 106, 109; genres in, 110–11; and indigenous-style *talempong*, 105, 110–12, 130; and indigenous practices, 109–12; Melayu focus of, 107; practical vs. theoretical training, 108–9; and professionalization, 109; and *sanggar*, 108, 112; and *talempong kreasi*, 110–12; and tourism, 108, 112
departments at, 99, 106, 115 (*see also* Department of Traditional Music; Department of Western Music)
establishment of, 4, 90–93, 95–98, 100
faculty at, 100, 113–17
goals of, 99–105
graduates of: and careers, 5, 103, 109, 127–30, 177, 185, 221; and dissemination of institutional

styles and skills, 110, 112, 116, 222; dispersal of, 5, 105, 110, 112–13, 130; as professional musicians, 218; and *sanggar,* 177, 185–86; and training of, 104–5, 115, 132, 218
and indigenous artists, 40, 102, 113–17, 122, 127; artist residencies, 40, 114–16; as faculty, 113–15 (see also *seniman*)
and indigenous practices, 95, 100–101, 109–12, 116, 131; pedagogy of, 113–18, 121–27
and KOKAR Surakarta, 93
and Minangkabau ethnicity, 89, 98, 130
in *nagari,* 115, 211
and national educational policies, 101–2, 105, 108, 116
and new epistemologies, 109, 117, 126, 219
outcomes, 219–20
pedagogical methods, 117–18, 121–27, 131; and analysis, 107, 118, 126, 219; implicit vs. explicit knowledge, 118–19, 126; and indigenous aesthetics, 120, 126–27; and musical competence 117–19; and notation, 109, 118, 120–24, *123–25,* 127, 131; vs. transmission in the *nagari,* 118–20
precedents of, 99–100
and the PRRI, 90
representation of indigenous practices, 221–22
research expeditions, 115–16, 120
as self-perpetuating system, 113–15
and *talempong:* from Bungo Tanjueng, 121–27; indigenous styles, 110–12, 120–27, 131–32; from Sialang, 121; *talempong goyang,* 209–12; *talempong kreasi,* 110–12; from Unggan, 120
instruments
aguang, 55, 57, *57,* 58, 65; part in Padang Alai *talempong pacik* ensemble, 62; technique in Paninjauan, 38, *54*
bansi, 46; in the curriculum, 106; and *orkes talempong,* 139, *143,* 144–45,

149–69, 170–71, *171;* and *sanggar,* 184; and *talempong goyang,* 202–3, 210; and *talempong kreasi,* 2, *187*
botol, 38, 55, *56,* 57, *57,* 65, 226n7
canang, 142–43; and *orkes talempong,* 142–43, 146; and *talempong kreasi,* 187, 189
djembe, 2, 188–89, 192
dol, 50 (see also genres: *gandang tambua*)
gambus, 29, 110
gandang, 55, *55,* 57, *57,* 58; in the curriculum, 106; in *talempong kreasi, 187*
gendang oyak, 210, 220
genggong, 119
giriang-giriang, 55, *56,* 57, *57* (see also instruments: tambourine)
gondang, 58 (see also instruments: *gandang*)
guitar, 30, 100
guitar, bass; and *talempong kreasi,* 2; and *talempong goyang,* 201–2, *201,* 208
guitar, electric, and *talempong goyang,* 199, 200–201, 208, 210
harmonica, 65, 66, 77, 83 (see also instruments: *sarunai bibia*)
kacapi, 46, 195
ogung, 58 (see also instruments: *aguang*)
pupuik batang padi, 226n5; in *talempong pacik* from Bungo Tanjueng, 63
pupuik gadang, 226n5; in the curriculum, 110; in *talempong pacik* from Bungo Tanjueng, 127, 191 (see also instruments: *pupuik batang padi*)
pupuik solo, 50, *51,* 226n5 (see also instruments: *pupuik batang padi* and instruments: *pupuik gadang*)
rabab darek, 46; at the institution, 110–12; and *sanggar* 195
rabab Pariaman, in the curriculum, 110
rabab Pasisia (see genres: *rabab Pasisia*)
rabano, 38, 55, 57, 63, 65 (see also genres: *dikia rabano*)

Index 263

rapa'i, 63, 127
saluang darek, 46; in the curriculum, 106, 110–12, 130–31
saluang panjang, 46; in the curriculum, 110
saluang Pauah, in the curriculum, 110
sampelong, 110
sarunai: in the curriculum, 106; and *orkes talempong,* 144; and *talempong goyang,* 202, 210; and *talempong kreasi,* 2, *187,* 191 (*see also* genres: *gandang sarunai*)
sarunai bibia, 66
sikatuntuang, 62
sirompak, 47; in the curriculum, 110
synthesizer, 5; and *orgen,* 28, 193, 197; and *talempong goyang,* 199, 202, 210–11; and *talempong kreasi,* 188
tambourine: in indigenous-style *talempong,* 38, 55, *56,* 57–58, 65; in *orkes talempong,* *143,* 145, *149–69;* in *saluang dangdut,* 221; in *talempong goyang,* 196, 202, 210; in *talempong kreasi,* 2, 192
tambua, 127
tasa, 50 (*see also* genres: *gandang tambua*)
tawak-tawak, 62
See also *saluang; saluang jo dendang; talempong,* instrument types
ISI Padang Panjang, 4, 95. *See also* institutionalization of the arts; institutions for the arts in West Sumatra

Jakarta, 1, 17, 180; Minangkabau population of, 13, 96; Minangkabau arts and artists in, 29, 31, 129–30, 196; and the PRRI, 96; and *sanggar,* 189, 194
Jambi, province of, 21
Jasril, 66, 70, 78, 120
Jenni Aulia, 42, 79, 85, 88, 227n16
Jensen, Joli, 33
jorong. See nagari

kaba, 46, 111. *See also* genres: *sijobang; rabab Pasisia*
Kafsir, Sidney, 84
Kahin, Audrey, 9, 19, 21–22, 95–96, 137
Kahn, Joel S., 33, 43
"Kaja-bakaja," 53
Kamal, Zahara, xi, 109
"Kambang Cari," 148, *149–69,* 172
"Kancang dayuang ilia," 48
"Kancang dayuang mudiak," 48
karawitan, 92; use of at the institution, 98–99. *See also* Department of Traditional Music
Kartomi, Margaret: and the institution, 91; and *orkes talempong* 135–6, 140, 142, 144–5, *145,* 147, *171,* 186; and *talempong* 26, 48, 58, 135; and tourism industry, 180
kebudayaan, 91, 97, 103, 218
"Kelok 44," 37
"Kelok Sembilan," 190, 203
keramaian, 77, 119, 148
kesenian 1, 3, 103, 218, 225n2
Kipp, Rita Smith, 178
KOKAR Bali, 93
KOKAR Minangkabau, 4, 89, 93, 128. *See also* institutionalization of the arts; institutions for the arts in West Sumatra
KOKAR Surabaya, 113, 135
KOKAR Surakarta, 92–3
Koto Kaciak, *nagari* of, 196
kreasi baru, 211; dance, 110; elsewhere in Indonesia, 135, 144, 147; in the *nagari,* 79. See also *talempong kreasi*
krismon, 116, 183, 194, 197
kulintang, 23
Kuntu, *nagari* of, 48

Lansano Entertaint, 1–2, 184, 188, 194–95
Limapuluh Kota, city of, 12, 110
Lokananta, 29–30
Loveman, Mara, 7
Lubuk Basung, town of, 73
"Lubuk Sao," 190
"Lupa-lupa ingat," 203

"Malam Bainai," 66
Maninjau, Lake, 37, 50, 219
marantau, 13–14
Mardiani, 38, *38,* 42, *54,* 65, 76–78

Mariani, 37, 38, 39, 52, 52, 65, 226n6
McIntosh, Johnathan, 183, 221
Mentawai, 12, 20, 178
Metro Minang, 195
middle class, 4, 129, 177, 183
migration, 12–15; and ethnicity 20, 23; and marriage, 69, 78; and *pop Minang*, 190
"Minangkabau," the piece, 187, *188–89*, 190
Minangkabau: aphorisms, 72–73, 75, 97, 106, 211; commonalities of, 18–20; demographics of, 11–13; diversity of music, 45–47; as historical social identity, 9, 43; and incorporation into the state, 20–22; and Islam, 16, 18–19; kinship system, 11, 68–69; multiplicity of, 6–7, 15–18, 32, 39, 214, 223–24; and mystical beliefs, 19, 27, 47, 68, 110. See also *adat*; ethnicity; migration
monetization, 33; of cultural practices, 34, 177; and music, 32–34; and new career paths, 34
Muaro Labuah, town of, 46, 110
"Muaro paneh," 49
Muchtar, Asril, 196–98, 203, 208
"Mudiak arau," 184, 190, 203
Murad, xi, 101, 114, 117; and *orkes talempong*, 137–40, 142, 146–47, 213
music and place, 45–47; in *saluang jo dendang*, 46–47; *talempong*, 48–49

nagari: and *adat*, 20; and agriculture, 43; and clans, 41–3; and community solidarity and spirit, 23, 75; definition of and life in, 40–45; economic life in, 81; histories of, 48; and *jorong*, 41–42; and kinship networks, 42, 67–69; and Minangkabau ethnicity, 23, 44–45; musicians in, 33; and regional autonomy, 41; and social identity, 43–44. See also Bungo Tanjueng; Durian Tinggi; Gunung Rajo; Ombilin; Padang Alai; Paninjauan; Sialang; Unggan
Naim, Mochtar, 13–4, 96

Navis, A. A., 29–30, 95–97, 100, 135
Nofrizal Dt. Simarajo, 41–43, 74, 76, 79, 87
North Sumatra, province of, 13, 114, 203
nostalgia 2, 31, 78, 190, 203–4
Nurlaili, 25

Oktavia, Rina, 204, 208
Ombilin, *nagari* of, 71
orgen (tunggal): costs of, 77; definition of, 28, 197; at weddings 76–79, 197; and Minangkabau ethnicity, 193, 205, 213; morals of, 77, 197–98; repertoire of, 197; and *sanggar*, 195
Orkes Gumarang, 29–30, 101, 136, 144, 174
orkes talempong, 4, 27, *145, 171;* and aesthetic appeal, 141; compared with gamelan, 140, 142, 144, 220; compared with *talempong kreasi*, 144, 176, 186–87; and cosmopolitans, 139–40, 147, 174; as culturally reformist, 137, 140–41, 144–48, 173; and *dendang*, 147–48, 171–73, *172;* and indigenous-style *talempong*, 138–39, 140, 144–46, 148, 169, 173; and the institution, 134–35, 137–38; instrumentation of, 142–45, *143, 171;* and Minangkabau ethnicity, 10, 14–15, 134–35, 139, 141–42, 146, 173–75; as modernist, 134–35, 140, 146, 173–74; orchestration of, 145–8, 170–3; and other indigenous practices, 139, 142, 148, 171–72; as presentational, 148; prototype of, 137–39; and PRRI, 134, 136–37, 174; and *saluang jo dendang*, 142, 172–73
otonomi daerah. See regional autonomy

Padang, city of: and *dendang Pauah*, 46, 110; and *gamaik*, 28; high school for the arts 5, 93–95, 114; music in, 28, 46, 72, 110; Office of Tourism and Culture 2, 194; and *sanggar*, 194; and *talempong goyang*, 196; tourism in, 179–80

Index 265

Padang Alai, *nagari* of, 16; ethnographic research in, 39, 226n2; future of, 87–88; *Gongs and Vocal Music,* 39; investment in local style, 86–88; and *talempong pacik,* 28, 50, 62, 72; and weddings, 28, 71–72

Padang Panjang, town of, 93, 193, 196, 207–8

Pangkalan, *nagari* of, 48

Paninjauan: *adat* and arts, 79; alternative ensemble to *talempong,* 65–66, *65,* 77, 83; and *gandang tambua,* 50, *51;* investment in their traditions, 78–79; *jorong* in, 41–42; *jorong* Paninjauan of, 41, 82; and *kreasi* arts, 79; *nagari* of, 37, 43; and *talempong duduak, 38,* 47, 51–57, *52;* —, access to instruments, 26, 81–82; —, economics of, 81–85; —, function of, 39, 77–78; —, future of, 88, 217; —, and gift economy, 82–85; —, and incorporation of *dendang* and pop songs, 65–66; —, and the institution, 81–83; —, monetization of the practice, 81–85; —, repertoire of, 39, 65, 77; —, and tuning, 58, *59,* 60, *61;* —, at weddings, 77–78; and *talempong pacik,* with *gandang tambua,* 50, *51;* "Tupai bagaluik," 53, *54,* 55, *57,* 63; and weddings, *67,* 72–74

pantun, 46

"Pararakan Kuntu," 48. *See also* Kuntu; music and place

Pariaman, regency of, 210; and *gandang tambua,* 50; and *indang,* 47; and *talempong,* 110. See also *indang; rabab Pariaman*

Pasaman, regency of, and *dendang,* 47

Pasisia, 46. *See also* genre: *rabab Pasisia*

Pauah, as region. *See* genre: *dendang Pauah; saluang Pauah*

Pauah, Paninjauan jorong of, 42, 83

Payakumbuh, the town, 16, 50, 88; and music, 46–47, 196

pelog scale, 58

Perlman, Marc, xi, 118

Pesisir Selatan, regency of: *dendang* of, 47; *talempong pacik* in, 62. *See also* Pasisia

Picard, Michel, 178–9

pop Minang, 2, 28–31; and Minangkabau ethnicity, 31–32, 136, 174, 223. *See also* indigenous-style *talempong; orgen; orkes talempong; sanggar; talempong duduak; talempong goyang; talempong kreasi; talempong pacik;* Unggan

professionalization of the arts, 33–35; career paths, 35, 91, 103–4, 108, 127–30; careers as civil servants, 103, 128; careers in culture industry, 103–28, 218; careers as faculty, 113, 128; careers as freelancers, 128–9, 194; careers in performance, 103, 128–29; careers as *sanggar,* 112, 128–29; careers in teaching, 109, 112, 128, 185; and indigenous arts outside the institution, 35, 103, 108–9, 128, 218; of indigenous-style *talempong,* 85–86; and *nagari* musicians, 86. *See also* monetization of music

professional musician: definition of, 34–35; framing of the act, 34–35, 86, 103–4, 217; institutional definition of, 102–3; outside the institution, 103

PRRI, 4, 21–22; consequences of, 22, 95–97, 99, 134, 136–37; and Minangkabau ethnicity, 136–37, 218; and *orkes talempong,* 173–74; and rebuilding the province, 96–97

Puti Limo Jurai, 193–94

Qureshi, Regula, 33

rabab Pasisia, 46; at the institution, 108, 110–12; as professional genre, 103, 108, 128, 218; and *sanggar,* 195; at weddings, 76

Radio Republik Indonesia, 29

Rahman, Yusaf, 138, 183

"Ramo-ramo tabang tinggi," 49
rantau, 12, 14, 18, 23, 47, 78, 136, 183, 203. See also *marantau*
Reformasi, 102, 116, 175–6, 180, 183
regional autonomy, 41, 180–81; and the arts, 181, 221; and tourism, 108, 176, 181
Riau, province of, 13, 21, 43, 48, 181, 226n2 (chap. 3)
Rice, Timothy, 6
Rosani, 37, *38, 52, 57, 65,* 74, 76, 83
Rugusman, 44
rumah gadang, 26, 47, 97, 144

Saayun Salangkah, 184, 189–90, 193–4
"Saibah," 200
Salisbury, David, 65, 135, 227n12
saluang, 2, 46; and *orkes talempong* 139, 142, *143,* 144–45, *149–69,* 170–73, *171;* and *pop Minang,* 31; and *sanggar,* 195; and *talempong goyang,* 202, 210; and *talempong kreasi, 187;* and *tukang saluang,* 102. See also genres: *saluang dangdut; saluang darek; saluang jo dendang; saluang panjang; saluang Pauah*
saluang jo dendang, 29, 46–47, 76, 103, 141, 148; in the curriculum, 111, 128; and *orkes talempong,* 142, 172–73; as professionalized, 103–4, 108, 128, 218; and *sanggar,* 184; and *talempong goyang,* 203–4
Samsinar, 38, *38, 56, 65,*
Sanday, Peggy Reeves, 33, 67, 69, 74
sanggar, 1, 177, 183–84; aesthetics of, 185; economics of, 193–95; and indigenous practices, 184, 191–92; indigenous vs. *sanggar* version, 191–92; and the institutions, 184–86, 191, 193; and Minangkabau ethnicity, 185; in private sector, 183, 193–94; repertoire of, 184–85, 190–91; and *talempong kreasi,* 184–5, 188–89; and tourism, 182, 193–94; in West Sumatra, 183–86. See also Gadih Ranti; Indojati; Lansano Entertaint; Metro Minang; Puti Limo Jurai; Saayun Salangkah; Satampang Baniah; Sofyani; Titian Aka
saron, 26, 142
Satampang Baniah, 185, 190–92, 194–95, 229n2
Sawahlunto-Sijunjung, regency of, 66
seniman, 102–3, 129, 217; vs. indigenous artists, 102–3
Seprinaldo, *200,* 208
Sialang, *nagari* of: extinction of *talempong* practice, 40, 217; at the institution 110, 121; parts in the ensemble, 52–53; and *talempong duduak* 50, 52–53, 58, *59, 61;* and tuning, 59
"Siamang tagogau," 48
"Singgalang ayak kapua": on indigenous *talempong* ensemble, 32; on *talempong goyang,* 32
Singingi River, 49
Singkarak, Lake, 32, 71
Siti Aisah, x, 26, 48–49, 60, 65–6, 68, 70, 81, 119–20; professional aspirations, 85–86, 218
Sjafei, Mohammad, 100
slendro scale, 58
SMKI Padang, 5, 95, 114, 222. See also institutionalization of the arts; institutions for the arts in West Sumatra
SMKI Sulawesi, 113
SMKN Padang, 5, 222. See also institutionalization of the arts; institutions for the arts in West Sumatra
social class, 14–16
Sofyani, choreographer, 138, 183
Sofyani, *sanggar,* 138, 183
Solo. See Surakarta
Solok, town of, 46
Spiller, Henry, 34, 198
Stamatov, Peter, 7
Stokes, Martin, 33, 84, 128, 206
STSI Padang Panjang, 4, *90,* 95, 107, 116, 222. See also institutionalization of the arts; institutions for the arts in West Sumatra
Suharto, 22, 90, 97–98, 102, 137, 177, 180, 190

Index 267

Sukarno, 22, 92, 137, 177
suku. See clans
Suryadi, 28, 31
Suryanti, 205
Sutton, R. Anderson, 117, 120, 131, 144; and institutions for the arts, 91–93, 98, 113, 121, 130, 135; and state cultural policies, 97, 182
Sweeney, Amin, 34–35, 86, 103
Syahrul Tarun Yusuf, 30–31

"Tak tontong" 147, 171–72, *172*, 228n3
"Talago Biru," 190
talempong, 23–28
talempong (as style), 3, 27; coexistence of styles, 27–28, 40, 216; diversity of styles, 27–28, 32, 216; history of, 48; newer styles of, 5, 27–28 (*see also* cosmopolitan-style *talempong*); older styles of, 27–28, 40, 49, 86 (*see also* indigenous-style *talempong*); styles in the *nagari*, 47–67. See also *orkes talempong; talempong bararak; talempong duduak; talempong goyang; talempong kreasi (baru); talempong pacik; talempong taleno*
talempong, cosmopolitan styles, indigenous attitudes toward, 49, 78. See also *orkes talempong; talempong goyang; talempong kreasi*
talempong, indigenous-style: aesthetic preferences for, 49, 63, 78, 86; aesthetics of, 49, 60, 64, 19; commonalities of, 49–50; and community identity, 23, 39, 40, 60, 63–64, 67, 72, 77–78, 80, 87; and contexts for performance, 80, 118–19; differences between *nagari*, 49–53, 55, 57–64; economics of, 81–86, 182; feelings toward, 31–32; future of, 28, 40, 87–88, 216–17; and gender, 47, 50, 57–58, 62–63, 70–71; and government officials, 66, 82; history of, 48; incorporation of *dendang* and pop songs, 32, 64–66, 87; at the institution vs. indigenous contexts, 118–27, 131–32; instrumentation of, 50–53, 55, 55–56, 57–58, 60, 62–63; as investment in the community, 45, 78, 80, 86–87; kin as performers of, 70, 83; and Minangkabau ethnicity, 39–40, 45, 132; and playing techniques, 50, 57–58; representing the *nagari,* 80, 87; terminology of parts, 50–51, 53, 55, 58, 62–63; transmission of, 118–20; and tuning, 50, 57–58, 59, 60, *61,* 63; at weddings, 68–78
talempong, instrument types: as kettle gong, 2, 23, *24; talempong batu,* 24; *talempong batuang,* 24–25; *talempong gadang,* 26; *talempong jao,* 26, *26, 61,* 120, 228n1; *talempong kayu,* 24, *25,* 26, 120; *talempong sambilu,* 26, 195
talempong bararak, 47. See also *talempong pacik*
talempong duduak: definition of, 27, 47; function of, 77; and gender, 47, 50, 57–58; importance at weddings, 68, 76, 78; and incorporation of *dendang* and pop songs, 64; and interlocking, 38, 52, 58, 63; and ostinati, 47, 51, 53, 55, 64; structure of tunes, 53, *54,* 119. See also Paninjauan; Sialang; Unggan
talempong goyang, 5, 27; and affective appeal, 204–5; compared with *talempong kreasi,* 195, 199, 210, 210; contexts for, 206; and cosmopolitans, 213–14; critique of, 205, 208–9, 212–13; and *dangdut,* 196–97, 202–4; defense of, 211–13; economics of, 77, 206–9; and emcee, 200, 205–6; incorporation of *dendang* and pop songs, 204, 213; and indigenous practices, 198–99, 203, 205; and the institutions, 182, 196, 202, 204, 207–12, 220; instrumentation of, 202–4, 210; and the market, 182, 200–201, 204, 212, 217; and Minangkabau ethnicity, 40, 205–12, 214, 220; Minangkabau identity of, 79, 205, 211; and morality, 198, 205; musicians

in, 206–7; in the *nagari,* 76–77, 79, 224; and *orgen,* 197–99, 202, 204–5, 213; origins of, 195–99; and pop, 196–99, 202–4, 210, 212–14; repertoire of, 202–5; and *saluang jo dendang,* 203–4; as tradition, 213; tuning of, 199, 202

talempong kreasi (baru), 2, 27, 186–93; and affective appeal, 190–91, 193; compared with *orkes talempong,* 186–87; compared with indigenous practices, 213; contexts for, 2–3; and cosmopolitans, 190, 192–93; and harmony, 187; and incorporation of *dendang* and pop songs, 184, 190, 195, 213, 222; at the institutions, 186–87, *187;* instrumentation at the institutions, 186–87, *187,* 210; instrumentation in *sanggar,* 188–90; and Minangkabau ethnicity, 3, 20, 193, 214, 222; orchestration of, 186–87, *188–89;* in the schools, 222; as traditional, 185, 192–93, 222; tuning of, 186

talempong pacik, 51, 62; and cyclical structure, 60; definition of, 27, 47; and *gandang tambua,* 50, *51;* and gender, 50, 62–63, 70–71; and incorporation of *dendang* and pop songs, 64; and interlocking, 60, 62–64, 123, 226n2, 227n12; and *nagari* variation, 60; and nondiatonic tuning, 60; and ostinati, 60; and processions, 28, 47–48, 70–72; and *sanggar,* 184, 191; as style, 49–50, 60, 62–63; in *talempong goyang,* 203; in *talempong kreasi,* 191; and variation, 124. *See also* Bungo Tanjueng; Padang Alai; Paninjauan; Unggan

talempong pambao, as part, 51, *52, 57*

talempong paningkah, as part, 52–53, *52, 55, 57, 57*

talempong taleno, 196

Taman Budaya, 128, 180–81, 228n7, 229n1

Taman Mini Indah Indonesia, 178, 222

tambo, 9, 18

Tanah Datar, regency of, 12

"Tari Barabah" 173, 229n3

"Tari Pasambahan," 79, 184, 190

tari piriang, 69, 191, 195

"Tari piring," 184, 190, 229n3

Taslimuddin Dt. Nan Tungga, 100

Teluk Bayur, 180

Timen, *200–201,* 208

Titian Aka, 185, 194

Tomi Chandra Putra, 85

tourism industry: as economic salvation, 1, 176, 180–81; in Indonesia, 179; and Minangkabau ethnicity, 182; and performances, 2, 178; and *sanggar,* 182; in West Sumatra, 179–80, 182

Tsing, Anna Lowenhaupt, 19, 178

tuning systems, indigenous Minangkabau compared with *gamelan,* 58. *See also* chromatic tuning; diatonic tuning; *slendro; pelog*

"Tupai bagaluik": *talempong* tune from Unggan, 48; *talempong* tune from Paninjauan, 53, *54,* 55, *57, 63*

Turino, Thomas, xi; and identity, 15–17; and cosmopolitanism, 16–17, 147; and professional musician, 34; and cultural reformism, 101, 140–41, 222; and Peircian semiotics, 174; and presentational music, 148

Unggan, *nagari* of, 42–43, 69; access to instruments, 26, 120; alternative instrumentation, 26, 120; *jorong* in, 42; legend of *talempong,* 48–49; and *orgen,* 78; prohibitions against *talempong,* 26–27, 68, 78, 120; and *talempong duduak:* censorship by government officials and community preferences, 66; —, diatonic tuning, 60; —, economics of, 81, 85–86; —, future of, 87, 217; —, on *Gongs and Vocal Music from Sumatra,* 39, 53; —, and incorporation of *dendang* and pop songs, 65–66, 87, 210, 217;

Index 269

Unggan (cont.)
—, at the institution, 110, 120, 131; —, and interlocking drums, 58; —, and keyboard, 58, 66; —, and tambourine, 58; —, and transmission methods, 119–20; —, and tuning, 59, 60, 61; —, and weddings, 70; and *talempong pacik*, in wedding processions, 68, 70; and weddings, 68–70, 72–73, 77
"Urang Halaban batimbang baju," 48. *See also* Halaban; music and place
"Urang tuo mancari pauah," 49
USU, 114
Utama, Edy, 72; and the institution, 113, 117, 212; and the PRRI, 136–37; and *talempong goyang*, 208, 212–13
Utama, Indra, 86; and the PRRI, 21, 96–97

Wardlow, Holly, 33, 84
weddings in the *nagari*, 67–80; and *adat*, 69; *baralek*, 69, 72–77; and community solidarity, 76; and food, 74–75; and gift economy, 74–76; and gifts, 70–71, 73–74; and invitations, 73; and kinship relationships, 67–69, 73–74; processions, 68, 69–72
Wegman, Rob, 33, 84
Weintraub, Andrew, 91, 135, 196–97
Weiss, Sarah, xi, 102
Western music (*musik barat*), 2, 99, 109, 117, 198, 200, 205, 225n1 (chap. 1); and *orkes talempong*, 134, 141, 147
West Sumatra, province of, 12, *13;* demographics of, 12; and Mentawai, 12; and Minangkabau, 10, 12

Yampolsky, Philip, xii, 29–30, 45–47, 92, 97, 101, 107, 178, 214; *Gongs and Vocal Music from Sumatra*, xi, 23, 39, 53, 135
Yusni, 26, *38,* 38–9, 52, 53, 65, 74, 76, 82–3, 88, 226n6, 227n14

Zain, Harun, 96–97, 137
Zoebir, Zuryati, x, 106, 113–14, 117
Zulkifli, x, 113, 137; as director of the institution, 130, 133, 211–12

www.ingramcontent.com/pod-product-compliance
Lightning Source LLC
Chambersburg PA
CBHW050626300426
44112CB00012B/1679